Friedrich Hölderlin

HYPERION
AND SELECTED POEMS

The German Library: Volume 22

Volkmar Sander, General Editor

Friedrich Hölderlin

HYPERION
AND SELECTED POEMS

Edited by Eric L. Santner

CONTINUUM · NEW YORK

1990
The Continuum Publishing Company
370 Lexington Avenue, New York, NY 10017

The German Library
is published in cooperation with Deutsches Haus,
New York University.
This volume has been supported by a grant from
the funds of Stifterverband für die Deutsche Wissenschaft
and The Princeton University Committee on Research
in the Humanities and Social Sciences.

Printed in the United States of America

Library of Congress Cataloging-in-Publication Data
Hölderlin, Friedrich, 1770–1843.
[Poems. English. Selections]
Hyperion and selected poems / Friedrich Hölderlin ; edited by Eric
L. Santner.
p. cm. — (The German library ; v. 22)
Includes bibliographical references (p.).
ISBN 0-8264-0333-6. — ISBN 0-8264-0334-4 (pbk.)
1. Hölderlin, Friedrich, 1770–1843—Translations, English.
I. Santner, Eric L., 1955– . II. Title. III. Series.
PT2359.H2A277 1990
831'.6—dc20   90-1759
                                         CIP

Acknowledgments will be found on page 305,
which constitutes an extension of the copyright page.

Contents

v

Contents • vii

Chronology

In preparing this chronology I have drawn on biographical information provided in: Adolf Beck, ed., *Hölderlin. Chronik seines Lebens* (Frankfurt a.M.: Insel, 1975); Pierre Bertaux, *Hölderlin* (Frankfurt a.M.: Suhrkamp, 1981); Thomas Pfau, trans., ed., *Friedrich Hölderlin. Essays and Letters on Theory* (Albany: SUNY Press, 1988); Richard Sieburth, trans., ed., *Hymns and Fragments by Friedrich Hölderlin* (Princeton: Princeton University Press, 1984); D. E. Sattler, ed., *Sämtliche Werke [Frankfurter Ausgabe]*, (Frankfurt a.M.: Verlag Roter Stern, 1975–); Friedrich Beissner, Adolf Beck, eds., *Sämtliche Werke [Grosse Stuttgarter Ausgabe]*, (Stuttgart: Kohlhammer, Cotta, 1943–77); Friedrich Beissner, Jochen Schmidt, eds., *Hölderlin. Werke und Briefe* (Frankfurt a.M: Insel, 1969).

1770   March 20. Johann Christian Friedrich Hölderlin is born in Lauffen on the Neckar (Swabia). He is the first child of Johanna Christiana Heyn (1748–1828) and Heinrich Friedrich Hölderlin (1736–72).

1772   Sudden death of father. Birth of sister Heinrike (Rike).

1774   Mother marries Johann Christoph Gok. Johanna Gok assumes full responsibility for the administration of her son's paternal inheritance. At no point will Hölderlin ever dispute his mother's authority in the distribution of monies from the estate.

1776   Hölderlin's stepfather becomes mayor of Nürtingen. Birth of Hölderlin's half brother Karl Gok. Hölderlin begins to attend school.

1779   Death of stepfather at the age of thirty. Twenty years later, Hölderlin will write to his mother: "Let me express, too, my heartfelt thanks for the sweet words about my dear departed father. . . . Believe me, I've thought . . . about his ever cheerful temperament, and that I might come to be like him. But neither are you, my dear mother, responsible for my tendency toward mournfulness, from which I have never quite been able to free myself. I see the whole of my life rather clearly, even back to my earliest days, and it is no mystery at which point my spirit took on this aspect. Perhaps you'll not believe me, but I remember it all too well. When my second father died, whose love for me I shall never forget, when I felt, with an incomprehensible pain, my orphaned state and saw, each day, your grief and tears, it was then that my soul took on, for the first time, this heaviness that has never left me and that could only grow more severe with the years."

1782–83   In preparation for entrance examinations, Hölderlin receives private instruction in, among other things, Hebrew, Latin, Greek, and rhetoric, and begins music lessons (piano, later flute). Beginning of friendship with Schelling, five years his junior, whom Hölderlin protects against abuse by older pupils. Lifelong love for travel literature most likely begins at this time with Georg Forster's *Journey Around the World 1772–75* and Admiral George Anson's *Voyage Round the World in the Years 1740–44*.

1784   Hölderlin enters the Lower Monastery School at Denkendorf, near Nürtingen, the beginning of formal training for the Lutheran ministry. First encounters with the poetry of Schiller and Klopstock; composes first verses. Earliest extant letter of Hölderlin, written to his former tutor, Nathanael Köstlin, expresses an anxious preoccupation with the maintenance of measure and harmony in relation to others and to God. Hölderlin seems very much aware of the precariousness of his emotional stability.

1786   Hölderlin enters the Higher Monastery School at Maulbronn. Falls in love with Luise Nast, youngest daughter of monastery administrator; friendship with her cousin, Immanuel Nast.

1787   Hölderlin begins to doubt his calling to the ministry. Expression of powerful poetic ambitions in the poem "Mein Vorsatz" ("My Project"), where the poet longs to attain "Pindar's flight" and "Klopstock-heights."

1788   Reads, on Luise Nast's recommendation, Schiller's *Don Carlos*. Eleven years later Hölderlin will write to Schiller: "It won't be easy to study *Carlos* in a rational way, since he was for so many years the magic cloud in which the good god of my youth enveloped me so that I would not see too soon the pettiness and barbarity of the world." Hölderlin enters, at the same time as Hegel, the Lutheran theological seminary *(Stift)* in Tübingen and is soon initiated into the poetry association of Ludwig Neuffer and Rudolf Magenau: "One Soul in Three Bodies!"

1789   Hölderlin breaks off engagement with Luise Nast: "I wish you happiness if you choose one more worthy than me, and then surely you will understand that you could never have been happy with your morose, ill-humored, sickly friend." End of friendship with Immanuel Nast. Meets the Swabian poet and publisher Gotthold F. Stäudlin in Stuttgart. Student activities at the Stift placed under close surveillance by Duke Karl Eugen. Hölderlin is punished by Stift administration for maltreatment of a local schoolteacher who failed to greet him appropriately. Expresses wish to study law but succumbs to pressure from his mother to stay on in the Stift.

1790   Passes his *Magister* exams. After Schelling enters the Stift, close friendship between Hegel, Schelling, and Hölderlin. Composition of first so-called Tübingen Hymns, philosophical verse inspired by Schiller's poetry and the spirit of the French Revolution. Reads Rousseau, Spinoza, Leibniz, Plato, but above all, Kant. As Magenau described the enthusiasm for Kant among students at the Stift: "Kant's philosophy made most of our heads spin, and the pulpit echoed of space and time." Hölderlin falls in love with Elise Lebret.

1791   First poems published (in Stäudlins *Musenalmanach fürs Jahr 1792*). Regarding this debut, Christian Schubart notes: "Hölderlin's muse is a solemn muse." Travels with friends to site of Rütli oath in Switzerland; meeting with Lavater in Zürich. Hölderlin still contemplates leaving the Stift. In a letter to his mother, Hölderlin complains of continuing headaches: "And then one's inner life no longer enjoys its youthful vigor."

1792   Hölderlin begins work on *Hyperion*. War between France and the Austro-Prussian coalition. Hölderlin writes to his sister: "Believe me, dear sister, we will face grim times, should the Austrians be victorious. The abuse of princely power will be terrible. You must believe me and pray for the French, the defenders of human rights."

1793   Hegel leaves Stift to assume a post as a private tutor in Bern. Hölderlin writes to his half brother: "My affections are now less directed toward particular individuals. The object of my love is the entire human race, though not, of course, as we so often find

it, namely in a condition of corruption, servility, and iner-
tia. . . . I love the race of coming centuries. For this is my
deepest hope, the faith that keeps me strong and vital: our
grandchildren will have it better than we, freedom must finally
come, and virtue will better flourish in the warmth of freedom's
sacred light than in the ice-cold zone of despotism. We live in
times when all things are working toward better days. These
seeds of enlightenment, these still wishes and strivings of iso-
lated individuals for the development of the human race will
spread and grow stronger and bear marvelous fruit. . . . This is
the sacred purpose of my wishes and my activity: that I might
stir the seeds of change that will ripen in a future age." Höld-
erlin meets Schiller in Ludwigsburg who recommends him
(with some reservations) to Charlotte von Kalb as a private tutor
for her son. Hölderlin assumes the post in Waltershausen at the
end of the year.

1794   Hölderlin begins his duties as a tutor with great ambition and
idealism: "To form my pupil into a full human being, this was
and is my goal." Continues to work on *Hyperion* and to study
Kant and Schiller. Friendship and possible love affair with
Wilhelmine Marianne Kirms, his employer's companion. Höld-
erlin travels with his pupil, Fritz von Kalb, to Jena where he
meets Herder and Goethe and attends Fichte's lectures. Regular
visits to Schiller who publishes the "Fragment of Hyperion" in
his *Neuer Thalia.*

1795   Hölderlin is increasingly frustrated in his rigorous pedagogical
ambitions, in part due to his pupil's habit of frequent and
perhaps compulsive masturbation. He writes to his mother in
January: "The impossibility of having a real influence on the
child and helping him had the most deleterious effects on my
health and spirit. The anxious wakefulness of the nightly vigils
destroyed my head and made me nearly useless for my daily
work." Hölderlin's increasing desperation forces Charlotte von
Kalb to terminate his employment. She provides him with
enough money to stay on in Jena for several months where he
continues his study of Fichte's philosophy. He writes to Hegel:
"His work regarding the reciprocal determinations of the 'I' and
the 'Not-I' is no doubt peculiar." Close friendship develops with
Isaac von Sinclair in whose garden house he lives for several
weeks. Sinclair is expelled from the university for participation

in student disturbances. Cotta agrees to publish the full version of *Hyperion*. Having rejected, the previous year, the idea of a marriage combined with a minister's position, he appeals to his mother to grant him "the undisturbed use of my powers which is just within reach for the very first time in my life." In June, Hölderlin suddenly leaves Jena in great emotional distress and returns to Nürtingen. Once home, he writes to Schiller: "I well knew that I would not be able to remove myself from your vicinity without doing damage to my inner being. I am able to confirm this more strongly with each new day. . . . I would never have been able to persuade myself to leave had not this very vicinity to you . . . been a source of great distress. I was always tempted to see you, and when I did the result was always the realization that I could be nothing to you." And in another letter to Schiller: "I am frozen and numb in the winter that is all around me. The heavens are as iron, and I am as stone." Philosophical discussions with Schelling in Tübingen and Nürtingen. Through the mediation of Johann Gottfried Ebel, Hölderlin is offered a position as private tutor in the home of the wealthy Frankfurt banker Gontard.

1796   Hölderlin assumes his post in January and soon falls deeply in love with his employer's young wife Susette, who becomes the "Diotima" of his poems and novel. In February, Hölderlin reports to his friend Immanuel Niethammer that "philosophy is once more my single occupation." Perhaps alluding to the overwhelming influence of Fichte and Schiller, he continues: "But the reverberations from Jena are still too strong . . . and the memory still too powerful for the present to restore me fully. My head is full of entangled threads and I am not capable of undoing them. . . . Philosophy is a tyrant, and it is more that I tolerate her power over me than give myself to her voluntarily." He promises his friend a series of philosophical letters, to be called "New Letters on the Aesthetic Education of Man," in which "I will find the principle that explains the divisions in which we think and exist, but one capable of making the opposition disappear, the opposition between subject and object, between our self and the world, even that between reason and revelation—theoretically, in intellectual intuition and without the aid of practical reason. But for this we are in need of aesthetic sense." The mutual attraction between Hölderlin and Susette blossoms into a clandestine romance. Toward the end of

June, Hölderlin writes to Neuffer: "I only hope that you are doing as well as I. I am in a new world. Once I thought I knew what was beautiful and good, but now that I see it I want to laugh at all my knowledge. My dear friend, there is a being in the world in whose presence my spirit can and will dwell for millenia. . . . At times I even find it impossible to think mortal thoughts in her presence, and for this reason it is so difficult to say anything about her." The war with revolutionary France forces Hölderlin, along with Susette and her children, to leave Frankfurt. In Kassel Hölderlin meets Wilhelm Heinse, a friend of the Gontards and author of the novel *Ardinghello*. Several years later, Hölderlin will dedicate the elegy "Brod und Wein" to him. Returns to Frankfurt in September. After a long silence on Schiller's part, Hölderlin writes an anxious letter to his former mentor: "Have you changed your opinion of me? Have you abandoned me? Forgive me such questions." Schiller responds with the advice that Hölderlin should avoid, at all costs, philosophical subjects and adhere more closely to the world of sense experience: "In this way you will avoid the danger of abandoning sobriety in the midst of enthusiasm."

1797   Despite his friend Ebel's words of disenchantment from Paris, Hölderlin continues to express hopes for radical change: "As for the general course of things, I do find one consolation, namely that every ferment and dissolution must lead either to annihilation or to a new organization of things. But there is no such thing as annihilation, and so the youth of the world must return out of our corruption and decay. . . . I believe in a coming revolution in the way we think, feel, and imagine, which will make the world as we have known it till now grow red with shame. And Germany can perhaps play a key role in all of this." Hegel arrives in Frankfurt where Hölderlin has found a post for him as tutor in the household of a wine merchant. The first volume of *Hyperion* appears in mid-April. At Schiller's behest, Goethe agrees to meet with Hölderlin in Frankfurt: "Yesterday Hölterlein paid a brief visit. He appears to be somewhat depressed and sickly, but he is actually quite amiable, the anxious humility of his openness even somewhat disarming. I urged him to work on short poems about particular objects of human interest." Toward the end of the summer Hölderlin begins plans for a tragedy based on the life and death of the philosopher Empedocles, who, Hölderlin writes, was "a sworn enemy of all one-sided existence and thus . . . dissatisfied . . . even in truly pleasant conditions simply because they are particular conditions."

1798   Toward the end of September, class and sexual tensions in the Gontard household culminate in Hölderlin's departure. In a letter to his mother he cites the daily humiliations he had to suffer as a "servant" of the wealthy bourgeoisie as the main reason for his break with the Gontards. Bettina von Arnim will later write to Karoline von Günderrode: "In Frankfurt you only have to mention his name and people cry out the most horrible things about him, all because he loved a woman so that he could write *Hyperion*." Hölderlin's former pupil Henry writes to him: "I can barely stand it that you have left." Sinclair persuades Hölderlin to take up residence in Homburg where he is a jurist in the service of the Landgrave of Hessen-Homburg. In November he writes to Neuffer: "My situation has changed since I wrote you last. . . . I have been here for a little over a month and have been using the quiet to work on my play, spend time with Sinclair, and enjoy the lovely autumn days. After the torment I have suffered, the pleasures of a little calm are like a gift from the gods." Hölderlin and Susette continue to meet and correspond secretly for the next two years. Sinclair introduces Hölderlin to acquaintances interested in political upheaval in Württemberg. Continues work on *Empedocles* tragedy.

1799   In a New Year's letter to his half brother in which he describes, at great length, the need for the political, philosophical, and above all aesthetic cultivation of the nation, Hölderlin writes that "if and when the realm of darkness breaks upon us with violence, so let us throw down our pens and go in God's name where . . . we are most needed." Along with his work on *Empedocles* Hölderlin studies Pindar and writes a number of his major essays dealing with philosophical and poetological matters, including the theory of the alternation of poetic tones. Friendship with the poet Böhlendorff, who writes of Sinclair and Hölderlin: "I have a friend here who is a republican with body and soul—also another friend who is one in spirit and in truth—which will emerge from the darkness when the time is right." Hölderlin interests a publisher in his plans for a journal of criticism and poetry, *Iduna,* and appeals to friends, above all Schiller and Schelling, for contributions. Lack of support kills the plan. Writing to Susette Gontard, he reports, "Only the uncertainty of my situation kept me from writing sooner. The journal project about which I wrote to you with so much—well-founded—confidence seems not to want to succeed. . . . Not only those men to whom I am more admirer than friend, but friends too, my dear one, friends who were not able to deny me support without becoming the most ungrateful of men, they too have left me until now without an answer. I have lived for a full eight weeks in this state of hope and expectation upon which my very existence depends to some degree. God only knows the cause of this reception. Are these people so totally ashamed of me?" Several months earlier he had already written her that he feels like a "living corpse." In October the second volume of *Hyperion* appears. In a letter to Susette accompanying the volume Hölderlin writes: "Here *our* Hyperion, my love! This fruit of our days of tenderness may still give you some pleasure. Forgive me Diotima's death. You remember that we couldn't fully agree about this back then. I felt that the whole conception of the work made it necessary." In the last letter he was to write to Neuffer, Hölderlin speaks of the impossibility of supporting oneself as a writer and contemplates searching for a post as vicar or private tutor.

1800 In May, last meeting between Hölderlin and Susette Gontard. Among her last words to him are: "Everything around me is mute and empty without you." Returns to Nürtingen before going to Stuttgart where he lives for several months with his friend Christian Landauer and supports himself with private lessons. In the biographical sketch accompanying the 1846 edition of Hölderlin's poems, Christoph Schwab writes of the poet's condition at this time: "His emotional condition seemed dangerous. His very appearance bore the marks of the transformation he had undergone over the last years; the inner struggles and suffering had taken such a toll on this once robust body that upon his return from Homburg one thought oneself to be in the presence of a ghost. Even more startling was his state of emotional agitation; an innocent word that had no connection to him could enrage him to the point that he would leave the company he was in and never return." Among the poetic fruits of this trying year are a number of odes and most of the major elegies, including "Bread and Wine." In December Hölderlin is offered a position as private tutor in the household of the merchant Anton von Gonzenbach in Hauptwil (Switzerland).

1801 Hölderlin assumes his new post in mid-January. The Treaty of Lunéville is signed in February. Hölderlin writes to his sister: "I am writing to you and our dear family at a moment when for us here everything is full of the news of the peace treaty. . . . I have faith that now the world is truly becoming a better place. I like to think of these days that are so near or of ancient times; everything fills my mind with these remarkable days, days of beautiful humanity, of goodness that is sure and unmarked by fear. . . . You see, my dear sister, I view my stay here as a man who has had his share of suffering in his youth and is now content and undisturbed enough to be deeply grateful for that which is." In the midst of these rare high spirits, Hölderlin works on the hymn "Celebration of Peace." In mid-April Gonzenbach relieves Hölderlin from his post for unknown reasons, issuing him a favorable letter of reference. The return to Swabia across Lake Constance is recalled in the elegy "Homecoming." In his final letter to Schiller he asks his former mentor for help in obtaining a position as lecturer on Greek literature in Jena: "You must have nearly abandoned all hopes for me, and so it might come as a pleasant surprise to see that the pressure of circumstances has not completely overwhelmed me. . . . And now I must write to you sooner than I had wanted. My wish to live in Jena in your vicinity has become nearly a life necessity, and having considered the pros and cons, I felt I needed a word from you, without whose approval I can do nothing, to authorize my choice." Schiller does not reply. An edition of Hölderlin's poetry promised for the following spring never sees print. Through the mediation of a friend, Hölderlin is offered a position as private tutor in Bordeaux in the household of Daniel Christoph Meyer, a wine merchant and consul of Hamburg. Before his departure he writes to Böhlendorff: "I am full of departure now. It's been a long time since I've cried. But it cost me bitter tears when I decided to leave my fatherland now, perhaps for good. For what is more dear to me in this world? But they have no use for me. Still, I shall and must remain German, even if the needs of my heart—and belly—drive me all the way to Tahiti." On December 10 he sets out on foot from his mother's house.

1802   Arrives in Bordeaux on January 28. His first letter to his mother reports: "I have experienced so much that I can barely speak of it now. For the last few days my journey has passed amidst a beautiful springtime, but just prior to this, on the fearsome snow-covered heights of the Auvergne, in the midst of storms and wilderness, in the icy night with my loaded pistol beside me in my rough bed—there I prayed the finest prayer of my life, and one I shall never forget. I've arrived in one piece—give thanks with me!"

        After only three months he returns to Germany, most likely by way of Paris. According to Hölderlin's first biographer, Wilhelm Waiblinger, he arrives in mid-June at the home of friends in Stuttgart "pale as a corpse, emaciated, with hollow wild eyes, long hair and beard, and dressed like a beggar." He returns to Nürtingen where his half brother recognizes "the obvious traces of mental derangement." Returns to Stuttgart and is informed by Sinclair of Susette Gontard's death on June 22. Back in Nürtingen, Hölderlin is placed in the care of a local physician. Travels with Sinclair to Regensburg where the latter's employer, the Landgrave of Homburg, informally commissions Hölderlin to write a work expressing true Christian piety. ("Patmos" will be dedicated to the Landgrave the following winter.) Sinclair will later write to Hölderlin's mother that he had "never seen him in a stronger mental and emotional state as back then." Back home, in the midst of his work on "Patmos" and other hymns, he writes to Böhlendorff: "It's been a long time since I wrote to you; I've been in France and have seen the mournful, lonely earth, the shepherds of southern France and things of beauty, men and women who have grown up with the fear of confused loyalties and of hunger. The mighty element, the fire from heaven and the tranquillity of the people, their life amidst nature, their simplicity and contentment, moved me to no end, and as it is said of heroes, I can well say, that Apollo has struck me."

1803   Contact with friends becomes more seldom. Continues work on hymns and translations of Pindar and Sophocles. Meets with Schelling in June, who writes to Hegel: "The saddest thing I saw during my stay here was Hölderlin. Since his trip to France . . . his spirit is totally shattered. Although he is to a certain extent still able to do some work—translating Greek, for example—he is otherwise totally withdrawn. The sight of him really shook me up: he neglects his appearance to a repulsive degree and although his manner of speaking would seem not to indicate madness, he has taken on the outward demeanor of those in that condition. There are no hopes for recovery if he stays here. I thought of asking you if you could look after him were he to come to Jena, which seems to be his wish." Hegel's reply is noncommittal and the matter pursued no further. In December Hölderlin sends his publisher Friedrich Wilmans the manuscript of his translations of *Oedipus* and *Antigone*, which appear the following April; he promises further a series of long poems concerned with history and the fatherland—the so-called *vaterländische Gesänge* (songs of the fatherland or patriotic songs)—as well as a group of shorter "nightsongs."

1804   Sacrificing some of his own salary, Sinclair arranges for Hölderlin to become (pro forma) librarian in the court of the Landgrave of Homburg. On the way to Homburg, Sinclair and Hölderlin participate in a series of informal meetings with Stuttgart radicals in which various possibilities of violent political action are discussed, including the assassination of the Elector of Württemberg. Final meeting with Schelling in Würzburg, who finds expressions of Hölderlin's "degenerated mental condition" in his Sophocles translations. Arrival in Homburg in June where Hölderlin takes up residence in the house of a French watchmaker. He receives a Virgil edition as a gift from the Landgrave and a piano from Princess Auguste of Hessen-Homburg.

1805   Sinclair is turned in to the authorities by a former acquaintance, Alexander Blankenstein, and charged with high treason for participation in a Jacobin conspiracy against the Elector of Württemberg. In his testimony, Blankenstein reports that Hölderlin knew of the conspiracy but soon "fell into a sort of madness, hurled insults at Sinclair and the Jacobins and cried out to the astonishment of all present: I am through with all Jacobins. Vive le roi!" Hölderlin is found to be mentally incompetent to stand trial. The physician brought in as an expert witness reported: "During the course of my visits his condition worsened and his speech became more unintelligible. Once his madness reached the point of a constant, wild agitation and his speech became a jumble of German, Greek, and Latin, one could no longer understand him at all." The previous year

Sinclair had written to Hölderlin's mother that "not only me, but 6–8 other people as well who have made his acquaintance, are convinced that what looks like mental confusion is . . . in fact a calculated act of simulation." Sinclair is released from prison after four months due to lack of sufficient evidence and returns to find Hölderlin in relative calm and at work on Pindar translations. Leo von Seckendorf, one of Sinclair's "co-conspirators" and friend of Hölderlin, pays a final visit to the poet before going into exile from Württemberg. He takes with him several poems he later publishes without Hölderlin's permission, including the first strophe of "Bread and Wine" (published as "The Night"), "The Rhine," "Patmos," and "Remembrance."

1806   Homburg is absorbed into the newly established Grand Duchy of Hessen-Darmstadt. Sinclair writes to Hölderlin's mother that he can no longer assume responsibility for her son's care. On September 11 Hölderlin is brought against his will to Tübingen where he is committed to the Autenrieth Clinic, one of the few hospitals that admitted the mentally ill at this time. The Landgravine Caroline von Hessen-Homburg writes to her daughter: "Poor Holterling was carried away this morning. . . . He tried desperately to throw himself from the carriage, but the man charged with his care held him back. Holterling believed that he was being abducted . . . and scratched the man with his long fingernails until the man was all bloody."

1807   After some seven months of observation and treatment, Hölderlin is released into the care of Ernst Zimmer, a carpenter and admirer of *Hyperion* who had visited the poet in the clinic. Though given only three years to live by Autenrieth, Hölderlin lives with the Zimmer family in a house on the Neckar river for more than thirty-five years. During this time he continues to write poetry; some fifty poems, which Hölderlin at times signed with the name Scardanelli, remain from this last period.

1808   Zimmer provides Hölderlin with a piano which, along with the flute and singing, is one of his main activities.

1822   Wilhelm Waiblinger begins to visit Hölderlin on regular basis. Seven years later he writes the essay, "Friedrich Hölderlin's Life, Poetry, and Madness." Second edition of *Hyperion* published.

1826   Publication of Hölderlin's *Selected Poems,* edited by Ludwig Uhland and Gustav Schwab.

1828   Death of Hölderlin's mother.

1842   Second edition of his poems published with a brief biographical sketch.

1843   Death of Hölderlin on June 7. Some hundred students march in the funeral procession in Tübingen.

Introduction

Reading Hölderlin in the Age of Difference

Not quite a hundred years after Hölderlin's death, the German critic and philosopher Walter Benjamin, himself a great admirer of Hölderlin and author of an important essay on his odes,[1] introduced a term that would inform all subsequent theorizations of modern experience and modernist aesthetics. It was a term appropriated from, of all places, Freud's speculative text *Beyond the Pleasure Principle*, and designates a class of experiences the radical proliferation of which Benjamin took to be coincidental with the advent of modernity: traumatic shock.[2] The central question raised in Benjamin's essay is in essence the question of the very possibility of the modern lyric as such: "The question suggests itself how lyric poetry can have as its basis an experience for which the shock experience has become the norm."[3] According to Benjamin, the answer to this question is to be found in Baudelaire's oeuvre. Here we find a poetry that has given itself over to a "heroism of modern life" that consists in the sobriety of a consciousness that, bereft of stable and consoling idealisms, must fight its way through the new urban spaces and their populations of displaced and anonymous masses. According to Benjamin, a life amid urban crowds is inherently traumatic because one is repeatedly confronted with eyes that do not return one's gaze: "What is involved here is that the expectation roused by the look of the human eye is not fulfilled. Baudelaire describes eyes of which one is inclined to say that they have lost their ability to look."[4] The shock of the chronic inhumanity of such eyes stands in contrast, as *spleen* to *idéal*, to the notion of *correspon-*

dances that signifies in Baudelaire a quasi-mystical familiarity and intimacy with the other even as it recedes into a distance that can never be mastered.[5] For Benjamin, the world of such "auratic" gazes is shaped by the social practices associated with premodern communal life and modes of production. Modernity, on the other hand, is seen as being organized according to the rationality of clock time and an ethos of self-interest, suggesting in turn yet another sense of the chronic inhumanity of modern life: here *kairos* has been displaced by *chronos,* here human beings are as isolated from one another as one discrete moment in time is from any other. As Benjamin says, "The *idéal* supplies the power of remembrance; the *spleen* musters the multitude of the seconds against it." What makes Baudelaire the preeminent modern poet is his apparent capacity to resist the seductions of regressive nostalgias for premodern "experience" (what Benjamin calls *Erfahrung*); rather, he becomes the first great lyric poet of modern "experience" (what Benjamin calls *Erlebnis*): "The poet who failed to found a family endowed the word *familier* with overtones pervaded by promise and renunciation. He has lost himself to the spell of eyes which do not return his glance and submits to their sway without illusions."[6]

Although it is rather difficult to associate such equanimity vis-à-vis the shock experiences that result from the breakdown of premodern social formations with the visionary Swabian poet Friedrich Hölderlin, the earlier poet was by no means a stranger to the radical disturbances and disorientations of an incipient modernity. One might even say that Hölderlin's oeuvre represents in its fragmented totality a sustained, if highly ambivalent, effort to master a series of personal, political, and, as it were, philosophico-theological traumas, the sum of which may be seen to lay down the terms of a social space that would indeed require a new, precisely modern, mode of heroism. Although Hölderlin's schizophrenic collapse undoubtedly attests to his failure to achieve such a heroism of modern life, this very failure allows us to read his work as a site where the contradictions, stresses, longings, and disenchantments that scar our own modern selves are passionately rehearsed.[7]

What exactly were the particular shocks that Hölderlin's work registers, thematically as well as in the formal patterns of words and sounds that make up his remarkable lyrics? There were, of course, the numerous personal traumas familiar from Hölderlin's biography: the loss of both father and stepfather early in life; Hölderlin's perpetual struggle with his mother over his refusal to enter the Lutheran ministry for which he had been trained at the Tübingen seminary; his for the most part failed efforts to establish himself in civil society and the resulting nomadic and often humiliatingly dependent existence as a private tutor in the houses of the wealthy bourgeoisie; the failure, due in large part to lack of support from his friends Schiller and Schelling, of his project to found a literary journal; and above all the abrupt ending of his love affair with Susette Gontard and her death in 1802. Beyond these more personal shocks there were what we might call the political traumas that left their marks on Hölderlin's life and literary production: the failure of progressive forces to introduce republican reforms in Swabia; the violent turn of the French Revolution and subsequent coup d'état; the Napoleonic Wars; and, closer to home, the arrest and trial of Hölderlin's closest friend, Isaac von Sinclair, for high treason, an affair which Hölderlin himself manages to escape only thanks to attestations by medical authorities of mental incompetence.

But what is it, exactly, that transforms a disturbing event, an experience of frustration or loss, a disappointment or disenchantment, into a shock or trauma? When and under what social, political, and psychological conditions does the experience of "the negative" cease to be merely a species of unpleasure and become traumatic? And what predisposes a particular individual to a special vulnerability to trauma, a vulnerability that may ultimately end, as it did in Hölderlin's case, in psychosis? These are questions that cannot be fully answered in the context of this introduction; in the following I would, however, like to sketch out the ways in which Hölderlin's work, perhaps more poignantly than any other poetic oeuvre, raises these questions. For it is here, in the terms in which Hölderlin experienced and named his own traumatizations, that we find most clearly adumbrated the core experiences of our own fragile modernity.

1

In Hölderlin's writings, the name of the trauma that the poet is constantly, even obsessively, trying to come to terms with, is *dif-*

ference and the resulting task of establishing the proper measure of distance and proximity to the other, whether it be nature, a friend or lover, the dead, another culture, or the gods. In the text of Hölderlin, all other disturbances, all other conflicts and struggles, are related back to what we might call the primal scenes of the opening up, the "differing" of difference. In an early philosophical fragment written in the theoretical register of the age of Kant and Fichte, Hölderlin conceives of difference as the primal separation between subject and object that "happens" in language, or more precisely, in the formation of judgment ("Urteil"): "In the highest and strictest sense [judgment] is the original separation of object and subject which are the most deeply united in intellectual intuition, that separation through which alone object and subject become possible, the arche-separation ["die Ur-Teilung"]."[8] As we see here, Hölderlin's concern, like that of so many of his intellectual contemporaries who together produced that body of thought we have come to call German Idealism, was an ancient one: the relationship between the One and the Many, unity and multiplicity, identity and difference.

More or less contemporaneous with this theoretical formulation, Hölderlin has the protagonist of his remarkable epistolary novel, *Hyperion,* reflect upon his passionate relationship with his friend Alabanda; here difference, the alterity of another human being and destiny, is experienced in a purely negative register, as a disabling condition of separateness: "The kingly youth! why was I born after him? why did I not spring from *one* cradle with him? I cannot bear the difference between us." With regard to the last sentence, a brief look at the German is of some interest. It reads: "Ich kann den Unterschied nicht leiden, der zwischen uns ist." "Leiden" can mean, and in this case no doubt primarily does mean, to bear or tolerate some negative state of affairs. But "leiden" can also mean to suffer or undergo something painful, a loss or ordeal of some sort. Reading the two significations together so that the tension between them constitutes a narrative, it is as if Hyperion were saying that he cannot tolerate difference because he has no means or context in which he might be able to suffer and work through the pain of difference and separateness. And indeed, the novel as a whole could be read as that "eccentric" textual process whereby differences and separations— from loved ones, from the dead, from past golden ages, from illusory redemptions, and, one might venture to say, from the "Unmediated" in a general sense—are worked through and come to be tolerated.

Hölderlin's work is full of evocations of the anxieties associated with difference. In the text of Hölderlin, difference is always on the brink of becoming a condition of brute isolation and abandonment. In Hölderlin's life and work, one might say that difference puts one in touch with the origins of madness. As I have already indicated, Hölderlin's novel would seem to be dedicated to the task of transforming its (autobiographical) protagonist's manic-depressive oscillations between nearly hallucinatory states of oneness with the other—nature, a friend, a lover—and states of complete and utter emptiness and abject isolation, into some sort of dialectic.[9] The typical cyclothymic rhythm of Hyperion's mood swings is identified quite early in the novel:

> To be one with all—this is the life divine, this is man's heaven. . . . To be one with all that lives, to return in blessed self-forgetfulness into the All of Nature—this is the pinnacle of thoughts and joys, this the sacred mountain peak, the place of eternal rest, . . . On this height I often stand, my Bellarmin! But an instant of reflection hurls me down. I reflect, and find myself as I was before—alone, with all the griefs of mortality, and my heart's refuge, the world in its eternal oneness, is gone; Nature closes her arms, and I stand like an alien before her and do not understand her.

This pattern of oscillation between oneness and abandonment is repeated in all of Hyperion's significant relationships but perhaps most forcefully and dangerously with Diotima, whose namesake was, after all, the great teacher of the meanings of erotic union in Plato's *Symposium*. Echoing Aristophanes' remarkable myth of the origins of Eros in that dialogue, Hyperion cries out:

> Ah! my heart was often torn to pieces by my sacred, ineffable longing, my love often raged in me as powerfully as an imprisoned Titan. Never before had my spirit strained so fervently, so implacably, against the chains that Fate wrought for it, against the iron, inexorable law that kept it separate, that would not let it be *one* soul with its adorable other half.

The psychological precariousness of Hyperion's erotic attachments is even more pronounced in the "Fragment of Hyperion" published by Schiller in 1794 in his *Neuer Thalia*. There Hyperion meditates anxiously about his disturbing emotional dependence on the woman he has fallen in love with (in this version she is called Melite):

> But what I was I was through her. The gracious one took pleasure in the light that seemed to emanate from me and it never occurred to her that it was only the reflection of her own brilliance. All too soon I felt how I became poorer than a shadow if she did not live in me, around me, and for me, if she did not become mine; that I was nothing when she withdrew from me. It was inevitable: with a deathly anxiety I had to watch every expression on her face, interrogate every utterance that came from her lips, follow every movement of her eyes, as if my life would flow from me should she divert her gaze toward heaven or to the earth.[10]

Here, as we saw in Benjamin's writings on Baudelaire, a traumatic "shock" is identified as the experience of eyes that do not return one's gaze. In Hyperion's case, however, it would seem that any interruption of a full specular reciprocity between himself and his other would be experienced as traumatic. And indeed, it is precisely this hypersensitivity to the occultation of the gaze of the other, the possibility and inevitability of which is coincident with the advent of alterity, that Hölderlin spent so much of his conscious adult life trying to overcome. His poetry and, more generally, what Hölderlin took to be the laws of a rigorous poetic process, was to be the primary site of these strivings.

While still working on the second book of his novel, Hölderlin wrote a letter to his old schoolfriend Christian Ludwig Neuffer in which, with a remarkable lucidity and honesty, he analyzed this hypersensitivity and the nature of the procedure he envisioned for mastering it. I would like to quote at length from this letter since it is no doubt one of the most important documents we have regarding the interrelationship between Hölderlin's psychological struggles and the development of his poetry and poetics:

Livingness in poetry is what now most preoccupies my mind and senses. I feel so deeply how far I am from attaining it, and yet my whole soul is struggling to do so, and often I am so overcome that I weep like a child when I feel in every way the lack in my work of one thing or another, and still I cannot wrest myself off the wrong poetic tracks on which I wander around. O the world has scared my mind back into itself ever since my youth, and I am still suffering from this. There is, to be sure, one honorable refuge for a poet who comes to grief like me: philosophy. But I cannot relinquish my first love and the hopes of my young days, and I would rather perish with nothing done than leave the sweet land of the Muses, out of which only chance has driven me. If you have any good advice, which would bring me to the truth as quickly as possible, then give it to me. I lack not so much power as ease, not so much ideas as nuances, not so much light as shadows, and all this for one single reason: I am too shy of what is common and ordinary in actual life. I am a proper pedant, if you like. And yet, unless I am mistaken, pedants are so cold and loveless, whereas my heart is so impatient to ally itself with sublunary people and things. I almost think that I am pedantic out of sheer love, I am not shy because I am afraid of being disturbed by reality in my self-absorbtion, but because I am afraid of being disturbed by reality in the inward communion with which I gladly attach myself to something else; I am afraid to chill the warm life in me with the icy history of common day, and this fear springs from my having been more sensitively receptive than others to any destructive thing which befell me, ever since my youth, and this sensitivity seems to be rooted in my being not firmly and indestructibly organized enough in relation to the experiences which I have had to undergo. I see that. Can my seeing it help me? A little, I think. Because I am more destructible than some other men, I must seek all the more to derive some advantage from what has a destructive effect on me, I must not take it as it is, but only in so far as it does service to my own truest life. Wherever I find such things, I must accept them in advance as indispensable material, without which my most inward being cannot ever entirely present itself. I must assimilate them, to arrange them eventually (as an artist, if I should wish to be one, and come to be one) as shadows to my light, to reproduce them as subordinate tones among which the tone of my soul springs out all the more livingly. What is pure can only be presented in terms of the impure, and if you try to give something of nobility without what is ordinary, then it will be most unnatural and discordant.[11]

This notion of an interplay of a fundamental tone with its subordinate tones, of shadows and light, the pure and the impure, the natural and the unnatural, origin and representation, contains the seeds of Hölderlin's difficult and often obscure theory of the alternation of tones and the relations of poetic genres. According to this theory, each genre (epic, tragic, lyric) is organized by a particular series of modulations of the three fundamental poetic tones, the naive, the heroic, and the ideal. Each tone is in turn associated with a *Grundstimmung,* a fundamental mood reflecting a particular state or level of attunement with the world. Moreover, each tone always occupies a position in relation to another, depending on the genre and the particular place in the alternating series. More specifically, the basic tone *(Grundton)* of any poetic utterance must always be mediated by way of an artistic effect *(Kunstcharakter)* associated with a contrasting tone; no tone can speak for itself, can make itself available in its utmost purity. According to this theory, every work of poetic art is a process whereby the tension between a fundamental tone and its signifying medium or artistic effect is elaborated. Every work thereby becomes the allegory—Hölderlin speaks of a *fortgesetzte Metapher* or extended metaphor—of what it cannot say directly and naturally if it is to remain the kind of work it is.[12] However, in the present context the complexity of the theory of tonal modulations is less important than the deep awareness expressed in this letter of Hölderlin's need to feel empowered and entitled to explore the heterogeneity, the impurity, of the material, historical world. Hölderlin seems also to be aware that such an entitlement can only come about by way of disturbing a compulsive and, as it were, pedantic intimacy that had heretofore governed his various "object relations." Hölderlin's mature years, right up to the final psychotic breakdown, were dedicated to the search for such empowering disturbances and strategies by which he might integrate them into his psychological makeup and poetic practice. And as the later hymns and fragments bear witness, the most important site of this homeopathic procedure, that is, these efforts to institute a properly dosed-out disturbance of an all too inward communion with the other, was in the relationship to the gods.

2

Perhaps the most poignant evocation of the task of establishing a proper measure of distance and difference vis-à-vis the sacred element is the early hymnic fragment "As On A Holiday. . . ." Here the poet's efforts end in failure. The hymnic voice is shattered at the very moment the poet insists on his capacity for full empathic participation in the inner life of the deity:

> The Father's ray, the pure, will not sear our hearts
> And, deeply convulsed, and sharing his sufferings
> Who is stronger than we are, yet in the far-flung
> > down-rushing storms of
> The God, when he draws near, will the heart stand fast.
> But, oh, my shame! when of
>
> My shame!
>
>
> And let me say at once
>
>
> That I approached to see the Heavenly
> And they themselves cast me down, deep down
> Below the living, into the dark cast down
> The false priest that I am, to sing,
> For those who have ears to hear, the warning song.
> There

The final strophe of "The Migration" intones the "warning song" from a somewhat safer distance:

> The handmaids of heaven
> Are miraculous,
> As is everything born of the gods.
> Try taking it by surprise, and it turns
> To a dream; try matching it by force,
> And punishment is the reward. . . .

In "The Rhine," a hymn that perhaps more successfully than any other enacts the modulation of the overstrained transcendental impulse—the refusal to suffer the alterity of the sacred—that for Hölderlin was the mark of all heroic excess, is associated with madness and self-destruction.

> that he shall destroy
> As his enemy, and under the rubble
> Bury his father and his child,
> If he should seek to be like them and not
> Allow inequality, the wild dreamer.

It is finally the gods themselves who contain and divert the "heroic" desire for merging—the desire for unboundedness—so often embodied in Hölderlin's poetry by the surging course of rivers:

> But a god desires to save his sons
> From flitting life, and he smiles
> When without restraint, but hemmed in
> By holy Alps, the rivers
> Rage at him in the depths as this one does.
> In such a furnace then
> All things freed of dross are shaped
> And beauty comes thereafter, when
> Leaving the mountains he meanders
> Quietly through German lands, content,
> And slakes his cravings
> In wholesome commerce, in husbandry,
> Father Rhine, feeding his beloved
> Children in towns that he has founded.

In a later fragment ("Greece"), the self-occultation of the gods is "clothed" in a familiar metaphor, and indeed, a metaphor of metaphor:

> Everyday but marvelous, for the sake of men,
> God has put on a garment.
> And his face is withheld from the knowing
> And covers the winds with art.
> And air and time cover

> The terrible one, so that not too much a man
> With prayers shall love him.

In "Mnemosyne," the failure to preserve this artful covering—the cloak of metaphor—is shown once again to have catastrophic consequences for human beings. This "failure" seems in its turn to be precipitated by a failure on the part of mortals to do their part in maintaining a necessary and mutual "infidelity" of gods and mortals[13]:

> On Kithairon
> Lay Eleutherai, city of Mnemosyne. And when
> God cast off his cloak, the darkness came to cut
> Her lock of hair. For the gods grow
> Indignant if a man
> Not gather himself to save
> His soul.

A somewhat less cryptic poetic performance of a (chastening) dialectic of desire may be found in the earlier ode "Voice of the People." Here it is once again a river's torrential current that stands in for the compulsion to undo the boundaries of individuation, a compulsion that can also overtake entire populations:

> So rivers plunge—not movement, but rest they seek—
> Drawn on, pulled down against their will from
> Boulder to boulder—abandoned, helmless—
>
> By that mysterious yearning toward the chasm;
> Chaotic deeps attract, and whole peoples too
> May come to long for death, and valiant
> Towns that have striven to do the best thing.

As we have seen, it is the gods who must intervene on behalf of mortals and block this self-destructive compulsion to efface difference:

> Yet they, the Heavenly, to men remain well-disposed,
> As we love them so they will return our love

And lest too briefly he enjoy the
Light, will obstruct a man's course to ruin.

And not the eagle's fledgelings alone their sire
Throws out of eyries, knowing that else too long
They'd idle—us the Ruler also
Goads into flight with a prong that's fitting.

Here, as in several of the other poems, one sees that it is in *oedipal*
terms that Hölderlin conceived of the process whereby differences
are instituted between self and other, here and there, now and
then—i.e., those differences that make something like human self-
hood possible and necessary. The process whereby an all too inward
communion with the other is (homeopathically) disrupted so as to
empower one to act in the world—in the "icy history of common
day"—unfolds under the auspices of a third term conceived as
paternal agency. That is, the ability to master the grief over the
taboos that interrupt the circuit of an excessive and, ultimately, self-
destructive desire is facilitated by an identification with the figure in
whose name these taboos were instituted in the first place. The
power to mourn successfully the primal "shock" of oedipal losses
derives, in other words, from the very origin of these losses: the
father, or as Lacan would have it, the Name-of-the-Father, the father
as idealized totemic figure. If successfully integrated, this totemic
metaphor may serve as a source of a soothing consolation, as guar-
antor of equipoise in this and all future experiences of loss, shock,
trauma. More precisely, once it has become an aspect of the self's
own structure, the paternal totem helps to prevent experiences of
loss, frustration, disenchantment, etc., from becoming full-fledged
traumas. To return for a moment to the terms of the discussion of
shock experience, it might be said that the successfully internalized
totem keeps loss or lack from resonating too violently "beyond the
pleasure principle."[14] The search for viable paternal totems will
come to figure in a central way in all of Hölderlin's mature poetic
works. In those visionary hymns and fragments that Hölderlin
referred to as his *vaterländische Gesänge* or patriotic songs and that
have quite rightly come to be seen as Hölderlin's greatest poetic
achievements, the poet's struggle for empowerment becomes more
and more assimilated to the larger task of tracing his literary and

world-historical filiation within the symbolic geography of a vast, greater European landscape.[15] Hölderlin's great hymns strive to establish a place for the Hesperidean or German successors to the cultural position once occupied by the poets and philosophers of Greek antiquity, and the law of this succession is fundamentally that of an oedipally structured, i.e., patriarchal, symbolic order.[16] One of the things that undoubtedly makes Hölderlin's writings so poignant for the modern reader is the fact that this oedipal process of succession—of the transmission of a paternal legacy from culture to culture—breaks down, leaving behind the stammerings of a schizophrenic discourse. Patriotic song proves, in the end, to be insufficient (and, perhaps, to contain too many double binds). The self is left exposed, protected by only the thinnest of membranes, subject to the multifarious shocks of the icy history of common day, the beginnings, perhaps, of what would become our modernity:

> And now
> I wish to sing the journey of the nobles to
> Jerusalem, and anguish wandering at Canossa,
> And Heinrich himself. If only
> My very courage does not expose me. This first we
> Must understand. For like morning air are the names
> Since Christ. Become dreams. Fall on the heart
> Like error, and killing, if one does not
>
> Consider what they are and understand.
> ("Patmos," Fragments of the Later Version)

For better or for worse, it is undoubtedly in the diction and texture of such lyrics that the modern reader recognizes him- or herself most powerfully. One might say that modernity begins where Hölderlin left off, in midsentence as it were. Without the security of ritually sanctioned psychic and social resources that guarantee a modicum of internal cohesion and equipoise for the nomadic passage through this world of names, signs, and differences, one is ever more at risk of losing oneself in the drift: "A sign we are, without meaning / Without pain we are and have nearly / Lost our language in foreign lands" ("Mnemosyne"). But it is, finally, also in the text of Hölderlin that one may perhaps come to sense the possibilities of new modes of discoursing and being, new modes of fortifying the self for its dialogue with the other.

3

This volume contains the full text of the final published version of Hölderlin's epistolary novel *Hyperion* and a representative selection of Hölderlin's mature poetic works: odes and epigrammatic poems, elegies, several of the so-called nightsongs, hymns, and unfinished drafts of hymns. I have also included one of the very late poems written during the long period of schizophrenic withdrawal. Limitations of space have made it impossible to include translations of the drafts of the tragedy "The Death of Empedocles" or any of Hölderlin's theoretical essays and letters, although I have made an effort to include significant passages from the letters in this introduction and in the brief chronicle of Hölderlin's life included in this volume.[17]

Regarding the translations, Willard R. Trask's rendering of *Hyperion* (New York: Frederick Ungar, 1965) has been adapted by David Schwarz with an eye toward preserving the jarring strangeness of Hölderlin's diction so that it strikes the American reader precisely as strange rather than merely foreign or archaic. By bringing linguistic strangeness closer to home, so to speak, it may become all the more uncanny. My choice of translations of poems has been guided in large part by principles taken from Hölderlin's own writings. In a now famous letter to his friend, the author Casimir Ulrich Böhlendorff, Hölderlin discusses the crucial differences between ancient Greek and modern German poetry:

> And I think that clarity of representation is to us originally as natural as the fire from heaven was to the Greeks. Precisely for this reason, they can be *surpassed* in comely passion . . . rather than in that Homeric presence of mind and gift for representing things. . . . It sounds paradoxical. But I say it again and offer it for your reflection and use: a peculiarly native quality becomes less salient as the cultivation of the mind proceeds. Therefore the Greeks are in less degree masters of holy pathos, because it was innate in them, whereas they excel, on the other hand, in the gift for representing things, from Homer onward, because

this extraordinary man had the profundity and greatness of soul to acquire for his Apollinian realm the occidental *Junonian restraint,* and thus truly to make the alien his own. . . . With us the opposite is the case. . . . But what is proper to oneself must be as well learned as what is alien. Therefore the Greeks are indispensable to us. It is simply that we shall not approach them in that which is proper and native to us, because, as I have said, the most difficult thing is the *free* use of what is proper to oneself.[18]

Of the three translators from whose fine work I have made my selections,[19] I would say that Richard Sieburth has tended to draw out more of the sobriety and "Junonian restraint," or to use the terms of Hölderlin's tonal theory, the epic-naive quality that becomes so crucial in the later hymns[20]; Christopher Middleton, on the other hand, has profiled more the ideal and heroic tonalities that Hölderlin associated with the sacred pathos native to the Greeks; finally, Michael Hamburger has tended to take more of a middle ground in this field of linguistic and stylistic tensions, producing what might be considered more "mimetic" renderings of the original. My hope is that this variety of approaches will lead to a deeper engagement with the work of one of the most remarkable poets of the Western tradition.

E. L. S.

Notes

1. Walter Benjamin, "Zwei Gedichte von Friedrich Hölderlin," in *Illuminationen* (Frankfurt a.M.: Suhrkamp, 1980), 21–41.
2. Benjamin discusses shock experience in his essay "On Some Motifs in Baudelaire," in *Illuminations. Essays and Reflections,* trans. Harry Zohn (New York: Schocken, 1969). I have cited English translations whenever possible.
3. Ibid., 162.
4. Ibid., 189.

5. See Benjamin's discussion of Baudelaire's sonnet "Correspondances" in "On Some Motifs," 181–85.

6. Benjamin, "On Some Motifs in Baudelaire," 183; 190.

7. In the context of this discussion, the ostensible discontinuities between modernity and postmodernity are less important than the continuities. For the purposes of this essay I thus include the present historical moment within the "modern."

8. Friedrich Hölderlin, "Judgment and Being," in *Friedrich Hölderlin. Essays and Letters on Theory,* ed. and trans. Thomas Pfau (Albany: SUNY Press, 1988), 37. I have given references for works by Hölderlin only if they are not included in this collection.

9. A provocative discussion of these patterns may be found in Jean Laplanche, *Hölderlin et la question du père* (Paris: Presses Universitaires de France, 1961).

10. Friedrich Hölderlin, "Fragment von Hyperion," in *Sämtliche Werke [Grosse Stuttgarter Ausgabe]*, ed. Friedrich Beissner, Adolf Beck, 7 vols. (Stuttgart: Kohlhammer, Cotta, 1943–77), 3: 170; my translation.

11. Letter to Neuffer, 12 November 1798, trans. Christopher Middleton, in *The Poet's Vocation: Selections from letters of Hölderlin, Rimbaud and Hart Crane,* ed. William Burford, Christopher Middleton (Austin: University of Texas Press, 1962), 15–16.

12. Still the best and most thorough discussion of Hölderlin's theory of tonal modulations is Lawrence Ryan's *Hölderlins Lehre vom Wechsel der Töne* (Stuttgart: W. Kohlhammer, 1960). For a succinct summary of the theory in English, see Theodore Ziolkowski's *The Classical German Elegy. 1795–1950* (Princeton: Princeton University Press, 1980), 119–21.

13. Regarding this notion of theological infidelity, see Hölderlin's notes to his translation of Sophocles' *Oedipus Rex,* "Remarks on 'Oedipus,'" in Pfau, *Friedrich Hölderlin,* 101–8.

14. That Hölderlin was deeply engaged in this task of modulating the resonances of the negative, of preventing the experience of unpleasure from destabilizing and fragmenting his self-cohesion—his sense of continuity with himself—is very clearly documented in a letter written to his half brother Karl Gok. Here Hölderlin expresses an awareness that he is as yet unable to experience *lack* in a delimited manner. Any particular experience of lack resonates for him uncontrollably, flooding out all other feeling and leaving him unable to imagine less than global strategies of reparation and recuperation: "and when I have reached that point where I have mastered the capacity to see and to feel in what

is in some way deficient the particular, momentary, specific lack it exhibits (and thus coming to appreciate the particular beauty and virtue of what is superior), rather than suffer the indefinite pain and general malaise I so often fall into when faced with something wanting—when I have mastered this, then my spirit will be calmer and my activity will attain a steadier progression. For when our experience of lack is without limits, we are naturally disposed to want to undo this lack in an absolute and total way, and in such cases our strength gets used up in a fruitless and exhausting struggle without direction, because we cannot see where the particular deficiency is and how precisely this lack might be corrected and rectified" (Letter of 4 June 1799; my translation).

15. Regarding this process of textual empowerment as it figures in the mourning-work that constitutes the self, Julia Kristeva has remarked: "We would follow the hypothesis according to which the infant prompted by separation . . . produces or utilizes objects or vocalizations that are the symbolic equivalents of that lacking. . . . Subsequently, and from the so-called depressive position, he tries to signify the sorrow that submerges him by producing in his own ego elements that, while alien to the exterior world, are to correspond to that lost or displaced exteriority. . . . We shall add . . . that such a triumph over sorrow is rendered possible by the ego's capacity to identify now no longer with the lost object but with a third instance: father, form, schema. . . . [T]his identification, that may be called phallic or symbolic, assures the subject's entry into the universe of signs and of creation. . . . Later, that essential moment in the symbol's formation . . . can, in the entirely different circumstances of, for example, literary creation, manifest itself by the constitution of a symbolic filiation (hence the recourse to proper names arising out of the subject's real or imaginary history, of which the subject presents himself as the inheritor or equal)" (Julia Kristeva, "The melancholic imaginary," in *Discourse in Psychoanalysis and Literature,* ed. Shlomith Rimmon-Kenan [London: Methuen, 1987], 109).

16. Here see once more the sixth strophe of "The Rhine" quoted above, where in the course of fourteen lines the raging river-youth accedes to the position of *Father* Rhine by way of a certain oedipal chastening. And as the so-called Frankfurt Plan of Hölderlin's unfinished Empedocles tragedy suggests, the refusal or failure to subject oneself to the patriarchal law of succession—to undergo, as it were, symbolic castration—may go hand-in-hand with a disavowal of a more generally conceived "law of succession," namely the temporality of linear time,

the noncoincidence of "now" and "then": "Empedocles, through his temperament and philosophy already filled with a hatred for culture, with a contempt for all particular affairs, all interests oriented toward particular objects, a sworn enemy of all one-sided existence and thus restless, dissatisfied, suffering even in truly pleasant conditions simply because they are particular conditions and are truly fulfilling only when they are felt to participate in a great harmony with all living things; because he cannot live, feel love in these conditions with the depth of a god's omnipresent heart; because as soon as his heart and mind attend to the concrete particular, he is bound by the law of succession" (StA 4,1: 145; my translation).

17. For a translation of the essays and a selection of letters, see Thomas Pfau's *Friedrich Hölderlin: Essays and Letters on Theory* cited above; for translations of other letters relevant to Hölderlin's poetics, see Middleton's *The Poet's Vocation* cited above.

18. Letter of 4 December 1801, trans. Christopher Middleton, in Bruford, Middleton, *The Poet's Vocation.*

19. *Friedrich Hölderlin, Eduard Mörike: Selected Poems,* trans. Christopher Middleton (Chicago: University of Chicago Press, 1972); *Friedrich Hölderlin: Poems and Fragments,* trans. Michael Hamburger (Cambridge: Cambridge University Press, 1980) (I am grateful to Michael Hamburger for sending me corrections of some of the translations taken from this volume); *Hymns and Fragments by Friedrich Hölderlin,* trans. Richard Sieburth (Princeton: Princeton University Press, 1984). With the exception of "Ages of Life," "Mnemosyne" and "The Fruits Are Ripe. . . ," which Sieburth based on D. E. Sattler's reconstructions of the poems in the introductory volume of his *Frankfurter Ausgabe,* all translations were based on the text of the poems in the *Grosse Stuttgarter Ausgabe.*

20. Regarding the increasing predominance of the naive tone in the later works, see Peter Szondi, "Gattungspoetik und Geschichtsphilosophie," in *Schriften I* (Frankfurt a.M.: Suhrkamp, 1978), 367–407, and my own *Friedrich Hölderlin. Narrative Vigilance and the Poetic Imagination* (New Brunswick: Rutgers University Press, 1986).

HYPERION, OR THE HERMIT IN GREECE

Volume One

Non coerceri maximo, contineri minimo, divinum est.

(Not to be confined by the greatest, yet to be contained within the smallest, is divine.)

Preface

I would be glad if I could promise this book the affection of the German people. But I fear that some of them will read it as a treatise and be too greatly concerned with the *fabula docet*, whereas others will take it too lightly, and that neither the former nor the latter will understand it.

He who merely inhales the scent of my plant does not know it, and he who plucks it merely in order to learn from it does not know it either.

The resolution of dissonances in a particular character is neither for mere reflection nor for empty pleasure.

The scene of the events which follow is not new, and I confess that I was once childish enough to try to alter the book in this respect, but I soon became convinced that it was the only scene appropriate to Hyperion's elegiac character and was ashamed that the presumable verdict of the public had rendered me so excessively pliable.

I regret that for the present it is not possible for everyone to judge of the plan of the book. But the second volume will follow as soon as possible.

Book One

Hyperion to Bellarmin

Once again the dear earth of my native country brings me joy and sorrow.

Now every morning I am on the heights of the Corinthian Isthmus; and often, like a bee among flowers, my soul flies back and forth between the seas that, to left and right, cool the feet of my glowing mountains.

One of the two gulfs would have delighted me especially, had I stood here a thousand years ago.

Then, surging on like a conquering demigod between the beautiful wilderness of Helicon and Parnassus where the red dawn plays among a hundred snow-covered peaks, and the paradisal plain of Sicyon, the shining gulf undulated toward the city of joy, youthful Corinth, pouring out the captured wealth of every region before its favorite.

But what is that to me? The cry of the jackal, changing his wild threnody amid the rubble of Antiquity, startles me from my dreams.

Fortunate the man whose native country flourishes to rejoice and strengthen his heart! For me, it is as if I were cast into a swamp, as if the coffin lid were being nailed shut over me, if anyone reminds me of mine, and whenever I hear myself called a Greek, it is as if I were being bound with a dog collar.

And see, my Bellarmin, often when such a remark escaped me, and perhaps anger brought a tear to my eye, too, the knowing gentlemen who so much enjoy raising their voices among you Germans, and for whom a grieving heart makes the perfect opportunity to drag out their old sayings, yes, they were in their element, they presumed to tell me: "Do not complain, act!"

Oh that I had never acted! By how many hopes should I be the richer!—

Yes, only forget that there are men, O famished, beleaguered, infinitely troubled heart! and return to the place from which you came, to the arms of Nature, the changeless, the quiet, the beautiful.

Hyperion to Bellarmin

I have nothing of which I may say that it is mine.

Distant and dead are my loved ones, and no voice brings me news of them anymore.

My business on earth is over. I set to work full of determination, I gave my blood to it, and made the world not a penny the richer.

Unknown and alone, I have returned to wander through my native country, which lies about me like a vast graveyard; and perhaps what awaits me is the knife of the hunter who preserves us Greeks for his sport even as he does the wild beasts of the forest.

Yet still do you shine, Sun of Heaven! Still do you grow green, sacred Earth! Still the rivers roar to the sea, and shady trees rustle under the noon of day. Spring's song of bliss sings my mortal thoughts to sleep. The fullness of the living universe feeds and satisfies my starving being with its intoxication.

O Blessed Nature! I know not how it is with me when I raise my eyes to your beauty, but all the joy of Heaven is in the tears that I weep in your presence, beloved of beloveds!

My whole being falls silent and listens when the delicate swell of the breeze plays over my breast. Often, lost in the wide blue, I look up into the ether and down into the sacred sea, and I feel as if a kindred spirit were opening its arms to me, as if the pain of solitude were dissolved in the life of the Divinity.

To be one with all—this is the life divine, this is man's heaven.

To be one with all that lives, to return in blessed self-forgetfulness into the All of Nature—this is the pinnacle of thoughts and joys, this the sacred mountain peak, the place of eternal rest, where the noonday loses its oppressive heat and the thunder its voice and the boiling sea is as the heaving field of grain.

To be one with all that lives! At those words Virtue puts off her wrathful armor, the mind of man lays its scepter down, and all thoughts vanish before the image of the world in its eternal oneness, even as the striving artist's rules vanish before his Urania, and iron Fate renounces her dominion, and Death vanishes from the confederacy of beings, and indivisibility and eternal youth bless and beautify the world.

On this height I often stand, my Bellarmin! But an instant of reflection hurls me down. I reflect, and find myself as I was before—alone, with all the griefs of mortality, and my heart's refuge, the world in its eternal oneness, is gone; Nature closes her arms, and I stand like an alien before her and do not understand her.

O! had I never gone to your schools! The knowledge which I pursued down its tunnels and galleries, from which, in my youthful folly, I expected confirmation of all my pure joy—that knowledge has corrupted everything for me.

Among you I became so truly reasonable, learned so thoroughly to distinguish myself from what surrounds me, that now I am solitary in the beautiful world, an outcast from the garden of Nature, in which I grew and flowered, and am drying up under the noonday sun.

Oh, man is a god when he dreams, a beggar when he thinks; and when inspiration is gone, he stands, like a worthless son whom his father has driven out of the house, and stares at the miserable pennies that pity has given him for the road.

Hyperion to Bellarmin

I thank you for asking me to tell you of myself, for making me remember earlier days.

What sent me back to Greece was wishing to live nearer to the places where I had played in my youth.

As the laborer into refreshing sleep, so my beleaguered being often sinks into the arms of the innocent past.

Peace of childhood! heavenly peace! how often do I pause before you in loving contemplation, and try to conceive of you! But our concepts are only of what has degenerated and been repaired; of childhood, of innocence we have no concept.

When I was still a child and at peace, knowing nothing of all that is about us, was I not then more than now I am, after all my trouble of heart and all my thinking and struggling?

Yes, divine is the being of the child, so long as it has not been dipped in the chameleon colors of men.

The child is wholly what it is, and that is why it is so beautiful.

The pressure of Law and Fate touches it not; only in the child is freedom.

In the child is peace; it has not yet come to be at odds with itself. Wealth is in the child; it knows not its heart nor the inadequacy of life. It is immortal, for it has not heard of death.

But this men cannot bear. The divine must become like one of them, must learn that they, too, are there; and before Nature drives it out of its paradise, men entice and draw it out into the field of the curse, so that, like them, it shall drudge its life away in the sweat of its brow.

But the time of awakening is beautiful, too, if only we are not awakened unseasonably.

Oh, they are sacred days, in which our heart first tries its wings, in which, bursting with swift, fiery growth, we stand in the glorious world, like the young plant when it opens to the morning sun and stretches its tiny arms toward the infinite sky.

How was I driven then to the mountains, to the seashore! O, how often I sat with throbbing heart on the heights of Tina and watched the falcons and the cranes, and the bold, rejoicing ships as they vanished below the horizon! "There," I thought, "there beyond the horizon you too will one day wander"; and I felt as the man dying of thirst feels when he flings himself into the cooling current and splashes the foaming water over his face.

Sobbing I would turn and go home then. "If only," I often thought, "my school years were over!"

Innocent boy! They are still far from over.

That in his youth a man thinks the goal is so near! It is the most beautiful of all the illusions with which Nature supports the weakness of our being.

And often, when I lay there among the flowers, basking in the delicate spring light, and looked up into the serene blue that embraced the warm earth, when I sat under the elms and willows on the side of the mountain, after a refreshing rain, when the branches were yet astir from the touch of the sky and golden clouds moved over the dripping woods; or when the evening star, breathing the spirit of peace, rose with the age-old youths and the other heroes of the sky, and I saw how the life in them moved on through the ether in eternal, effortless order, and the peace of the world surrounded and rejoiced me, so that I was suddenly alert and listening, yet did not know what was befalling me—"Do you love me, dear Father in Heaven," I whispered, and felt his answer so certainly and so blissfully in my heart.

O you to whom I cried, as if you were above the stars, whom I named Maker of Heaven and Earth, kindly idol of my childhood, do not be angry that I forgot you!—Why is the world not poor enough to make us seek Another outside of it?*

Oh, if glorious Nature is the daughter of a Father, is not the daughter's heart his heart? Her inmost being, is it not He? But then, do I possess it? do I know it?

It is as if I saw, but afterward I am filled with fear again, as if what I saw had been my own shape; it is as if I felt it, the Spirit of the World, like a friend's warm hand, but I awake and realize that I was holding my own finger.

Hyperion to Bellarmin

Do you know how Plato and his Stella loved each other?

So I loved, so was I loved. Oh, I was a fortunate boy!

It is pleasant when like and like meet in friendship; but it is divine when a great man draws lesser men up to him.

A gracious word from a valiant heart, a smile under which the searing glory of the spirit hides itself, is little and is much, is like a magical password that conceals death and life in its simple syllable, is like living water that comes welling from the inmost recesses of the

---

*It is scarcely necessary to say that no one can justly take offense at such expressions, which are no more than manifestations of a state of mind. (Hölderlin's note.)

mountains, imparting the secret strength of the earth to us in each of its crystal drops.

How I hate all the barbarians who imagine that they are wise because there is no more heart left in them! all the self-important monstrosities who slay and desecrate beautiful youth a thousand times over with their petty, meaningless discipline!

God in heaven! this is owls undertaking to drive eaglets from the nest and show them the way to the sun!

Forgive me, spirit of my Adamas, for mentioning these creatures before I speak of you. That is all the profit that we gain from experience—to be able to think of nothing excellent without thinking of its distorted opposite.

Oh! if only you were ever before me, with all that is akin to you, grieving demigod of whom I fondly think! He whom you, O warrior and champion, enfold in your stillness and strength, he whom you encounter with your love and wisdom—let him either run away or become like you! Meanness and weakness cannot survive beside you.

How often you were close to me when you were far from me and long had been, how often you illumined me with your light, warmed me so that my numbed heart moved again, like the frozen spring when heaven's ray touches it! Oh, how I wished I could flee to the stars with my happiness, that it might not be debased by what was around me!

I had grown up like a grapevine without a prop, and the wild shoots trailed aimlessly over the ground. You know how many a noble power perishes in us because it is unused. I wandered like a will-o'-the-wisp, caught at everything, was caught by everything, but only for a moment, and my unskilled powers wore themselves out for nothing. I felt that I was missing something everywhere, yet I could not find my goal. Such was I when he found me.

He had long applied all his patience and his art to his material, the so-called cultivated world; but his material had been and had remained stone and wood, even if under compulsion it outwardly assumed the noble form of man; but that meant nothing to my Adamas. He wanted men, and he had found his art too poor to create them. Once upon a time they had existed, those whom he sought, those whom his art was too poor to create—this he knew for a certainty. Where they had existed he also knew. He resolved to go there and search under the rubble for their genius and thus to occupy his lonely days. He came to Greece. Such he was when I found him.

I still see him come walking toward me, looking at me and smiling; I still hear his greeting and his questions.

As a man stands before a plant whose peace soothes his struggling spirit, and simple content returns to his soul—so he stood before me.

And I—was I not the echo of his quiet inspiration? did not the melodies of his being repeat themselves in me? What I saw, I became; and what I saw was divine.

How ineffectual is the best-intentioned diligence of men compared with the power of pure inspiration!

It does not stop at the surface, does not take hold of us here or there, needs no time and no means, has no use for command and coercion and persuasion; from all sides, at every level of depth and height, it seizes us instantly, and before we know it is there, before we can ask what is befalling us, it transforms us through and through, in all its beauty and bliss.

Well for him whom a noble spirit has thus encountered in early youth!

Oh, those are golden, unforgettable days, filled with the joys of love and sweet activity!

Soon Adamas led me, now into Plutarch's world of heroes, now into the magical land of the Greek gods; now he quieted my youthful impatience with arithmetic and geometry, now he climbed among the mountains with me—by day for field flowers and woodland flowers and the wild moss that grows on cliffs, by night that we might gaze at the sacred stars above us, and understand them as men may.

There is a precious sense of well-being in us when our inner life thus draws strength from what is its material, differentiates itself, and establishes truer inner relationships, and our mind gradually comes of age to bear arms.

But with threefold force did I feel him and myself when, like shades from a time long past, in pride and joy, in rage and grief, we climbed Mount Athos and from there sailed across to the Hellespont, then down to the shores of Rhodes and the mountain gorges of Taenarum, through all the quiet islands; when longing drove us from the coasts inland to the somber heart of ancient Peloponnesus, to the lonely banks of the Eurotas (ah! the valleys, lifeless now, of Elis and Nemea and Olympia!); when, leaning against a pillar of the temple of the forgotten Jupiter, with oleander and periwinkle all around us, we gazed into the wild riverbed, and the life of spring and the ever-young sun bade us think that once man was there and now is gone, that man's glorious nature, if it remains there at all, remains but like a shattered fragment of a temple, or only in memory, like the image of one dead—and there I sat, playing sadly beside him, scraping the moss from a demigod's pedestal, digging a marble hero's shoulder out of the rubble, cutting the brambles and heather from the half-buried architraves, while my Adamas sketched the landscape that embraced the ruin, kindly and comforting: the wheat-covered hillock, the olive trees, the flock of goats hanging from the mountain's cliffs, the forest of elms dropping down from the peaks to the valley; and the lizard played at our feet and the flies buzzed about us in the silence of noon—Dear Bellarmin, I want to tell you of it all, point by point like Nestor; I move through the past like a gleaner over the stubblefield when the landowner has harvested; he gathers up every straw. And when I stood beside him on the heights of Delos, what a day it was that dawned for me as I climbed the ancient marble steps with him up the granite wall of Cynthus. Here once the Sun God lived, amid the divine festivals at which all Greece shone round him like a sky of golden clouds. Here the youth of Hellas plunged into full tides of joy and exaltation, as Achilles plunged into Styx, and came forth invincible as the demigod. In the groves, in the temples, their souls awoke and echoed musically in one another, and every youth faithfully guarded the treasure of that enchanting harmony.

But why do I speak of this? As if we still have even an inkling of those days! Oh, not even a beautiful dream can flourish under the curse that weighs upon us! Over the flowers of our spirit the present blows like a howling north-wind, blasting them even in the bud. And yet it was a golden day that wrapped me there on Cynthus! It was still gray dawn when we stood on the summit. Now he rose, the ancient Sun God, in his eternal youth; at peace and effortlessly as ever, the immortal Titan soared up with the thousand joys that are his, and smiled down on his devastated country, on his temples, his pillars, which fate had thrown down before him like withered rose petals that a child heedlessly tore from the branch as it passed and scattered over the ground.

"Be you like him!" Adamas cried, and grasped my hand and held it up toward the god; and it seemed to me that the winds of morning bore us along with them in the train of the divine being who now, in all his kindness and greatness, rose to the summit of the heavens, and in splendor filled the world and us with his spirit and his power.

My inmost heart still mourns and rejoices over every word that Adamas spoke to me then, and I cannot understand how I can feel destitute, when I often feel as he must then have felt. What is loss, when a man finds himself in his own world? In us is all. Why should a man be miserable if a hair falls from his head? Why does he struggle so fiercely for servitude, when he could be a god? "You will be lonely, dear child!" This, too, Adamas said to me then. "You will be like the crane whose brothers leave him behind in the harsh time of the year, while they go to seek spring in a far country!"

And there it is, dear friend! It is this that makes us poor among all wealth, that we cannot be alone, that, so long as we live, love does not perish in us. Give me my Adamas again, and come with all who are akin to me, that the old, beautiful world may be renewed among us, that we may join together and be one in the arms of our divinity, Nature—and lo! I shall know nothing of lack.

But let no one tell me that Fate parts us! It is we, we ourselves! we delight in flinging ourselves into the night of the unknown, into the cold strangeness of any other world and, if we could, we would leave the realm of the sun and rush headlong beyond the comet's track. Ah! for a man's wild heart no home is possible; and as the sun's ray shrivels the very plants of earth that it has brought to bloom, so man kills the sweet flowers that flourish in his heart, the joys of kinship and love.

I seem to be chiding my Adamas for forsaking me, but I am not. Oh, he meant to come back!

A people of rare capacity is said to be hidden somewhere in the depths of Asia; there his hope drove him.

I went with him as far as Nio. Those were bitter days. I have learned to bear pain, but I have no strength for such a parting.

With every moment that brought the last hour nearer, it became more apparent how deeply this man was woven into the very texture of my being. As one dying clings to his fleeing breath, so did my soul cling to him.

A few more days we passed at Homer's grave, and Nio became the most sacred of islands to me.

Finally we tore ourselves away. My heart had struggled until it was exhausted. I was calmer at the last moment. I knelt before him, embraced him for the last time with these arms. "Give me a blessing, my father," I cried softly up to him, and he smiled; there was greatness in his smile, his brow widened in the light of the morning stars, his eye pierced the depths of the heavens—"Guard him for me," he cried, "you spirits of a better age! and draw him up to your immortality; and all you kindly powers of Earth and Heaven, be with him!"

"There is a god in us," he added more quietly, "who guides destiny as if it were a river of water, and all things are his element. Above all else, may he be with you!"

So we parted. Farewell my Bellarmin!

Hyperion to Bellarmin

How could I escape from myself, if I had not the sweet days of my youth?

Like a shade that finds no rest by Acheron, I return to the forsaken scenes of my life. All things age and are rejuvenated. Why are we excepted from this beautiful circling of Nature? Or does it rule us, too?

I should believe so, were it not for *one* trait that is in us—the gigantic striving to be all things, which, like Aetna's Titan, rages up from the depths of our being.

And yet, who would not rather feel it within him, like seething oil, than acknowledge that he was born for the whip and the yoke? A raging battlehorse, or a workhorse with hanging ears—which is the nobler?

Dear friend! there was a time when my heart, too, basked under the sun of great hopes, when the joy of immortality pulsed in my every vein, when I roved among beautiful projects as through the half light of a vast forest, when, happy as the fish in the sea in my boundless future, I pressed on, farther, ever farther.

How boldly, blessed Nature! did the youth leap from your cradle! how he rejoiced in his untried weapons! His bow was drawn, his arrows rattled in the quiver, and the immortals, the high spirits of Antiquity, led him on, and his Adamas was among them.

Wherever I went, wherever I stopped, their glorious presences were with me; in my thought the high deeds of all the ages were mingled together, and as those gigantic forms, the clouds of heaven, united in *one* exultant storm, so the hundredfold victories of the Olympiads were united in me, so did they become *one* never-ending victory.

Who can abide it, whom does it not lay low, as a hurricane lays low young woods, when the terrifying splendor of Antiquity seizes him as it seized me, when, as for me, the surroundings are lacking in which he might gain a strengthening self-reliance?

Oh, as for me, the greatness of the ancients bowed my head like a storm, swept the bloom from my face, and often I lay where no eye saw me, weeping a thousand tears, as a fallen fir tree lies by a stream and hides its faded crown in the water. How gladly would I have paid with blood for one moment from the life of a great man!

But what use was that? No one wanted me!

Oh, it is pitiful to see oneself so reduced to nothing; and let him who does not understand this ask no more but give thanks to Nature who made him, like the butterflies, for joy; let him go and never in his lifetime speak again of pain and unhappiness.

I loved my heroes as a moth loves the light; I sought their perilous presence, and fled, and sought it again.

As a bleeding stag plunges into the stream, so I often plunged into the whirlpool of pleasures, to cool my burning breast and bathe away the raging, glorious dreams of fame and greatness, but what use was that?

And when, as often toward midnight, my empassioned heart drove me down into the garden under the dewy trees, and the lullaby of the fountain and the sweet air and the moonlight soothed my thoughts, and the silver clouds moved in such freedom and peace above me, and from far away the fading voice of the sea came faintly, how graciously then did all the great phantoms that it loved play with my heart!

"Farewell, you heavenly spirits!" I often said in thought, when above me the melody of the dawn's light began softly sounding. "You glorious dead, farewell! Would that I could follow you, would that I could cast off all that my century has given me, and make my way into the freer realm of the shades!"

But I languish on the chain and snatch with bitter joy the miserly bowl that is offered to my thirst.

* * *

Hyperion to Bellarmin

My island had become too cramped for me, now that Adamas was gone. For years, in fact, Tina had bored me. I wanted to go out into the world.

"Go to Smyrna first," said my father; "master the arts of navigation and war there, learn the speech of cultivated peoples and their political constitutions, their views, their manners and customs, investigate everything, and choose the best!—Go on from there, if you will."

"Learn a little patience, too," my mother added, and I accepted the advice gratefully.

To take the first step beyond the circle of youth is pure enchantment; it is as if I were thinking of my birthday when I think of my departure from Tina. There was a new sun above me, and I enjoyed land and sea and air as if for the first time.

The ardor and activity with which I now pursued my education in Smyrna, and my speedy progress, did not a little to calm my heart, and I remember, too, many a blissful holiday evening from that time. How often I walked under the evergreen trees on the bank of the Meles, by the birthplace of my Homer, and picked an offering of flowers and cast them into the sacred stream! Then in my peaceful dreams I approached the nearby grotto where, they say, the old man sang his Iliad. I found him. Every sound in me was stilled by his presence. I opened his divine poem, and it was as if I had never known it, so differently did it now come to life in me.

I like to remember, too, my wanderings through the countryside around Smyrna. It is a radiant land, and a thousand times I have wished I had wings, that *once* a year I might fly to Asia Minor.

From the plain of Sardis I climbed up the rock cliffs of Tmolus.

I had spent the night in a hospitable hut at the foot of the mountain, among myrtles and the scent of the labdanum-bearing cistus, where in the golden stream of Pactolus the swans played beside me, where an ancient temple of Cybele looked out from the elms into the clear moonlight like a shy ghost. Five lovely pillars mourned over the rubble, and a kingly portal lay fallen at their feet.

Now my path passed upward through a thousand blossoming shrubs. Whispering trees leaned down from the rugged slope, dropping their delicate floss on my head. I had set out with the morning. By noon I reached the summit of the mountain. I stood, looking happily about me, relishing the purer airs of the sky. They were blessed hours.

Like a sea, the countryside from which I had climbed up lay spread before me, youthful, filled with living joy; spring's heavenly, unending play of colors greeted my heart; and, even as the Sun in the heavens found itself again in the thousand changes of light that the Earth sent back to him, so my spirit recognized itself in the fullness of life that was all about it, that beset it from every side.

To the left the stream, an exulting giant, plunged down into the woods from the marble cliff that hung over me, where the eagle played with his fledglings, where the snow-crowned peaks glittered up into the blue ether; to the right storm clouds came rolling over the forests of Sipylus; I did not feel the rushing wind that bore them on, I felt only a faint breeze in my hair; but I heard their thunder as we hear the voice of the future, and I saw their flames, like the distant light of dimly apprehended divinity. I turned southward and walked on. Now there lay before me the whole paradisal countryside through which the Caystrus flows in so many an enchanting meander, as if it could not linger long enough amid the profusion and loveliness that surrounds it. Like the zephyrs, my spirit wandered blissfully from beauty to beauty, from unknown, peaceful villages lying deep at the foot of the mountain, on to where the chain of Messogis was dimly visible.

I came back to Smyrna like a drunken man from a feast. My heart was too full of pleasant things not to impart some of its abundance to mortal existence; Nature had yielded me too happy a treasure of her loveliness for me not to make good the deficiencies of human life with it. My paltry Smyrna clad herself in the colors of my enthusiasm and stood before me like a bride. Her flocking citizens attracted me. The absurdity of their ways amused me like a children's prank; and since by nature I was above their established forms and customs, I played with them all, putting them on and taking them off like carnival costumes.

But what I now found giving some flavor to the insipid fare of daily life was the well-proportioned faces and figures that compassionate Nature still sends, here and there, like stars into our darkness.

What heartfelt pleasure I took in them! With what faith did I read those smiling hieroglyphics! But I had almost the same experience with them that I had had long ago with birches in spring. I had heard of the sap of these trees and was amazed at the thought of what a precious drink their graceful stems must yield. But there was neither strength nor life enough in it.

And, oh! how irredeemably wanting was everything else that I heard and saw!

As I went now here, now there, among these people, it seemed to me that human nature had resolved itself into the multifarious species of the animal kingdom. As everywhere, so here, too, the men were especially demoralized and corrupted.

Some animals howl when they hear music. But my more mannerly humans laughed when the conversation turned to beauty of spirit and virtue of heart. Wolves run away when you strike a light. When these men saw a spark of reason, they turned their backs like thieves.

If ever I happened to say a warm word for ancient Greece, they yawned and said that after all a man had to live in this day and age; and—someone else added sententiously—good taste had not perished from the earth.

And so I saw: one would crack jokes like a sailor, another puffed out his cheeks and delivered old sayings.

Yet another, to demonstrate what an advanced thinker he was, would snap his fingers at Heaven and cry that he had never worried about the birds in the bush, give him birds in the hand! Yet when death was mentioned he would at once clasp his hands, and as the conversation went on, would manage to put in that it was a very dangerous thing that our priests no longer had any influence.

The only people from whom I sometimes profited were the story-tellers, the living gazettes of foreign cities and countries, the speaking peep-boxes in which one can see potentates on chargers and church steeples and markets.

At last I grew weary of wasting myself, of looking for grapes in the desert and flowers on a glacier.

I now lived more determinedly alone, and the sweet spirit of my youth had almost vanished from my heart. The incurable corruption of my century became so apparent to me from so many things that I tell you and do not tell you, and my beautiful faith that I would find my world in *one* soul, that I would embrace my whole kind in one sympathetic being—that, too, was denied me.

Dear friend! What would life be without hope? A spark that leaps from coal and goes out, a blast of wind in the dreary time of the year, heard for a moment and then still forever—would it be so with us?

Even the swallow seeks a more hospitable country in winter, the wild beasts run here and there in the heat of the day, their eyes search for the stream. Who tells the babe that its mother will not deny it the breast? And yet it seeks for it!

Nothing would live if it did not hope. My heart now shut away its treasures, but only to keep them safe for a better time, for the unique, the sacred revelation of fidelity that surely, at some epoch of my existence, would come to my thirsting soul.

How blissfully I often clung to it when, in hours of veiled anticipation, it played about me softly as moonlight, soothing my brow. Even then I knew you; even then, maiden, you looked down at me from the clouds like a Genius—you who in time to come rose before me out of the turbid sea of the world in all the peace of beauty! Then this heart struggled and burned no more.

As a lily sways in newly stilled air, so my being moved in its element, in my ravishing dreams of her.

Hyperion to Bellarmin

Smyrna had lost all attraction for me now. Altogether, my heart had grown gradually wearier. At moments, to be sure, the wish could still take me to travel through the world, or to turn soldier and fight in some war, or to find my Adamas and burn my discontent to ashes in his fire; but that was as far as it ever went, and my meaningless, parched life refused to be renewed.

Soon summer was over; I already anticipated the sullen days of rain, and the whistling winds, and the roar of storm-swollen streams, and Nature, which had surged up into every plant and tree like a foaming fountain, now stood before my darkened apprehension fading and closed and turned in upon itself, just as I was.

Yet I wanted to take with me what I could of all this fleeting life; everything outward to which I had become attached, I wanted to preserve within me, for I knew well that the returning year would not find me among these trees and mountains, so now I walked and rode more than ever before through the countryside.

But what most impelled me to go out was my secret longing to see a man whom for some little time I had come upon every day when I passed under the trees outside the city gate.

Like a young Titan, this noble stranger strode resplendent among that race of dwarfs, who fed upon his beauty in joyous dread, measured his tall stature and his strength, and with covert glances regaled themselves on the Roman majesty of his shining face, as upon forbidden fruit. And it was a glorious moment each time that this man's eye, for whose glance the ether seemed too narrow, put off all pride and searched until, with an effort, it found its way to mine and, blushing, we gazed at each other and passed on.

One day I had ridden deep into the forest on Mount Mimas and did not start back until late in the evening. I had dismounted and was leading my horse down a steep, wild path, over roots and stones. As I was thus making my way through the underbrush into the gulf that now opened before me, a pair of Karaborniote robbers suddenly fell on me, and for a moment it was hard to fight off the two drawn sabers; but they were already tired from other work, so I managed. I quietly mounted my horse again and rode on.

At the foot of the mountain, between woods and soaring cliffs, a little meadow opened before me. It grew light. The moon had just risen over the dark trees. Some distance away I saw horses lying stretched out and men beside them on the grass.

"Who are you?" I cried.

"That is Hyperion!" cried a voice that rang like a hero's, in happy surprise. "You know me," the voice continued; "I see you every day under the trees outside the city gate."

My horse flew to him like an arrow. The moon shone bright on his face. I recognized him; I sprang to the ground.

"Good evening!" he cried, charming in his youthful vigor, and looked at me with his wild eyes subdued to tenderness, while his sinewy hand grasped mine so that the touch of it penetrated to my inmost being.

Oh! now my meaningless life was at an end!

Alabanda (such was the stranger's name) now told me that he and his servant had been set upon by robbers, that the two I had come upon had been sent about their business by him, that he had missed the path out of the woods, and so had been obliged to stay where he was until I arrived. "It has cost me a friend," he added, and pointed to his dead horse.

I turned mine over to his servant, and he and I set out together on foot.

"It served us right," I began, as, arm in arm, we made our way out of the wood; "why did we hesitate so long and pass each other by, until misfortune brought us together?"

"But it was you, I must tell you," answered Alabanda, "who were most to blame; you were the colder. I rode after you today."

"Noble youth!" I cried, "wait and see! You shall never surpass me in love!"

We became ever more intimate and happier together.

Near to the city we passed a well-built caravansary, set peacefully among murmuring brooks and fruit trees and sweet-scented meadows.

We decided to spend the night there. For a long time we sat on together by the open window. The high silence of spirit enveloped us. Earth and ocean were blissfully silent, like the stars that hung above us. It was much if even a breeze flitted into the room from the sea and played delicately with the candle, or if the stronger tones of more distant music penetrated to us, while the thunderclouds lulled themselves to sleep in the bed of the ether, now and again to sound distantly, as a sleeping giant breathes more heavily in his dreaded dreams.

Our souls were impelled toward each other all the more strongly because they had come together against our will. We met like two brooks that, pouring from a mountain, throw off their burden of earth and stone and rotten wood and the whole sluggish chaos that holds them back, determined to clear the way to each other, to burst through until, clasping and clasped with equal force, they set out, mingled in *one* majestic stream, on their long journey to the sea.

He, driven by fate and human barbarity from his own home to wander among strangers, embittered and unguided from early youth, and yet with his inmost heart full of love, full of longing to break out of the coarse husk and win through into a congenial element; I, already so profoundly cut off from everything, so utterly and determinedly a stranger and alone among men, with the most precious melody of my heart so absurdly accompanied by all the world's tinkling bells; I, the scorn and aversion of all the lame and the blind, and yet in my own judgment only too lame and blind, so intolerably burdensome to myself by everything in me that was even distantly akin to worldly wisdom and pseudo-reason, to the barbarians and the would-be wits—and so full of hope, so single-mindedly awaiting but one thing, a more beautiful life—

Was it not inevitable that these two youths should embrace each other in such joyous and impetuous haste?

O my friend and brother-in-arms, my Alabanda! where are you? I almost believe that you have made your way to the unknown land, to rest, have become again what once we were as children.

Sometimes, when a storm passes over me, dispensing its divine powers among woods and sown fields alike, or when the waves of the sea play together, or a choral train of eagles soars about the mountain peaks among which I am wandering, my heart can stir as if my Alabanda were not far away. But more visibly, more presently, more unmistakably does he live in me—the whole man—as once he stood, stern and aglow and terrible, denouncing the sins of this century. How my spirit awoke in its depths! how the thundering words of implacable justice rolled on my tongue! Like messengers of

Nemesis, our thoughts journeyed over the whole earth, purifying it until no trace of a curse remained.

We summoned the past, too, before our bar of justice, and proud Rome did not cow us with its splendor nor Athens corrupt us with its youthful bloom.

As storms, exulting in their unwearied play, travel on through forests, over mountains, so our souls drove ever forward in colossal projects—not that we effeminately created our world as by a magic spell and, childishly inexperienced, expected no resistance; Alabanda was too intelligent and too brave for that. But even spontaneous enthusiasm is often militant and shrewd.

One day is especially present to me.

We had gone to the country together and were sitting with our arms trustfully around each other in the dark shade of an ever green laurel, looking at our Plato—the passage where he speaks with such wondrous sublimity of aging and rejuvenation, and from time to time we rested, looking out over the mute, leafless landscape, where the sky, playing with clouds and sunlight, was more than ever beautiful among the autumnally sleeping trees.

We then spoke much of Greece as it is today, both of us with bleeding hearts, for the desecrated soil was Alabanda's native country too.

Alabanda was moved to a degree most unusual in him.

"When I see a child," he cried, "and think how shameful and stultifying is the yoke that it will bear, and that it will starve as we do, look for men as we do, search after truth and beauty as we do, will waste away in barren pining because it is alone as we are, that it— O men of this land! take your sons from the cradle and cast them into the river, that at least they will be spared your ignominy!"

"Surely, Alabanda," said I, "surely, it will not always be so."

"What can change it?" he answered. "Our heroes have lost their fame, our wise men their pupils. Great deeds, when there is no people to understand them, are no more than a powerful blow on an unresponsive brow, and high words, when they do not echo in high hearts, are like a dying leaf rustling down onto dung. What are you going to do?"

"I will take a shovel and throw the dung into a pit. A people among whom spirit and greatness no longer engenders any spirit and any greatness has nothing in common with other peoples who are still men, has no more rights, and it is an empty farce, sheer superstition, to go on honoring such will-less corpses as if a Roman heart beat in them. Away with them! The withered, decaying tree shall not stand where it stands, it steals light and air from the young life that is ripening for a new world!"

Alabanda flew to me and embraced me, and his kisses penetrated to my soul. "Companion in the fight!" he cried, "dear brother! oh, now I have a hundred arms!

"I have heard my melody at last," he continued, in a voice that stirred my heart like a battle cry; "it is enough! You have spoken a glorious word, Hyperion. What! shall the god be dependent upon the worm? The god in us, for whose road infinity lies open—shall he stand and wait until the worm crawls out of his way? No! no! We do not ask if you are willing, you slaves and barbarians! You are never willing! Nor will we try to make you better, for that is useless! We will but make certain that you get out of the way of humanity's victorious career! Oh! let someone light a torch for me, that I may burn the weeds from the field, let someone lay me the mine with which I can blow the dull clods from the face of the earth!"

"When possible, we should but gently push them aside," I interrupted.

Alabanda was silent for a while.

"I find my joy in the future," he began again at last, and ardently seized both my hands. "Thank God, I shall come to no common end! To be happy means to be sleepy, in the language of slaves. Happiness! it is as if I had pap and lukewarm water in my mouth when they talk to me of happiness. So vapid and so irredeemable is all for which you slaves give up your laurel crowns, your immortality!

"Oh, holy light, which, moving tirelessly above us, fills all its immense realm with its power and imparts its soul even unto me in the rays that I drink—may your bliss be mine!

"The children of the sun live by their deeds; they live by victory; their own spirit rouses them, and their strength is their joy."

The spirit of this man often laid hold of me with such force that I might well have felt ashamed of being snatched up and carried away like a feather.

"O Heaven and Earth!" I cried, "this is joy!—This is another age, this is no voice from my infantile century, this is not the soil on which the heart of man pants under the oppressor's whip.—Yes! yes! by your glorious soul, O man! you will save my fatherland!"

"So I will," he cried, "or perish."

From that day on we became ever more sacred, ever dearer to each other. A gravity of purpose that was indescribably profound had arisen between us. Each of us lived only in the eternal fundamental tones of his being, and we moved austerely from one great harmony to another. Our life together was filled with glorious sternness and courage.

"Whatever has made you so tongue-tied?" Alabanda once smilingly asked me. "In the tropical regions, nearer the sun," said I, "the birds do not sing either."

But everything is now up, now down in this world, and man, for all his gigantic powers, holds on to nothing. I once saw a child put out its hand to catch the moonlight; but the light went calmly on its way. So do we stand trying to hold back ever-changing Fate.

Oh, that it were possible but to watch it as peacefully and meditatively as we do the circling stars!

The happier one is, the less it takes to destroy one, and such blissful days as Alabanda and I were living are like a steep cliff where your traveling companion has but to touch you to fling you involuntarily down over the jagged edge into the lightless depths.

We had made a glorious voyage to Chios, had found a thousand joys in each other. Like breezes over the plain of the sea, the kindly enchantment of Nature had played about us. We looked at each other in happy surprise, without speaking, but our eyes said: I have never seen you like this. So gloriously transfigured were we by the powers of Earth and Heaven.

We had argued, too, gaily and ardently, over many things during the voyage; as so often before, I had taken the most heartfelt delight in watching that spirit on its bold, erratic course, following its path in such unconstrained gladness still for the most part so unfalteringly.

No sooner had we landed than we hastened to be alone.

"You cannot persuade anyone," I cried with fondest love; "you convince men, you win them over, before you begin. When you speak, none can doubt; and he who does not doubt is not persuaded."

"Proud flatterer!" he cried in answer. "You lie! But you have given me a timely reminder. Only too often have you made me forsake reason! Nor for the world and all its crowns would I be freed of you, but it often troubles me that you are so indispensable to me, that I am so bound to you. And since," he continued, "you possess me so entirely, it is time that you knew me entirely! Amid all these splendors and all our joys, we have not thought of looking back at the past."

And he told me the story of his life; I felt as if I were watching a young Hercules battling with Megaera.

"Now will you forgive me," he ended the tale of his adversities, "will you take it more calmly if I am often harsh and offensive and intolerable?"

"Be silent, silent!" I cried, moved to the depths; "it is wonder enough that you are still here, that you kept yourself alive for me!"

"Yes, for you!" he cried, "and it rejoices my heart that I am still a palatable dish for you. And if I sometimes taste like a crab apple to you, squeeze me in the press until I am fit to drink."

"Let me be! let me be!" I cried; I strove in vain, the man turned me into a child, and I could not hide it from him; he saw my tears, and woe to him if he had not the right to see them!

"We are rioting in pleasures," Alabanda began again; "we are wasting time in drunkenness."

"We are celebrating our betrothal," I cried gaily, "it is only right that it should sound as if we were in Arcadia.—But to return to what we were talking of earlier!

"You accord the state far too much power. It must not demand what it cannot extort. But what love gives, and spirit, cannot be extorted. Let the state leave that alone, or we will take its laws and whip them into the pillory! By Heaven! he knows not what his sin is who would make the state a school of morals. The state has always been made a hell by man's wanting to make it his heaven.

"The state is the coarse husk around the seed of life, and nothing more. It is the wall around the garden of human fruits and flowers.

"But is the wall around the garden of any help when the soil lies parched? Only the rain from heaven helps then.

"O rain from heaven! O inspiration! you will bring us the springtime of peoples again. The state cannot command your presence. But let it not obstruct you, and you will come, come with your all-conquering ecstasies, will wrap us in golden clouds and carry us up above this mortal world; and we shall marvel and wonder if this is still we, we who in our poverty asked the stars if a spring bloomed for us among them.—Do you ask me when this will be? It will be when the darling of Time, the youngest, loveliest daughter of Time, the new Church, will arise out of these polluted, antiquated forms, when the awakened feeling of the divine will bring man his divinity, man's heart its beautiful youth again, when—I cannot prophesy it, for my eyes are too dim to surmise it, but it will come, that I know for certain. Death is a messenger of life, and that we now lie asleep in our infirmaries testifies that we shall soon awaken to new health. Then, and not till then, shall we exist, then, then will our spirit's element have been found!"

Alabanda was silent and gazed at me for a moment in astonishment. I was carried away by boundless hopes; divine forces bore me on like a summer cloud—

"Come!" I cried and grasped his garment, "come! who can any longer abide in the prison that darkens around us?"

"Come where, my enthusiast?" Alabanda answered drily, and a shadow of mockery seemed to pass over his face.

I was as if fallen from the clouds. "Go!" I said, "you are a small man!"

At that moment some strangers entered the room. They were striking figures, haggard and pale for the most part, so far as I could see by the moonlight, and calm, but there was something in their countenances that pierced the soul like a sword, and it was as if one were standing in the presence of omniscience; one would have doubted that this was the outward form of creatures subject to needs, if here and there slain emotion had not left its traces.

One of them struck me especially. The stillness of his features was the stillness of a battlefield. Wrath and love had raged in this man, and understanding shone over the wreckage of feeling like the eye of a hawk perched upon ruined palaces. Profound contempt was on his lips. One felt that this man was bent upon no insignificant purpose.

Another appeared to owe his calm rather to a natural hardness of heart. He showed almost no trace of violence perpetrated either by his own will or by Fate.

A third seemed rather to have wrested his coldness from life by the force of his conviction, and still to be often at odds with himself; for there was a concealed contradiction in his being, and I thought that he had to keep a tight rein on himself. Of them all, he spoke the least.

As they entered, Alabanda sprang up like bent steel.

"We have been seeking you," one cried.

"You would find me," he said with a laugh, "if I were hidden at the center of the earth. They are my friends," he added, turning to me.

They seemed to scrutinize me with a certain severity.

"He, too, is one of those who would see the world a better place," Alabanda cried after a moment, and pointed to me.

"Are you serious in this?" one of the three asked me.

"It is no joking matter to better the world," said I.

"You have said much in little!" cried one. "You are our man!" added another.

"Are you of the same mind as I?" I asked.

"Ask what we are doing," came the answer.

"And if I asked?"

"We would tell you we are here to purge the earth, that we clear the stones from the field and break up the hard clods with the mattock and draw furrows with the plow, that we grasp the rank growth by the roots, cut it through at the roots, and tear it up by the roots, so that it shall wither in the burning sun."

"Not that we may reap," another interrupted; "the reward of our labors will come too late for us; the harvest will not ripen in our time.

"We are at the evening of our days. We often went wrong, we hoped much and did little. We ventured rather than deliberated. We were eager to have done and trusted to luck. We spoke much of joy and sorrow and loved and hated them both. We played with fate, and fate with us. It tossed us high and low, from beggar's staff to crown. It swung us as one swings a glowing censer, and we glowed until the coals turned to ashes. We have ceased to speak of good and evil fortune. We have grown beyond the midpoint of life, where it is green and warm. But it is not the worst in man that outlives youth. The cold sword is forged from hot metal. They say that grapes grown on burned-out, dead volcanoes yield no bad cider."

"We say this not for our sake," another now cried in more hurried tones, "but for yours! We do not go begging for mens' hearts. For we need neither their hearts nor their wills. For men are in no case against us, since everything is for us, and the fools and the cunning, the simple and the wise, and all the vices and virtues of incivility and good breeding are at our service without hire and blindly help us on toward our goal—we only hope that some might be found to know the joy of it, and so, among our thousand blind helpers, we choose out the best, that we may make them into seeing helpers—but if no one wants to live where we have built, it is neither our fault nor our loss. We did what was for us to do. If no one wants to reap where we plowed, who can blame us for that? Who upbraids the tree when its fruit falls into the mire? I have often said to myself, 'You are sacrificing to decay,' and yet I finished my day's work."

"These are traitors!" the very walls dinned into my sensitive heart. I felt like one suffocating in smoke, breaking open doors and windows to escape—so did I thirst for air and freedom.

They soon saw, too, how uneasy I felt, and broke off. Day was already dawning when I stepped out of the boat where we had been together. I felt the morning breeze like balsam on a burning wound.

I was already too irritated by Alabanda's mockery not to be completely confused by his having these mysterious friends.

"He is evil," I cried, "yes, evil! He feigns unbounded trust, and consorts with such as these—and hides it from you!"

I felt like a girl who learns that her betrothed is secretly living with a whore.

Oh, it was not the grief that one can cherish, that one carries in one's heart like a child, that sings in sleep with the voice of the nightingale!

Like a raging snake that, gliding implacably up legs and loins to coil round every limb, sinks its poisonous fangs now into its victim's chest, now into his back—so it held me in its terrible embrace. I summoned all the courage of my heart to my aid, and struggled for noble thoughts, that I might remain calm; for a few moments I succeeded, but now I had gained strength enough for fury, and now, as if it were arson, I killed every spark of love in me.

"He must," I thought, "yes—for these are his friends—he must be conspiring with them against you! But what did he want with you? What could he have been trying to get from you and your enthusiasm? Oh, had he but gone his way! But these people have a strange desire to take up with their opposite! to have some peculiar animal in their stables suits them to perfection!"—

And yet I had been unspeakably happy with him, had so often sunk into his embraces only to awaken from them with my heart invincible, had so often been hardened and refined in his fire like steel!

On one serene midnight, when I pointed out the Dioscuri to him, Alabanda laid his hand on my heart and said: "These are but stars, Hyperion, by which the name of the heroic brothers is written in the sky; but they are in us, living and true, with their courage and their divine love, and you! you are the son of a God and share your immortality with your mortal Castor!"—

When once I wandered through the forests of Ida with him, and we made our way down into the valley that we might ask the silent grave mounds there to tell us of their dead, and I said to Alabanda that one among them might perhaps belong to the spirit of Achilles and his beloved, and Alabanda confided to me that he was often childish enough to think that we would fall together in *one* battle-torn valley and rest together under *one* tree—who then would have thought what was to come?

I reflected with all the power of thought that remained to me, I accused him, defended him, accused him again all the more bitterly; I struggled against my emotions, determined to be cheerful, and thereby only plunged myself in blackest darkness.

Ah! my eye was already so sore from many blows, was only just beginning to heal—how could it see more healthily now?

Alabanda visited me the next day. My heart boiled when he entered, but I controlled myself, however much his pride and imperturbability agitated and infuriated me.

"The air is glorious," he said at last, "and it will be a very beautiful evening; let us go up to the Acropolis together!"

I accepted. For a long time we said not a word. "What do you want?" I at last asked.

"Can you ask me that?" the tameless youth answered, with a melancholy that pierced my soul. I was stricken, bewildered.

"What am I to think of you?" I began again at last.

"What I am," he answered calmly.

"You must cleanse yourself," I said in a changed voice, and looked at him proudly, "cleanse yourself! absolve yourself!"

That was too much for him.

"How does it happen," he cried indignantly, "that this fellow can twist me as he pleases?—True enough, I was turned out of school too early. I had dragged all chains and I had broken them, only *one* remained, only *one* was still to be snapped, I had not yet been chided by a weathercock of a fellow—stop your muttering, I have kept silent long enough!"

"O Alabanda, Alabanda," I cried.

"Be still," he answered; "and use not my name as a dagger against me."

Now anger raged uncontrolled in me, too. We did not rest until any turning back was well-nigh impossible. We violently destroyed the garden of our love. Often we stopped and stood silent, and oh so gladly, so joyously would we have fallen on each other's necks; but accursed pride stifled every tone of love that rose from our hearts.

"Farewell!" I cried at last, and rushed away. But against my will I looked back, and against his will Alabanda had followed me.

"A strange beggar, is he not, Alabanda?" I cried; "he throws his last penny into the bog!"

"If he does, then let him go hungry!" he cried, and left me.

I staggered away, stupefied. Then I was standing by the sea, gazing at the waves—ah! it was beneath them that my heart longed to be, there beneath them, and my arms flew toward the unfettered tide; but soon, as if from heaven, a gentler spirit came over me and restrained my unruly, sorrowing heart with its peaceable rod; more tranquilly now, I reflected on the course of my life, my belief in the world, my cheerless experiences, I considered men, as I had felt them and known them from my early youth, men of the most various upbringing, and everywhere I found but false notes, muffled or strident; only in the simple confines of the child did I find pure melodies—"It is better," I said to myself, "to become as the bee and build one's house in innocence, than to rule with the masters of the world and howl with them as with wolves, than to dominate peoples and befoul one's hands with that unclean material." I wanted to go back to Tina and live for my gardens and fields.

Smile if you will! I was utterly serious. If the life of the world consists in an alternation between opening and closing, between going forth and returning, why is it not even so with the heart of man?

To be sure, I found this new lesson hard to accept; to be sure, I dreaded turning from the error of my youth—who gladly tears off his wings?—but it had to be so!

I went through with it. I took ship. A fresh wind from the mountains drove me out of the harbor of Smyrna. In a miraculous peace, exactly like a child that knows nothing of the instant to come, I lay in my bark and gazed at the trees and mosques of the city, my eyes traced my green walks along the shore, the path by which I climbed the Acropolis, I saw them and let them go, recede farther and farther; but now, as I came out into the open sea, and everything slowly sank down behind me, like a coffin into a grave, suddenly it was as if my heart had broken—"O Heaven!" I cried, and all the life in me awoke and strove to hold back the fleeing present, but it was gone, gone!

Like a mist it lay before me, the divine land where, like a deer free of the meadow, I had wandered far and wide through valleys and mountains, and brought the echo of my heart to springs and streams, to the distances and depths of the earth.

There inland I had climbed Tmolus in solitary innocence; down there where Ephesus once stood in its happy youth and Teos and Miletus, up there in the sacred, mourning Troad, I had wandered with Alabanda, with Alabanda! and there like a god I had ruled him, and like a tender, confiding child I had obeyed his eye in joy of soul, with the most intense delight in his being, always happy, whether I held his horse for him or, carried above myself, I met his soul in glorious resolves, in daring thoughts, in the fire of eloquence!

And now it was all over, now I was nothing, now I had been so irremediably deprived of everything, had become the poorest of men, and did not myself know how.

"O eternal labyrinth!" I thought, "when will man escape from your chains?"

We speak of our hearts, of our plans, as if they were ours; yet there is a power outside of us that tosses us here and there as it pleases until it lays us in the grave, and of which we know not whence it comes nor where it is bound.

We want to grow upward, and spread wide our branches and twigs, yet soil and weather bring us to whatever is to be, and when the lightning strikes your crown and splits you to the roots, poor tree! what part do you have in it?

So I thought. Are you displeased, my Bellarmin? There is yet more that you must hear.

The sad thing, dear friend, is that our mind so eagerly assumes the posture of our erring heart, so fondly clings to passing grief, that thought, which should heal sorrows, itself sickens, that the gardener, charged with planting rosebushes, so often tears his hand on them—oh! this has made a fool of many a man before others whom, but for this, he would have ruled like an Orpheus, this has so often made the noblest nature a laughingstock to such fellows as can be found in every street, this is the hidden reef for the favored of Heaven—that their love is strong and tender like their spirit, that their hearts are often stirred to motions swifter and more impetuous than the waves that the God of the Sea governs with his trident; and so, my friend, let none be proud!

Hyperion to Bellarmin

Can you listen, will you understand, if I tell you of my long sickness of grief?

Accept me as I present myself, and consider that it is better to die because one has lived than to live because one never lived! Envy not the carefree, the wooden images who want nothing because their souls are so lacking in everything, who do not ask if the sun will shine or the rain fall, because they have nothing to cultivate.

Yes: yes! it is very easy indeed to be happy and at peace, with a shallow heart and a narrow mind. Let them enjoy it; who goes into a passion if the wooden target does not cry when the arrow strikes it, if the empty pot gives such a hollow sound when someone throws it against the wall?

Only, dear people, you must resign yourselves, and hold your tongues and wonder, if you cannot understand that others are not so happy as you are nor so self-satisfied; you must beware of making your wisdom law, for obedience to you would be the end of the world.

I was now living very quietly and unpretentiously in Tina. I really succeeded in letting the shows of the world pass by like mists in autumn, and laughed sometimes too with tears in my eyes—at my heart, when it went flying off to regale itself like the bird that pecks at painted grapes, yet I remained unsoured and unperturbed.

I grudged no one his opinions or his improprieties. I was converted, I no longer wished to convert others; it only saddened me when I saw that people believed that I did not interfere with their clownish behavior because I esteemed it as highly as they did. I was not willing actually to subject myself to their nonsense, but I tried to let it pass wherever I could. "It is all the pleasure they have," I thought, "it is their life!"

Often I was even pleased to join in with them, and yet, however apathetically and unspontaneously I made the effort, not one of them ever noticed, not one of them was aware of any lack in me, and had I asked them to excuse me, they would have stood there wondering and asked: "But what have you done to us?" What forbearance they showed!

Often in the morning when I stood at my window and the busy day began to pour in upon me, I could even forget myself for a moment, I could look about me as if I were going to undertake something in which my being could still find delight, as once it did; but then I would rebuke myself, I would recollect myself like one who inadvertently utters a word of his mother tongue in some country where no one understands it—"Where are you going, my heart?" I enjoined myself prudently, and obeyed.

"What is it for which man so immeasurably longs?" I often asked myself; "what is eternity doing in his breast? Eternity? Where is it? who has ever seen it? Man wants more than he is capable of! that seems to be the truth of it! Oh, you have experienced it often enough! And as it is, so it must be. This it is which bestows the sweet, rapturous sense of power, that our powers do not flow forth as they will; this it is, and nothing else, which creates our fair dreams of immortality and all the enticing, all the colossal phantoms that ravish men a thousand times over; this it is which creates his Elysium and his gods for man, that the line of his life does not run straight, that he does not speed to his goal like an arrow, that a power outside of him stops him in his flight.

"The heat's surging wave would not foam up so beautifully and become spirit, did not the ancient cliff of Fate stand silently opposing it.

"Yet, even so, the impulse dies in our breast, and with it our gods and their heaven.

"The fire leaps up in shapes of joy from the dark cradle in which it slept, and its flame rises and falls, is gone and comes laughing back again, until that on which it fed is consumed; now it smokes and struggles and dies; what remains is ashes.

"So it is with us. This is the heart of all that the wise teach us in forbidding and enticing mysteries.

"And you? why do you concern yourself? That now and again something rises up in you, and in *one* instant, like a dying man's mouth, your heart opens itself to you with such power and closes again—that is precisely the fatal symptom.

"Only be still and let things take their course! Stop devising! Stop childishly trying to add a foot to your height!—It is as if you wanted to create another sun and new creatures for it to nourish, to bring forth an earth and a moon."

So I dreamed on. Patiently, little by little, I took leave of everything.—O you who live in this age with me! seek not counsel of your doctors nor of your priests when your hearts wither away!

You have lost all faith in anything great; you are doomed, then, doomed to perish, unless that faith returns, like a comet from unknown skies.

Hyperion to Bellarmin

There is a forgetting of all existence, a hush of our being, in which we feel as if we had found everything.

There is a hush, a forgetting of all existence, in which we feel as if we had lost everything, a night of our soul, in which no glimmer of any star nor even the fire from a rotting log gives us light.

I had become quiet. No longer did anything drive me from bed at midnight. No longer did I singe myself in my own flame.

Now I looked straight before me, alone and impassive, nor did my eyes roam over the past and the future. No longer now did far and near jostle together in my mind. Unless men forced me I did not see them.

Once this century lay before my mind's eye like the eternally empty cask of the Danaïdes, and my soul poured itself out with prodigal love, to fill the void; now I saw no more void, now the ennui of life no longer oppressed me.

Never now did I say to the flower, "You are my sister," and to the springs, "We are of *one* race." Now, like an echo, I faithfully gave each thing its name.

Like a river past arid banks, where no willow leaf mirrors itself in the water, the world flowed past me untouched by beauty.

Hyperion to Bellarmin

Nothing can grow, nothing so utterly wither away, like man. He often compares his woe with the darkness of the abyss, his bliss with the ether, and how little does that tell of either?

But nothing is more beautiful than when, after a long death, it begins to dawn in him and sorrow goes like a brother to meet distantly dawning joy.

Oh, it was with a heavenly anticipation that I now greeted the returning spring! Like the far music of the beloved's lyre in windless air when all is asleep, so spring's soft melodies sounded about my breast; as if from distant Elysium, so I felt its coming, when the dead twigs stirred and a soft air brushed my cheek.

Lovely sky of Ionia! Never had I so looked to you; but never had my heart been so like you as then in its playful gaiety, its playful tenderness.—

Who does not long for the joys of love and for high deeds when spring returns to the eye of Heaven and the bosom of Earth?

I rose as from a sickbed, quietly and slowly, but my breast trembled so blissfully with secret hopes that I quite forgot to ask what this might mean.

More beautiful dreams now wrapped me when I slept, and when I woke they were in my heart, like the trace of a kiss on the cheek of the beloved. Oh! the morning light and I—we went to meet each other now like newly reconciled friends when they still hold back and yet already bear in their souls the coming, endless moment of their embrace.

Now once again my eye truly opened—not, to be sure, as once it did, armed and filled with strength from within me; it had become more entreating, it begged for life, but in my heart of hearts it was as if I could be again what once I had been, and better.

I looked at men again as if I, too, was to work among them and rejoice with them. I cordially and sincerely committed myself everywhere.

Heavens! what a sight for them to gloat over—the proud nonconformist brought low, become one of themselves! What a joke: the wild deer of the forest driven by hunger to come running into their barnyard!—

Ah! I looked for my Adamas, for my Alabanda, but neither of them appeared to me.

Finally, I even wrote to Smyrna, and, as I wrote, it was as if all the tenderness and all the strength of humanity were concentrated in that *one* moment; three times I wrote thus, but no answer came, I implored, threatened, evoked all our hours of love and courage, but no answer came from him of imperishable memory, from him whom I loved beyond life—"Alabanda!" I cried, "O my Alabanda! you have pronounced my death sentence. You kept me from falling, you were the last hope of my youth! Now I want nothing more, now it is sworn and sealed!"

We pity the dead as if they felt death, yet the dead have peace. But the pain, the pain that no pain equals, is the incessant feeling of utter annihilation when our life loses its meaning, when our heart bids itself "Down! into the depths! there is nothing left of you; you have planted no flower, built no hut, so that you might but say: I leave a trace behind me on earth." Yet, oh! the soul can always be so full of longing, even when it is so cast down!

I still sought for something, but I did not dare to raise my eyes in the presence of men. I went through hours when I feared the laughter of a child.

Yet for the most part I was perfectly quiet and patient, I even had a strangely superstitious belief in the healing power of many things, from a dove that I bought, a row that I took, a valley that the mountains hid from me, from these I could hope for comfort.

Enough! enough! Had I grown up with Themistocles, had I lived among the Scipios, my soul would never have come to know itself in this light.

Hyperion to Bellarmin

At times some energy would even yet waken in my spirit. But only for destruction!

What is man?—so I might begin; how does it happen that the world contains such a thing, which ferments like a chaos or moulders like a rotten tree, and never grows to ripeness? How can Nature tolerate this sour grape among her sweet clusters?

To the plants he says: I, too, was once like you! and to the pure stars: I shall become like you in another world!—meanwhile he falls to pieces and keeps practicing his arts on himself, as if, once it had come apart, he could put a living thing together again like a piece of masonry; but it does not disconcert him if nothing is the better for all his efforts; yet what he does will always be but artifice.

Oh, you wretches who feel all this, who, even as I, cannot allow yourselves to speak of man's being here for a purpose, who, even as I, are so utterly in the clutch of the Nothing that governs us, so profoundly aware that we are born for nothing, that we love a nothing, believe in nothing, work ourselves to death for nothing only that little by little we may pass over into nothing—how can I help it if your knees collapse when you think of it seriously? Many a time have I, too, sunk into these bottomless thoughts, and cried out: Why do you lay the axe to my root, pitiless spirit?—and still I am here.

Oh, once, my brothers in darkness, it was otherwise. Then all was so fair above us, all so fair and joyous before us; our hearts, too, overflowed before the distant, blessed phantoms, our spirits, too, strove upward bold and exulting and broke the barriers—and, when they looked about, alas, there was only endless emptiness.

Oh, I can fall to my knees and wring my hands and pray—but to whom?—for other thoughts. But I cannot overcome it, the scream-ing truth. Have I not twice convinced myself? When I look at life, what is last of all? Nothing. When I arise in spirit, what is highest of all? Nothing.

But be still, my heart! This is your last strength that you are wasting! Your last strength? and you—you would storm heaven? then where are your hundred arms, Titan, where your Pelion and Ossa, your stairway to the city of the Father of the Gods, that you may climb it and throw down the God and his divine banquet and the summit of Olympus, and preach to mortals: Remain below, children of the moment! seek not to reach these heights, for there is nothing here above.

You may well leave off watching what governs others, my heart. Your new knowledge is meant for you. Sure enough, before you and above you there is emptiness and desolation, because there is emp-tiness and desolation within you.

To be sure, if you other men are richer than I am, you might just help a little.

If your garden is so full of flowers, why does not their breath rejoice me too?—If you are so filled with divinity, give me to drink of it. At feasts no one starves, not even the poorest. But only *one* holds his feast among you: that is Death.

Sorrow and Fear and Darkness are your lords. They separate you, they drive you together with blows. You call hunger love, and where you see nothing more, there dwell your gods. Gods and love?

Oh, the poets are right, there is nothing so little and of so little account that man could not know rapture by it.

So I thought. How all this came to be in me, I still do not understand.

Book Two

Hyperion to Bellarmin

I now live on Ajax's island, dear Salamis.

I love all of this Greece. It wears the color of my heart. Wherever you look, a joy lies buried.

And yet there is so much that is delightful, so much that is great, about one.

On the promontory I have built a hut of mastic branches, and planted moss and trees about it, and thyme and every kind of shrub.

There I spend my favorite hours, there I sit evening after long evening, gazing across at Attica, until finally my heart beats too strongly; then I gather up my gear, go down to the bay, and catch fish.

Or, up on my hill, I read of the ancient, magnificent sea fight that once blazed up at Salamis in wild but skillfully controlled confusion, and I rejoice in the mind that could guide and master the fierce chaos of friends and foes as a rider does his horse, and I feel deeply ashamed of my own career as a soldier.

Or I gaze out over the sea and reflect upon my life, its heights and its depths, its bliss and its sorrow, and often my past comes back to me like the sound of a lyre on which the master runs through every tone, blending discord and harmony in obedience to a hidden plan.

Today up here it is especially beautiful. Two gracious days of rain have cooled the air and the weary earth.

The ground has turned greener, the fields are more open. The golden wheat stands endless, mingled with joyful cornflowers, and a thousand hopeful crowns rise from the depth of the grove. Each faint or bold line of the distance is conveyed through space; one behind the other, the mountains rise unbroken to the sun, like a flight of steps. The whole sky is pure. The white light is but breathed over the ether, and like a little silver cloud the shy moon goes floating across the bright day.

Hyperion to Bellarmin

It is long since I have been as now I am.

As Jupiter's eagle listens for the song of the Muses, so I listen for the marvelous, unending euphony in me. Undisturbed in mind and soul, strong and joyous and smilingly serious, I play with Fate and the Three Sisters, the holy Parcae. Full of divine youth, my whole being rejoices over itself, over all things. Like the starry sky, I am calm and moved.

I have waited long for such a holiday time, that I might write to you once again. Now I am strong enough; now let me tell on.

In the midst of my dark days, a friend from Calaurea invited me over to visit him. I must come to his mountains, he insisted; life there was freer than anywhere else, and there, too, amid the pinewoods and the enchanting streams, there were lemon groves and palms and lovely herbage and myrtles and the sacred grape. He had planted a garden high in the mountains and built a house; close-set trees shaded it from behind, and cooling airs played softly about it in the burning days of summer; from it, like a bird from the top of a cedar, one looked down into the low country, over the villages and green hills and peaceful homes of the island, lying like children about the glorious mountain and drawing their nourishment from its foaming brooks.

That roused me a little, even then. It was on a bright, blue April day that I sailed over. The sea was unusually beautiful and pure, the air as light as in higher regions. In the gliding bark we left the earth behind, as one leaves a delicious dish when the sacred wine is handed round.

My dark moods strove in vain against the influence of sea and air. I surrendered myself, cared neither about myself nor others, sought for nothing, thought of nothing, let the boat rock me half asleep, and imagined that I was lying in Charon's bark. Oh, it is sweet so to drink from the cup of oblivion.

My cheerful skipper wanted to strike up a conversation with me, but I was very monosyllabic.

He kept pointing to islands right and left, but I did not look long, and the next minute I was back in my own sweet dreams.

Finally when he pointed out quiet peaks in the distance and said that we should soon reach Calaurea, I became more attentive, and my whole being opened to the marvelous power that, sweet and still and inexplicable, suddenly played upon me. Wide-eyed, astonished and happy, I gazed out into the secrets of the distance, my heart trembled a little, my hand escaped me and hastened to grasp my skipper affectionately.—"What!" I cried, "is that Calaurea?" And as he turned to look at me in surprise, I was myself at a loss what to make of myself.

I greeted my friend with the greatest fondness. My whole being was full of sweet unrest.

That very afternoon I set out to explore part of the island. The woods and secret valleys attracted me indescribably, and the charming day lured everything out.

It was so plain to see that all living things crave more than daily bread, that the bird, too, has its festal banquet, and the beast.

It was enchanting to look at! As when a mother cajolingly asks where her dearest pet has got to, and all her children come rushing to her lap and even the littlest reaches out its arms from the cradle, so every life flew and leaped and struggled out into the divine air, and beetles and swallows and doves and storks circled together in joyous confusion in its depths and heights, and the steps of all that were earthbound became flight, the horse charged over the furrows and the deer over the hedges, the fish came up from the bottom of the sea and leaped over the surface. The motherly air affected the hearts of all, uplifted all and drew them to her.

And men came out of their doors, and wonderfully did they feel the ethereal breeze as it lightly moved the fine hairs over their foreheads, as it cooled the sun's ray, and happily they loosed their garments to receive it upon their chests, and breathed more sweetly, felt more gently touched by the light, cool, soothing sea in which they lived and moved and had their being.

O Sister of the spirit that lives in us and rules us with fiery power, holy Air! how beautiful it is that, no matter where I wander, you accompany me, all-present, immortal one!

It was with the children that the high element played most beautifully.

One hummed happily to himself, a little rhythmless song rose from another's lips, a shout of joy from another's open throat; one stretched, one leaped high; another strolled about, lost to the world.

And all this was the language of a *single* sense of well-being, all was *one* answer to the caresses of the ravishing breezes.

I was filled with indescribable longing and peace. An uncanny power ruled me. Kindly Spirit, I said to myself, where are you calling me? to Elysium, or where?

I went up through a wood, following purling waters as, here, they trickled down a cliff, there glided innocently over pebbles; and little by little the valley grew narrower and became an arcade, and the light of high noon played solitary in the still darkness—

Here—would that I could speak, my Bellarmin! would that I could write to you calmly.

Speak? Oh, I am a novice in joy, I want to speak!

Does not silence dwell in the Land of the Blessed? Above the stars the heart forgets its needs and its language.

I have guarded it sacredly! I have carried it within me like a palladium—the divine that appeared to me! and if henceforth Fate lays hold of me and casts me from abyss to abyss and drowns all powers in me and all thoughts: yet shall this unique revelation outlive myself in me and shine in me and rule me, in eternal, indestructible brightness!—

So did you lie poured out, sweet life, so did you look up, and arise, and stand there before me in delicate completeness, divinely calm, and with your heavenly face filled with the serene ecstasy in which I disturbed you!

Oh, he who has looked into the stillness of those eyes, he for whom those sweet lips have opened—of what else can he speak?

Peace of beauty! divine peace! he whose raging life, whose doubting spirit, has once been soothed by you, what else can avail him?

I cannot speak of her; but there are hours when the best and most beautiful appears as in clouds, and the heaven of crowning perfection opens before the surmise of love; in such a moment, Bellarmin, think of her being, in such a moment go down on your knees with me and think of my bliss! but forget not that I had what you only surmise, that I saw with these eyes what appears to you only as in clouds.

That men will sometimes say they are happy! Oh, believe me, you who speak thus, you have had no faintest inkling of what happiness is! Not the shadow of its shadow has yet appeared to you! O blindmen, depart, and speak not of the blue ether!

That one can become as children are, that still the golden age of innocence returns, the time of peace and freedom, that *one* happiness, *one* place of rest remains upon earth!

Does not man grow old and shrivelled, is he not like a fallen leaf that finds not its branch again and is driven here and there by the winds, until the sand buries it?

And yet his spring returns!

Weep not, when the best fades, it will soon revive! Mourn not, when the melody of your hearts falls silent, soon will a hand be found to tune it again!

How was it with me, then? Was I not like a shattered lyre? I sounded a little still, but they were tones of death. I had sung a mournful swan song for myself! Gladly would I have woven myself a funeral wreath, but I had only winter flowers.

And where, then, was it now—the deathly silence, the darkness and emptiness of my life? all that paltry mortality?

True enough, life is wretched and lonely. We live here below like the diamond in the mine. In vain we ask where we went astray, that we may find the way upward again.

We are like fire that sleeps in the dry branch or in the coal, and ever we struggle and seek for an end to our cramped confinement. But they come, they make up for aeons of struggle, the moments when we are set free, when the divine shatters the prison, when the flame bursts from the wood and flies up over the ashes, ah! when it is with us as if, its sorrows and its servitude forgotten, the unshackled spirit were returning in triumph to the halls of the Sun.

Hyperion to Bellarmin

Once I was happy, Bellarmin! Am I not so still? Should I not be happy even if the sacred moment when first I saw her had been the last?

I have seen it *once*, the one thing that my soul sought, and the perfection that we put somewhere far away above the stars, that we put off until the end of time—I have felt it in its living presence. There it was, all that is highest! in this circle of human nature and of things, it was there!

I no longer ask where it may be; it was in the world, it can return into it, it is in the world now, only more hidden. I no longer ask what it is; I have seen it, have known it.

O you who seek the highest and the best, whether in the depths of knowledge, in the turmoil of action, in the darkness of the past, in the labyrinth of the future, in graves or above the stars! do you know its name? the name of that which is one and is all?

Its name is Beauty.

Did you know what you were looking for? I know it not yet, but I surmise it as from afar, the new kingdom of the new divinity, and I hasten toward it and seize upon others and take them with me, as the river the rivers to the ocean.

And you, you showed me the way! With you I began. They are not worth speech, the days when yet I knew you not—

O Diotima, Diotima, divine being!

Hyperion to Bellarmin

Let us forget that time exists and cease to reckon the days of our lives!

What are centuries compared to the moment when two beings thus divine and approach each other?

I still see the evening when Notara took me to visit her for the first time.

She lived only a few hundred paces from us, at the foot of the mountain.

Her mother was a thoughtful, tender being, her brother a simple, happy lad, and both of them, in all that they did, gladly acknowledged that Diotima was the queen of the household.

Ah, everything was blessed and beautified by her presence. Wherever I looked, whatever I touched, the rug beside her chair, her cushion, her little table—they were all mysteriously allied to her. And, oh, the first time she addressed me by my name, that she came so close to me that her innocent breath touched my listening being!—

We spoke to each other very little. Speech abashes. Music alone would serve: to become all music and united with each other in *one* celestial melody!

And of what were we to speak? We saw nothing but each other. Of that we did not dare to speak.

In the end we spoke of the life of the Earth.

Never has a hymn at once so ardent and so childlike been sung to her.

It did us good to bestrew our kindly Mother's lap with what overbrimmed our hearts. We felt relieved, as the trees do when the summer wind shakes their fruitful branches and pours their sweet apples over the grass.

We called Earth one of the flowers of Heaven, and Heaven the infinite garden of life. As roses gladden one another with golden dust, we said, even so does the heroic sunlight gladden Earth with its rays; she is a glorious living being, we said, alike divine when raging fire or sweet clear water pours from her heart; even happy, whether she be nourished by dewdrops, or by thunderclouds that she prepares for her delight with the sky's aid; she is the ever more faithfully loving mate of the Sun God, perhaps in the beginning more intimately united with him but then divided from him by some all-powerful Fate, so that now she seeks him, approaches him, draws away, and, between joy and sorrow, ripens to the highest beauty.

So we spoke. I give you the gist, the essence of it. But what is that without the life?

Twilight fell, it was time to go. "Good night, you angel eyes!" I thought in my heart. "Appear to me soon again, you beautiful, divine spirit, with your peace and your abundance!"

Hyperion to Bellarmin

Some days later they came up to visit us. We walked about the garden together. Diotima and I found ourselves ahead of the others, absorbed; tears of ecstasy often rose to my eyes for the holiness that walked so unpretentiously beside me.

Now we were standing close to the summit's rim, gazing out into the endless East.

Diotima's eyes opened wide, and softly, as a bud unfolds, that sweet face unfolded under the airs of heaven, became pure speech and soul, and, as if beginning to rise among the clouds, her whole figure stood drawn gracefully up in gentle majesty, her feet scarcely touching the ground.

Oh, could I have caught her under the arms, as the eagle grasps his Ganymede, and flown away with her over the sea and the islands!

Now she stepped yet farther forward, and gazed down the precipitous rock wall. She found a pleasure in gauging the terrifying depths and losing herself in the night of the woods that raised their lustrous crowns from among fallen rocks and foaming, storm-swollen streams.

The balustrade against which she was leaning was rather low. So I dared to hold the charming being a moment, while thus she leaned forward. Ah! hot, trembling rapture coursed through my being, my every sense reeled and was confounded, my hands burned like coals, when I touched her.

And then the profound joy of standing so familiarly beside her, and my tender, childish fear that she might fall, and my delight in the glorious maiden's enthusiasm!

What is all that men have done and thought over thousands of years, compared with *one* moment of love? But in all Nature, too, it is what is nearest to perfection, what is most divinely beautiful! There all stairs lead from the threshold of life. From there we come, to there we go.

Hyperion to Bellarmin

The one thing that I should forget is her singing, only that music from the soul should never return into my unending dreams.

We do not know the proudly sailing swan when it sits asleep on the bank.

Only when she sang could one know the sweet, silent one who was so reluctant to speak.

Only then did that divinely uncomplaisant maiden appear in her majesty and her charm; then, then did her tender, blossoming lips breathe now cajolery and flattery, now the sternness of a divine decree. And what a quickened heart there was in that divine voice, how all pride and all humility, all the joy and sorrow of life appeared beautified in the nobility of those tones!

As the swallow catches bees in flight, so she ever seized us all.

It was not delight, not wonder that arose among us, it was the peace of heaven.

A thousand times have I said it to her and to myself: the most beautiful is also the most sacred. And such was everything in her. Like her singing, even so was her life.

Hyperion to Bellarmin

Her heart was at home among flowers, as if it were one of them.

She named them all by their names, or out of her love for them gave them new and more beautiful ones, she knew exactly which was the happiest season for each of them.

Like a sister when a dear brother or sister comes running to her from every corner, and each would be greeted first, so was her quiet being busy with hand and eye, blissfully distracted, when we walked to the meadows or the woods.

And all this was so utterly unaffected and uncalculated in her, it was so much a part of her own growth.

It is eternally true, it is visible everywhere: the more innocent, the more beautiful a soul is, the more familiarly will it live with those other happy beings to which men deny souls.

Hyperion to Bellarmin

A thousand times in the joy of my heart have I laughed at people who imagine that a noble spirit cannot possibly know how to cook a vegetable. At the proper time Diotima could speak stoutly of the hearth, and surely there is nothing nobler than a noble maiden who tends the all-beneficent flame and, like Nature herself, prepares the food that gladdens the heart.

Hyperion to Bellarmin

What is all the artful knowledge in the world, what is all the proud autonomy of human thought, compared with the unstudied music of this spirit, which knew not what it knew or what it was?

Who would not rather choose the full, fresh grape-cluster as it sprang from the root, than the picked and dried grapes that the merchant presses into a box and sends out into the world? What is the wisdom of a book compared with the wisdom of an angel?

She always seemed to say so little, and said so much.

One late twilight I was taking her home; like dreams, dewy mists were gliding over the fields, the blessed stars looked down through the twigs like watchful spirits.

Rarely was a "How beautiful!" heard from her lips, even though her reverent heart left no whispering leaf, no purling brook unheard and unheeded.

But this time she said it aloud to me: "How beautiful!"

"Perhaps it is so to please us!" I said casually, as children say something, neither in jest nor in earnest.

"I can imagine that it is as you say," she answered; "I like best to think of the world as of life in a household of which each member, without exactly thinking about it, adapts himself to all the others, in which all live pleasing and rejoicing one another simply because that is what springs from their hearts."

"A happy and noble truth!" I cried.

She was silent for a while.

"Then we, too, are children in such a household," I finally resumed; "we are, and shall be."

"Shall ever be," she answered.

"Shall we?" I asked.

"In this," she continued, "I trust Nature, as daily I trust her."

Oh, how I wished that I could have been Diotima as she said this! But you do not know what she said, my Bellarmin! You neither saw it nor heard it.

"You are right," I cried. "Eternal Beauty—Nature—suffers no loss as she suffers no addition. Her ornaments are different tomorrow from what they were today; but she cannot dispense with what is best in us, with us, with us ourselves, and least of all with you. We believe that we are eternal because our souls feel the beauty of Nature. She will be a mere patchwork, she will be neither divine nor complete, if ever you are lacking to her. She does not deserve your heart if she must blush before your hopes."

Hyperion to Bellarmin

Such freedom from wants, such divine content I have never found before.

As the ocean swell about the shores of happy islands, so the peace of the heavenly maiden flowed about my restless heart.

I had nothing to give her except a mind full of wild contradictions, full of bleeding memories, I had nothing to give her except my boundless love with its thousand cares, its thousand furious hopes; but she stood before me in changeless beauty, effortless, in smiling perfection, and all the visions, all the dreams of mortality, ah! all that the Genius presages of higher regions in golden morning hours—it was all fulfilled in that *one* calm soul.

Men say that the battle will die away beyond the stars; only after our lees have sunk, they promise us, will fermenting life be changed into the noble vintage of joy; men look no more on this earth for the heart-whole rest of the blessed. I know otherwise. I have taken the shorter way. I stood before her, and heard and saw the peace of Heaven, and in the very midst of this sighing chaos, Urania appeared to me.

How often have I stilled my grieving before that image! how often have arrogant life and the striving mind been pacified when, sunk in blessed contemplation, I looked into her heart, as one looks into a spring when it trembles silently under the touch of the sky that trickles down on it in drops of silver!

She was my Lethe, her soul my sacred Lethe, from which I drank forgetfulness of existence, so that I stood before her like an immortal and joyously rebuked myself and, as if after oppressive dreams, could not but smile at all the chains that had hung heavy on me.

Oh, I could have become a happy man, an admirable man with her!

With her! But that failed, and now I wander about in what is before me and in me, and beyond, and know not what to make of myself and other things.

My soul is like a fish cast up out of its element on the sand of the beach, and it writhes and flings itself about until it dries up in the heat of the day.

Ah! were there but something left in the world for me to do! were there work for me, a war for me—that would refresh me!

Boys torn from their mother's breasts and cast out into the wilderness were once, so they say, suckled by a she-wolf.

My heart is not so fortunate.

Hyperion to Bellarmin

I can speak only here and there a word about her. I have to forget what she is in her completeness if I am to speak of her at all. I have to trick myself into believing that she lived long, long ago, that I know only a little about her from hearsay, if her living image is not so to overwhelm me that I perish in rapture and woe, if I am not to die of delight in her and die of grief for her.

Hyperion to Bellarmin

It is in vain; I cannot hide it from myself. Wherever I flee with my thoughts, be it up to the heavens or into the abyss, to the beginning and to the end of Time, even if I turn to that which was my last refuge, which consumed every other grief in me, which burned up every other joy and woe of life for me in the flame in which it revealed itself, even if I cast myself into the arms of that glorious, secret Spirit of the World, plunge into its depths as into the boundless ocean—there, even there the sweet terror finds me, the sweet, bewildering, fatal terror, that Diotima's grave is near me.

Do you hear? do you hear? Diotima's grave!

Yet my heart had grown so quiet, and my love was buried with the dead one whom I loved.

You know, my Bellarmin, that for a long time I did not write to you of her, and when I wrote, I wrote to you calmly, or so I think?

So what is it now?

I go down to the shore and look across to Calaurea, where she rests—it is that.

Oh, may no one lend me his boat, may no one have pity on me and offer me his oars and take me across to her!

May the kindly sea not remain calm, that I may not cut myself a piece of wood and swim across to her. But let me plunge into the raging sea and ask its waves to cast me on Diotima's shore!

Dear brother! I comfort my heart with all sorts of imaginings, I pour myself many a sleeping potion; and surely it would be nobler to free oneself forever than to make do with palliatives; but who does not do likewise? So I am content to have it so.

Content! that would be a fine thing! that would be the help that is needed where no god can help.

Now, now! I have done what I could! I call on Fate to give me back my soul.

Hyperion to Bellarmin

Was she not mine, you Sisters of Fate, was she not mine? I summon the pure springs to witness, and the innocent trees that saw and heard us, and the light of day and the ether! was she not mine? at one with me in all the tones of life?

Where is the being that knew her as mine did? In what mirror, as in me, were all the rays of that light concentrated? was she not joyously terrified by her own splendor when first she became conscious of it in my joy? Ah! where is the heart that filled her and was filled by her like mine, that existed only to embrace hers, as the eyelash exists for the eye.

We were but *one* flower, and our souls lived in each other, like the flower when it loves and hides its tender joys in its closed cup.

And yet, and yet, was she not torn from me like a crown usurped, and laid in the dust?

Hyperion to Bellarmin

Before either of us knew it, we belonged to each other.

When, with all the homage of my heart, blissfully conquered, I stood before her, saying nothing, and all my life offered itself up in the gaze of my eyes that saw only her, embraced only her, and she in turn looked at me in tender uncertainty, not knowing where my thoughts had come to rest; when often, absorbed in delight and beauty, I watched her at some charming task, and about her slightest movement, as the bee about the swaying twig, my soul darted and flew, and when then she turned to me in calm thought, and, startled by my joy, had to hide my joy from herself, and sought for peace in her dear task again, and found it—

When in her miraculous omniscience, she caught every harmony, every dissonance in the depths of my being and revealed them to me before I was even aware of them, when she saw every shadow of a cloud on my brow, every shadow of melancholy, of pride, on my lips, every spark in my eyes, when she listened for the ebb and flow of my heart, and sadly foreboded troubled hours as my spirit spent itself too intemperately and prodigally in exuberant speeches, when the dear being showed me every change in my face more faithfully than a mirror, and often in loving concern reproved me for my unstable being and scolded me as one scolds a cherished child—

Ah! when once, innocent being, you counted on your fingers the steps that led down from our mountain to your house, when you showed me your walks, the places where you had often sat, and told me how the hours had passed for you then, and said at last that now it seemed to you as if I had always been there too—

Had we not then long since belonged to each other?

Hyperion to Bellarmin

I dig my heart a grave, that it may rest; I spin a cocoon about myself, because it is winter everywhere; I wrap myself against the storm in blissful memories.

One day we were sitting in Diotima's garden under blossoming almond trees, with Notara (that was the name of the friend in whose house I was living) and a few others who, like ourselves, were among the nonconformists in Calaurea, talking, among other things, about friendship.

I had scarcely joined in the conversation; for some time I had avoided saying much about things that lie closest to the heart, so taciturn had my Diotima made me.—

"When Harmodius and Aristogiton were alive," someone cried at last, "friendship still existed in the world." That pleased me too much for me to remain silent.

"We should twine you a wreath in reward for those words!" I cried. "But have you really any notion, any image, of the friendship between Aristogiton and Harmodius? Forgive me! But, by the

Ether! one must be Aristogiton to have a sense of how Aristogiton loved, and surely he must not fear lightning who would be loved with Harmodius' love, for I am mistaken in everything if the terrible youth did not love with all the sternness of Minos. Few have come off successfully in such a test, and it is no easier to be the friend of a demigod than, like Tantalus, to sit at the table of the gods. But by the same token there is nothing more glorious on earth than when such a proud pair as they are so sovereign over each other.

"This is my hope, too, my longing and my joy in solitary hours, that such noble tones, yes, and nobler, must yet sound again in the symphony of the world's course. Love brought to birth millenniums filled with living men; friendship will give birth to them again. Once upon a time the peoples set forth from the harmony of childhood; the harmony of spirits will be the beginning of another history of man. Men began and grew from the happiness of the plant, grew until they ripened; from that time on they have been in ceaseless ferment, inwardly and outwardly, until now mankind lies there like a Chaos, utterly disintegrated, so that all who can still feel and see are dizzied; but Beauty forsakes the life of men, flees upward into Spirit; the Ideal becomes what Nature was, and even though the tree is dried out and weatherworn below, a fresh crown has still sprung from it and flourishes green in the sunlight as the trunk did once in its days of youth; the Ideal is what Nature was. By this, by this Ideal, this rejuvenated divinity, the few recognize one another and are one, for one thing is in them; and from them, from them, the world's second age begins—I have said enough to make it clear what I think."

You should have seen Diotima then, springing up and giving me both her hands and crying: "I have understood it, beloved, much as it means, understood it all.

"Love bore the world, friendship will bear it again.

"Therefore, O you of the future, you new Dioscuri, therefore linger a little when you pass by the place where Hyperion sleeps, linger in sympathy over the forgotten man's ashes, and say: He would be like one of us, were he here now."

This I heard, my Bellarmin! this was granted to me, and shall I not willingly go to my death?

Yes! yes! I have already had my reward; I have lived. A god could bear more joy, but not I.

Hyperion to Bellarmin

Do you ask how it was with me at that time? As with one who has lost all to gain all.

To be sure, I often came from Diotima's trees like one intoxicated with victory, often I had to hurry away from her lest I betray any of my thoughts; so did joy rage in me, and my pride and my boundless rapture in believing that Diotima loved me.

Then I sought out the highest mountains and their air, and like the eagle whose bleeding pinion has healed, my spirit moved in freedom, spread itself over the visible world as if the world belonged to it; strange to tell, I often felt as if the things of earth were purified and fused together like gold in my fire, and something divine arose from them and me, so did joy rage in me; and oh! how I picked up the children and clasped them to my throbbing heart! how I greeted the plants and the trees! I could have wished that I possessed a spell to gather all the shy deer and the wild birds of the forest like a happy family about my prodigal hands—in such blissful folly did I love all things!

But not for long, and all this was extinguished in me like a light, and speechless and mournful as a shade I sat and sought for the life that had vanished. I felt no wish to complain, no wish to console myself. I cast away hope as a lame man casts away his broken crutch; I was ashamed to weep; I was ashamed to exist. Yet in the end my pride burst out in tears, and the pain that I would have disowned became dear to me, and I took it to my breast like a child.

"No," cried my heart, "no, my Diotima! it does not hurt. Preserve your peace, and let me go my way. Let it not disturb your quietude, pure star! that there is ferment and murk below you.

"Oh, let not your rose fade, blessed springtime of the gods! Let not your beauty age in the trials of earth. This, this is my joy, sweet life! that you bear carefree Heaven within you. You are not made to become a pauper, no, no, you shall not see yourself destitute of love."

And when again I went down to her—I would have liked to ask the breeze and try to divine from the drift of the clouds how it would be with me in an hour! And how happy I was when some friendly face met me on the way and called "A lovely day!" to me not too mechanically.

When a little girl came out of the woods and held out a bunch of strawberries for me to buy, but with a look as if she wanted to give them to me, or when a farmer, sitting in his cherry tree picking as I passed, called down to me from among the branches and asked if I would not like a handful to taste—those were good omens to my superstitious heart!

If one of Diotima's windows stood wide open toward the road by which I came down, what good that did me!

Perhaps she had been looking out of it not long before.

And now I stood before her, breathless and wavering, and pressed my crossed arms against my heart that I might not feel its trembling, and as the swimmer struggles out from the clutching tide, so my spirit strove and struggled not to drown in endless love.

"What shall we talk about, I wonder?" I would cry. "It is often difficult, finding a subject from which one's thoughts will not stray."

"Are they off into the air again?" my Diotima answered. "You must fasten lead to their wings, or I will tie a string to them as a boy does to a kite, so that we shall not lose them."

The dear girl was trying to help us both out by jesting, but it was little use.

"Yes! yes!" I cried, "whatever you say, whatever you think best— shall I read aloud? Your lute is probably still in tune from yesterday and I really have nothing to read—"

"You have more than once promised," she said, "to tell me of your life before we came to know each other—will you not do it now?"

"True," I said; my heart plunged into it eagerly, and I told her, as I have told you, of Adamas and my lonely days in Smyrna, of Alabanda and how I was parted from him, and of the strange sickness that afflicted my being before I came over to Calaurea—"Now you know all," I told her calmly when I had ended, "now you will find me less objectionable; now you will say," I added with a smile, " 'Do not laugh at this Vulcan if he limps, for the gods have twice flung him down from heaven to earth.' "

"Be still," she cried in a choked voice, and hid her tears in her handkerchief, "oh, be still, and do not mock your destiny, your heart! for I understand them better than you do.

"Dear—dear Hyperion. You are indeed hard to help.

"Do you not know," she continued, raising her voice, "do you not know what you are starving for, the one thing that you lack, what you are seeking as Alpheus his Arethusa, what you mourn for in all your sorrow? It did not vanish years ago, it is impossible to say exactly when it was there, when it went, but it was, it is—it is in you! It is a better age, that is what you seek, a more beautiful world. It was that world alone that you embraced in your friends, with them you were in that world.

"It rose for you in Adamas; with him it set for you. In Alabanda its light appeared to you for the second time, but more fiercely and searingly, and so it was like midnight about your soul when you found him gone.

"Now do you see, too, why the least doubt of Alabanda could not but become despair in you? why you repudiated him, only because he was not quite a god?

"It was no man that you wanted, believe me, you wanted a world. The loss of all golden centuries, crowded together, as you felt them, in *one* happy moment, the spirit of all spirits of a better time, the strength of all the strength of heroes—you wanted one man to take their place for you!—Do you not see now how poor, how rich, you are? why you must be so proud and so downcast? why joy and sorrow visit you in such dreadful alternation?

"It is because you have everything and nothing, because the phantom of the golden days that must come belongs to you and yet is not here, because you are a citizen in the regions of Justice and Beauty, are a god among gods in the beautiful dreams that steal upon you by day, and when you awaken you find yourself standing on the soil of modern Greece.

"Twice, did you say? Oh, in a *single* day you are flung from heaven to earth seventy times. Shall I say it? I fear for you, you can ill endure the destiny of this age. You will yet attempt many things, you will—

"Oh, God! and your last refuge will be a grave!"

"No, Diotima," I cried, "by Heaven, no! So long as *one* melody still sounds for me, I fear not the deathly stillness of the wilderness under the stars; so long as the sun shines, and Diotima, there is no night for me.

"Let the death bell toll for every virtue; yet I hear you, you, the song of your heart, O you whom I love! and find immortal life, while all other things must die and fade away."

"Hyperion," she cried, "what are you saying?"

"I say what I must. I can no longer, no longer hide all my bliss and fear and anxiety—Diotima!—Yes, you know it, must know it, you have long since seen that I perish if you do not reach out your hand to me."

She was astonished, bewildered.

"And is it I," she cried, "is it I in whom Hyperion would seek support? yes, I wish—now for the first time I wish—that I were more than a mortal maiden. But I am to you what I can be."

"Oh, then you are all to me!" I cried.

"All? wicked hypocrite! what, then, of humanity, your last and only love?"

"Humanity?" I said; "let humanity make Diotima its watchword and paint your picture on its banner and say: 'Today shall the divine have victory!' Angel from heaven! what a day that would be!"

"Go," she cried, "go, and show heaven your transfiguration! It must not be so close to me.

"You will go, will you not, dear Hyperion?"

I obeyed. Who in my place would not have obeyed? I went. Never before had I gone from her thus, O Bellarmin! it was joy, serenity of life, divine peace, heavenly, wondrous, unfathomable joy!

Words avail not here, and he who would seek her like has never known her. The one thing that could express such a joy was Diotima's own singing when it floated between height and depth, in the golden mean.

O you meadows on the banks of Lethe! you sunset paths to the woods of Elysium! you lilies by the valley's streams! you garlands of roses about the hill! I believe in you in this gracious hour and say to my heart: There you will find her again, and all the joy that you lost.

Hyperion to Bellarmin

I will tell you more and yet more of my happiness.

I will try the temper of my heart on the joys of the past until it is like steel; I will exercise myself upon them until I am invincible.

Ha! do they not often fall upon my soul like a sword-stroke? but I play with the sword until I am used to it, I hold my hand in the fire until I can bear it as if it were water.

I will not faint; yes; I will be strong! I will hide nothing from myself, will conjure up the bliss of all blisses from the grave.

It is incredible that a man should fear the most beautiful; yet it is so.

Oh, have I not fled a hundred times from these moments, this mortal ecstasy of my memories, turned away my eyes as a child does from lightning! Yet in the luxuriant garden of the world there grows nothing lovelier than my joys, neither in heaven nor on earth does anything nobler flourish than my joys.

But only to you, my Bellarmin, only to a pure, free soul like yours, do I tell it. I will not be as lavish as the sun with its rays; I will not cast my pearls before the lowly multitude.

After that last conversation in which our souls met, I knew myself less every day. I felt there was a holy secret between me and Diotima.

I wondered, dreamed. As if a blessed spirit had appeared to me at midnight and chosen me to be his companion—such was the state of my soul.

Oh, it is a strange mixture of bliss and melancholy when it becomes apparent to us that we are forever outside of ordinary existence.

After that, I never managed to see Diotima alone. There was always some third person to intrude on us, separate us, and the world lay between her and me like an unbounded emptiness. Six days of mortal dread passed in this way, during which I had no knowledge of Diotima. It was as if the others about us paralyzed my senses, as if they killed my entire outward life, so that there was no way by which my imprisoned soul could reach her.

If I tried to find her with my eyes, night fell around me; if I tried to approach her with a word, it stuck in my throat.

Ah! my heart was often torn to pieces by my sacred, ineffable longing, my love often raged in me as powerfully as an imprisoned Titan. Never before had my spirit strained so fervently, so implacably, against the chains that Fate wrought for it, against the iron, inexorable law that kept it separate, that would not let it be *one* soul with its adorable other half.

The star-bright night had now become my element. Then, when all was still, as in the depths of the earth where gold grows in secret, then the more beautiful life of my love began.

Then my heart indulged its poetic right. It told me how Hyperion's spirit had played with his dear Diotima in the Elysium of the unborn before it came down to earth, in divine childhood innocence, beside the music of the fountain and under branches that were like earthy branches when we see them reflected, beautified from the golden water.

And, like the past, the gates of the future opened within me.

We flew, Diotima and I; we wandered from one springtime of the world to another, through all the Sun's wide realm and beyond, to the other isles of heaven, to the golden shores of Sirius and Arcturus' vale of spirits—

Oh, it is so to be desired to drink the joy of the world from *one* cup with the beloved!

Intoxicated by the blissful lullaby that I sang to myself, I fell asleep amid those glorious phantoms.

But when the life of the earth was kindled again by the rays of morning, I looked up and sought for the dreams of the night. Like the lovely stars, they had vanished, and only the joy of grief bore witness to them in my soul.

I mourned; but I believe that there is such mourning among the blessed, too. It was the messenger of joy, this grief, it was the graying dawn in which countless roses bud in the red of morning.

The burning summer day had now driven all things to seek refuge in the deepest shade. In Diotima's house, too, all was now still and empty, and the envious curtains stood in my way at every window.

I lived in thoughts of her. Where are you, I thought, where shall my lonely spirit find you, sweet maiden? Do you stare aimlessly and muse? Have you laid your work aside to sit with elbow on knee and your head on your little hand, giving yourself to lovely thoughts?

Let nothing disturb her peace if my quiet one is refreshing her heart with sweet fancies, let nothing touch this cluster of grapes and graze the quickening dew from its delicate berries.

So I dreamed. But while my thoughts were looking for her inside the walls of the house, my feet sought her elsewhere, and before I knew it I was walking under the arcades of the sacred wood behind Diotima's garden, where I had seen her for the first time. But what was this? Since then I had so often mingled among those trees, had become familiar with them, more at peace under them; now a power laid hold of me, it was as if I stepped within Diana's shadow and must die from the presence of the goddess.

Meanwhile I walked on. With every step the wonder within me grew stronger. I wanted to fly away, but it was as if my feet were weighted with lead. My soul had hurried on before and forsaken my earthly limbs. I heard no more, every shape grew dim and tremulous before my eyes. My spirit was already with Diotima; the tree top played in the light of morning while the lower branches still felt the chill of dawn.

"Ah! my Hyperion!" a voice now called to me; I flew toward it; "My Diotima! O my Diotima!"—beyond that I had no words and no breath, no consciousness.

Vanish, vanish, mortal life, paltry commerce, in which the lone spirit looks ever and again at the pennies it has gathered together and counts them over; we are all called to the bliss of the gods!

There is a gap in my existence here. I died, and when I awoke I was lying against the heart of the heavenly maiden.

O life of love! in what a ravishing, perfect flowering did you appear in her! as if lightly sung to sleep by blessed geniuses, the enchanting head lay on my shoulder, smiling sweet peace, raising eyes the color of the ether to me in happy, innocent amazement, as if they were even now looking at the world for the first time.

Long did we stand thus, ourselves forgotten in lovely contemplation, neither of us knowing what was happening to us, until at last joy increased in me too greatly and my lost speech broke forth in tears and cries of delight and roused my rapt, silent Diotima back to life.

At last we looked around us again.

"O my old, kindly trees!" cried Diotima, as if she had not seen them for a long time, and the memory of her earlier solitary days played over her joys, as charmingly as shadows upon virgin snow when it reddens and glows in the joyous light of sunset.

"Angel from heaven," I cried, "who can conceive of you? who can say that he has wholly understood you?"

"Are you surprised," she answered, "that I am so fond of you? O my proudly humble beloved! Am I, then, one of those who cannot believe in you? have I not fathomed you, not recognized the genius among his clouds? Hide yourself as much as you will, refuse to see yourself; I will conjure you forth, I will—

"But he is already here, he has come forth like a star; he has broken through the husk and stands there like spring; like a crystal stream from a dark cavern, so has he come forth; this is not the somber Hyperion, this is no longer the wild mourning—O my own, my glorious boy!"

All this was like a dream to me. Could I believe in such a miracle of love? could I? the joy of it would have killed me.

"Divine creature!" I cried, "is it to me that you speak? can you thus deny yourself, deny your blissful self-sufficiency! can you thus rejoice in me? Oh, now I see, now I know, what I have dimly surmised so often: man is a garment that a god often wears, a cup into which heaven pours its nectar, that its children may taste of the best."—

"Yes, yes!" she interrupted me, smiling raptly, "your namesake, the glorious Hyperion of heaven, is in you."

"Let me," I cried, "let me be yours, let me forget myself, let all the life of body and spirit in me fly but to you; but to you, in blissful, endless contemplation! O Diotima! so did I once stand, too, before the shadowy divine image that my love created for itself, before the idol of my lonely dreams; I nourished it faithfully; I animated it with my life, with my heart's hopes I refreshed it, warmed it, but it gave me nothing save what I had given, and when I had become impoverished, it left me poor; and now! now I have you in my arms and I feel the breath of your breast, and feel your eyes in my eyes, your beautiful presence flows into all my senses, and I can bear it, now I possess all that is most glorious, and tremble no longer, yes! truly I am not he who I was, Diotima! I have become like you, and divinity plays with divinity like children playing together."—

"But try to be a little calmer," she said.

"You are right, my lovable one!" I cried joyously; "if I am not, the Graces do not appear to me; if I am not, I do not see the sweet, subtle movements of Beauty's sea. Oh, I will yet learn to overlook nothing of you. Only give me time!"

"Flatterer!" she cried, "but this must be the end for today, dear flatterer! the golden cloud of evening has given me warning. O be not sad! Preserve this pure joy for you and for me! Let it echo in you until tomorrow, and kill it not with discontent! the heart's flowers need gentle care. Their roots are everywhere, but they themselves flourish only in fair weather. Farewell, Hyperion!"

She freed herself. My whole being flamed up in me, as she vanished from me in her glowing beauty.

"O you!" I cried, and ran after her and gave my soul into her hand in endless kisses.

"God!" she cried, "what will come of this?"

That struck home. "Forgive me, divine creature!" I said, "I go. Good night, Diotima! Only think of me a little!"

"I will," she cried, "good night!"

And now not another word, my Bellarmin. It would be too much for my longsuffering heart. I feel I am shaken. But I will go out among the plants and trees and lie down among them and pray that Nature may bring me to a quiet like theirs.

Hyperion to Bellarmin

Our souls now lived ever more freely and beautifully together, and everything in us and around us fused into golden peace. It seemed as if the old world had died and a new were beginning with us, so pure and strong and loving and light had everything become, and we and all that has being floated together in blissful union, like a chorus of a thousand inseparable tones, through the endless ether.

Our conversations glided on like a sky-blue stream from which the golden sand gleams now and again, and our silence was like the silence of the mountain peak, where, in glorious, lofty solitude, high above the realm of storms, only the air of heaven still murmurs through the bold traveler's hair.

And the wondrous, sacred grief, when the hour of parting tolled through our exaltation, and I often cried: "Now we are mortal again, Diotima!" and she said: "Mortality is illusion, is like the colors that quiver before our eyes when they have long looked at the sun!"

Ah! and all the gracious pastimes of love! the cajoling words, the misgivings, the sensitivities, the sternness and indulgence.

And the all-embracing knowledge with which we saw through each other, and the infinite trust with which we glorified each other!

Yes! man is a sun, all-seeing and all-illuminating, when he loves; loving not, he is a dark house in which a smoking lamp burns.

I should be silent, should forget and be silent.

But the bewitching flame tempts me until I plunge into it and, like the moth, perish.

Amid all this blessed, unrestrained giving and taking, I one day felt that Diotima was becoming more and more quiet.

I questioned, I implored; but that seemed only to make her yet more distant; finally she implored me to question her no more, to go, and, when I returned, to talk of something else. That cast me, too, into a painful silence, which I found hard to bear.

It was as if an unbelievably sudden fate had vowed the death of our love, and all life was gone, from me and from all else.

I was ashamed of this feeling; I knew very well that chance did not govern Diotima's heart. But what she was remained a mystery to me, and my pampered, disconsolate spirit ever demanded manifest and present love; for it, hidden treasures were lost treasures. Ah! in my happiness I had come to forget hope, at that time I was still like those impatient children who cry for the apple on the tree as if it were not there at all unless it is kissing their lips. I knew no rest, again I implored, violently and meekly, in tenderness and anger, love armed me with all its invincible, humble eloquence, and now—O my Diotima! now I had it, the enchanting confession, I have it now and shall keep it, until the tide of love brings me, too, with all that I am, back to our ancient home, to the bosom of Nature.

The innocent being! not yet did she know the power and richness of her heart, and sweetly terrified by the wealth within her, she buried it in the depths of her breast—and when now, with oh! what sacred ingenuousness, she confessed, confessed with tears, that she loved too much, and took leave of all that she had until then cradled against her heart, and cried: "I have become unfaithful to May and summer and autumn, and heed not day and night as once I did, belong no more to Heaven and Earth, belong but to one, to one; but the bloom of May and the flame of summer and the ripeness of autumn, the brightness of day and the solemnity of night, and Earth and Heaven are united for me in that one! so do I love!" and when now, in utter content of heart she looked at me, when, in brave, holy joy she took me into her beautiful arms and kissed my forehead and my mouth, ha! when that divine head, dying in bliss, sank down against my bared throat, and the sweet lips rested on my beating breast and her lovely breath touched my soul—O Bellarmin! my senses fail me, and my spirit flees.

I see, I see how it must end. The rudder has dropped into the tide and the ship, like a child caught by the feet, is seized and flung against the cliffs.

Hyperion to Bellarmin

Life has great hours. We gaze up at them as at the colossal figures of the Future and of Antiquity; we fight a glorious fight with them, and if we hold our own against them, they become like sisters and never forsake us.

Once we were sitting together on our mountain, on a stone of the city that anciently stood on this island; we were talking together of how the lion Demosthenes found his end here, how by a sacred, self-sought death, he here made his way out of Macedonian chains and daggers to freedom.—"That glorious spirit departed from the world with a jest," cried one. "Why not?" I said; "there was nothing left for him here; Athens had become Alexander's whore, and the world was being hounded to death like a deer by the great huntsman."

"O Athens!" cried Diotima; "I have more than once mourned when I looked out and the phantom of the Olympieion rose before me from the blue twilight!"

"How long a crossing is it?" I asked.

"A day's journey, more or less," answered Diotima.

"A day's journey!" I cried, "and I have not yet been there? We must go across together at once."

"Indeed yes!" cried Diotima; "we shall have a calm sea tomorrow, and everything is still in its time of greenness and ripeness.

"The eternal sun and the life of the immortal earth are essential for such a pilgrimage."

"Tomorrow, then!" I cried, and our friends assented.

We started early, the roosters were still crowing as we passed out of the roadstead. The world shone fresh and bright, and so did we. In our hearts was the golden peace of youth. The life in us was like the life of a newborn ocean island, with its first spring just beginning.

Under Diotima's influence, my soul had long since attained more equipoise; today I felt this with threefold clarity, and my dispersed and roving powers were all concentrated in *one* golden mean.

We talked of the excellence of the ancient Athenians, of whence it arose and in what it consisted.

One said that the climate had produced it; another: art and philosophy; a third: religion and form of government.

"Athenian art and religions, and philosophy and form of government," said I, "are flowers and fruits of the tree, not soil and root. You take the effects for the cause.

"But let him who tells me that the climate produced all this consider that we still live in it ourselves.

"Left more undisturbed in every way, freer from ruthless interference than any other people on earth, so did then Athenian people grow to manhood. No conqueror weakens them, no success in war intoxicates them, no foreign religion stupefies them, no rash wisdom urges them to premature ripeness. Left to itself, like the forming diamond—such is their childhood. Almost nothing is heard of them until the times of Pisistratus and Hipparchus. They took but a small part in the Trojan War, which, as in a hothouse, too early heated and stimulated most of the Greek peoples.—An extraordinary destiny never begets men. The sons of such a mother are great, are giants, but they never become beings of beauty or, what is the same thing, men—or else not until late, when the opposing forces in them battle too savagely not to make peace at last.

"In exuberant vigor Lacedaemon rushes ahead of the Athenians, and for that very reason would have dissipated and dissolved itself, had not Lycurgus come and, for all its overweening nature, held it together by his discipline. From then on everything in the Spartan was an achievement, every excellence was laboriously conquered, bought at the price of conscious effort, and if in a certain sense we can speak of Spartan simplicity, still the true simplicity of the child was completely lacking in them. The Lacedaemonians too early transgressed the order of instinct, they degenerated too soon, hence discipline, too, had likewise to begin for them too early; for every discipline and art begins too early when man's nature has not yet become mature. Nature must have developed to perfection in the human child before he goes to school, so that the image of childhood may show him the way back from school to the perfection of Nature.

"The Spartans forever remained a fragment; for he who was not once a perfect child is hard put to it to become a perfect man.—

"It is true, too, that Heaven and Earth did their part for the Athenians, as for all the Greeks, gave them neither poverty nor superfluity. The rays of Heaven did not fall on them like a rain of fire. Earth did not pamper them, intoxicate them, with caresses and excessive gifts, as the foolish Mother sometimes does elsewhere.

"To add to this, came Theseus' prodigious act, his voluntary limitation of his own royal power.

"Oh! such a seed sown in the hearts of the people cannot but bring forth an ocean of golden ears, and even at this late hour it still visibly operates and flourishes among the Athenians.

"I say it again! That the Athenians grew up so free from every kind of ruthless interference, on so moderate a diet—it was this that made them so outstandingly excellent, and only this could do it!

"Leave the human being undisturbed from the cradle on! do not force him out of the close-wrapped bud of his being, the small house of his childhood! Do not do too little, lest he make shift without you, and hence distinguish you from himself; do not do too much, lest he feel your power or his own, and hence distinguish you from himself; in short, let him not learn until late that there are men, that there is something else outside of himself, for only thus will he become a man. But man is a god as soon as he is man. And once he is a god, he is beautiful."

"How strange!" cried one of our friends.

"You have never yet spoken so deeply from my soul," cried Diotima.

"It comes to me from you," I answered.

"It is so that the Athenian was a man," I continued; "and so he could not but become a man. Beautiful he came from Nature's hands, beautiful in body and soul, as the saying goes.

"The first child of human, of divine Beauty is art. In art the divine man rejuvenates and repeats himself. He wants to feel himself, therefore he sets his Beauty over against himself. Thus did man give himself his gods. For in the beginning man and his gods were one, when, unknown to itself, eternal Beauty *was*. I speak mysteries, but they exist.—

"The first child of divine Beauty is art. Thus it was among the Athenians.

"Beauty's second daughter is religion. Religion is love of Beauty. The wise man loves Beauty herself, eternal, all-embracing Beauty; the people love her children, the gods, who appear to them in multifarious forms. So it was, too, among the Athenians. And without such a love of Beauty, without such a religion, every state is a dry skeleton without life and spirit, all thought and action is a tree without a top, a column whose crown has been cut off.

"That this was indeed the case among the Greeks, and especially the Athenians, that their art and their religion were the true children of eternal Beauty—perfect human nature—and could only spring from perfect human nature, is clearly apparent if we will but look with unprejudiced eyes at the productions of their sacred art and at the religion with which they loved and honored them.

"Shortcomings and false steps are to be found everywhere, and hence here too. But it is certain that, even so, in most of the productions of their art we find man in his maturity. Here there is neither the pettiness nor the colossality of the Egyptians and the Goths, here there is human intelligence and human proportions. They run less than other peoples to the extremes of the metaphysical and the physical. Their gods remain more nearly in the golden mean of humanity than others.

"And even as the productions of their art were, so was their love. Not too servile, and not too familiar!—

"This beauty of mind and spirit in the Athenians inevitably produced the indispensable sense of freedom.

"The Egyptian impassively bears the despotism of arbitrary power, the son of the North unprotestingly bears the despotism of law, injustice in the form of codes of justice; for the Egyptian is born from the womb with an urge to do homage, to idolatrize; in the North, men believe too little in the pure, free life of Nature not to cling superstitiously to legality.

"The Athenian cannot tolerate arbitrary power, because his divine nature refuses to be intruded upon, he cannot tolerate legality everywhere because he does not need it everywhere. Draco is not for him. He insists on being treated gently, and he is right to do so."

"Well and good!" someone interrupted me; "I understand this, but I do not see how this poetic and religious people also comes to be a philosophical people."

"The fact is," I answered, "that without poetry they would never have been a philosophical people!"

"What has philosophy," he answered, "what has the cold sublimity of philosophical knowledge, to do with poetry?"

"Poetry," I answered, confident of my argument, "is the beginning and the end of philosophical knowledge. Like Minerva from the head of Jupiter, philosophy springs from the poetry of an eternal, divine state of being. And so in philosophy, too, the irreconcilable finally converges again in the mysterious spring of poetry."

"What a paradoxical man!" cried Diotima; "yet I understand him. But you two digress. We are talking of Athens."

"The man," I resumed, "who has not at least *once* in his life felt full, pure beauty in himself, when the powers of his being merged like the colors in the rainbow, who has never felt the profound harmony that arises among all things only in hours of exaltation— that man will not even be a philosophical sceptic, his mind is not even capable of tearing down, let alone of building up. For, believe me, the sceptic finds contradiction and imperfection in all that is thought, because he knows the harmony of perfect beauty, which is never thought. The dry bread that human reason well-meaningly offers him, he disdains only because he is secretly feasting at the table of the gods."

"Visionary!" cried Diotima. "So that is why you, too, were a sceptic. But the Athenians!"

"I am close upon them," I said. "The great saying, the εν διαφερον εαυτω (the one differentiated in itself) of Heraclitus, could be found only by a Greek, for it is the very being of Beauty, and before that was found there was no philosophy.

"Now classification became possible, for the whole was there. The flower had ripened; now it could be dissected.

"The moment of beauty was now well known to men, it was there in life and thought, the infinitely one existed.

"It could be analyzed, taken apart in men's minds, it could be reconstituted from its components, and so the being of the highest and the best could be increasingly known, and the knowledge of it be set up as the law in all the multifarious realms of the spirit.

"Do you see now why the Athenians in particular could not but be a philosophical people too?

"Not so the Egyptian. He who does not live loving Heaven and Earth and loved by them in equal measure, he who does not live at one in this sense with the element in which he has his being, is by his very nature not so at one with himself as a Greek, at least he does not experience eternal Beauty as easily as a Greek does.

"Like a grandiose despot, the East in its power and splendor casts its inhabitants to the ground and, before man has learned to walk, he is forced to kneel, before he has learned to speak, he is forced to pray; before his heart has attained an equipoise it is forced to bow, before his spirit is strong enough to bear flowers and fruit, Fate and Nature drains all his strength through torrid heat. The Egyptian is devoted before he is a whole, hence he knows nothing of the whole, nothing of Beauty, and what he calls the highest is a veiled power, an awesome enigma; the dumb, dark Isis is his first and last, an empty infinity, and out of that nothing reasonable has ever come. Even the most sublime nothingness gives birth to nothingness.

"The North, on the contrary, too early turns its nurslings in upon themselves, and if the spirit of the fiery Egyptian hurries forth too eagerly to journey through the world, in the North the spirit begins to return into itself even before it is ready to travel.

"In the North one must be judicious before one's capacity for feeling has fully developed, one thinks oneself guilty of everything even before ingenuousness has achieved its beautiful end; one must be reasonable, must become a conscious intelligence before one is a man, be a shrewd man before one is a child; the oneness of the whole man, Beauty, is not allowed to thrive and ripen in him before he cultivates and develops himself. Pure intellect, pure reason are always the kings of the North.

"But pure intellect has never produced anything intelligent, nor pure reason anything reasonable.

"Without beauty of spirit, intellect is like a willing journeyman who constructs the fence out of rough timber as it has been sketched out for him and nails the sawn and planed posts together for the garden that his master intends to plant. The entire business of intellect is makeshift. By its ability to sort out, it saves us from folly, from injustice; but to be safe from folly and injustice is, after all, not the highest level of human excellence.

"Reason without beauty of spirit and heart is like an overseer whom the master of the house has set over the servants; he knows as little as they do what will come of all their endless toil, he only shouts: 'Get busy,' and is almost sorry to find the work being accomplished, for in the end he would have nothing more to oversee, and his part would be played.

"Mere intellect produces no philosophy, for philosophy is more than the limited perception of what is.

"Mere reason produces no philosophy, for philosophy is more than the blind demand for ever greater progress in the combination and differentiation of some particular material.

"But once the light of the divine εν διαφερον εαυτω, which is struggling reason's ideal of Beauty, shines out, it does not demand blindly, it knows why and to what end it demands.

"If the sun of the Beautiful shines for intellect at its work, as a May day shines into the artist's workshop, it does not go running out and leave its work of makeshift unfinished, though it thinks fondly of the holiday when it will rove abroad in the rejuvenating light of spring."

Thus far had I discoursed, when we landed on the shores of Attica.

Ancient Athens was now too much in our minds for us to engage in anything like an orderly conversation, and I now felt surprised myself at the sort of things I had been saying. "How did I ever come," I cried, "to be on the arid mountain peak on which you saw me just now?"

"It is ever thus," Diotima answered, "when we feel at our best. Exuberant strength seeks something to do. Young lambs butt their heads together when they are sated with their mother's milk."

We made our way to the summit of Lycabettus, and, though pressed for time, we stopped now and again wrapped in thought, preparing ourselves for wonders to come.

It is beautiful that man finds it so hard to convince himself of the death of what he loves, probably no one has ever visited a friend's grave without some faint hope of really finding his friend there. The beautiful phantom of ancient Athens took possession of me like the figure of a mother returning from the realm of the dead.

"O Parthenon!" I cried, "pride of the world! Neptune's kingdom lies at thy feet like a subjugated lion, and around you the other temples cluster like children, and the eloquent Agora and the Grove of Academe—"

"Can you thus transport yourself to ancient times?" asked Diotima.

"Remind me not of time!" I answered; "it was a divine life and in it man was the center of Nature. Spring, when it blossomed about Athens, was like a modest flower on a maiden's bosom; the sun rose red with shame before the glories of earth.

"The marble cliffs of Hymettus and Pentelicus leaped from their slumbering cradle like children from their mother's lap, and attained form and life under the loving hands of Athenians.

"Nature bestowed honey and the most beautiful violets and myrtles and olives.

"Nature was a priestess and man her god, and all life in her and her every form and sound were but a single rapt echo of that glorious *one* to whom she belonged.

"Him did she celebrate, to him only did she sacrifice.

"And he was worthy of it, whether he sat fondly in the sacred workshop clasping the knees of the divine image that he had fashioned, or lay at ease among his listening students on Sunium's green promontory, whiling away the time with high thoughts, or ran in the

Stadium, or, from the orator's tribune, sent rain and sunshine and thunder and golden clouds, like the Storm God—"

"Oh, look!" Diotima suddenly cried to me.

I looked, and could have fainted, so mighty was the spectacle.

Like an immense shipwreck, when the gales have been hushed and the sailors have fled and the corpse of the shattered fleet lies on the sandbank unrecognizable, so before us lay Athens, and the forsaken pillars stood before us like bare treetrunks of a wood that at evening was still green and, the same night, went up in flames.

"Here," said Diotima, "one learns to accept one's own fate in silence, be it good or bad."

"Here," I continued, "one learns to accept all things in silence. Had the reapers who mowed this grainfield enriched their barns with its stalks, nothing would have been lost, and I should be content to stand here as a gleaner—but who was the winner?"

"The whole of Europe," answered one of our friends.

"Oh, yes!" I cried, "they have dragged away the columns and statues and sold them to one another, they have put no small price on those noble forms—for their rarity, as one prizes parrots and monkeys."

"Say not so," the same man answered; "if it is indeed true that the spirit of all beauty is not among them, it is because it could not be carried away, could not be bought."

"Yes!" I cried, "yes! That spirit had perished even before the destroyers descended on Attica. Not until houses and temples have been deserted do the wild beasts dare to venture into gateways and streets."

"For him who possesses that spirit," said Diotima consolingly, "Athens still stands like a blossoming fruit tree. The artist can easily restore the torso for himself."

The next morning we set out early, saw the ruins of the Parthenon, the site of the ancient Theater of Dionysus, the Temple of Theseus, the sixteen still-standing pillars of the divine Olympieion; but what struck me most was the ancient gate that in times past afforded passage from the old city to the new, where once a thousand beautiful men and women must have greeted each other in a *single* day. Now the gate gives passage to neither the old nor the new city, it stands there silent and empty, like a dried up fountain from whose conduits clear, cool water once poured with a welcoming splash.

"Ah!" said I as we walked about, "Fate makes brave sport here, throwing down temples and giving their shattered stones to children to play with, turning disfigured gods into benches before peasants' huts, and tombs into resting places for pasturing cattle; such prodigality is more royal than Cleopatra's whim of drinking dissolved pearl—but alas for all that beauty and greatness!"

"Dear Hyperion!" cried Diotima, "it is time for you to go from here; you are pale, your eyes are tired, and you seek in vain to sustain yourself with new thoughts. Come out where it is green! out among the colors of life! That will do you good."

We went out into the nearby gardens.

The others, having fallen into talk with two English scholars who were reaping a harvest from the antiquities of Athens, were not to be budged. I was glad to leave them.

My whole being revived when I found myself alone with Diotima again; she had fought a magnificent fight against the sacred chaos of Athens. As the lyre of Urania above the discordant elements, so Diotima's quiet thoughts ruled above the ruins. As the moon out of a tenuous cloudbank, so her spirit rose out of her beautiful sorrow; the divine maiden stood there in her grief like the flower that breathes forth its loveliest perfume in the dark of night.

We walked on and on, and at last had not walked in vain.

O you groves of Angele, where the olive tree and the cypress, whispering together, cool each other with pleasant shade, where the golden fruit of the lemon tree glimmers from among dark leaves, where the swelling grape grows luxuriantly on the stake, and the ripe bitter-orange lies by the wayside like a smiling foundling! you sweet-scented, hidden paths, you peaceful seats, where the reflection of the myrtle smiles out of the spring! never shall I forget you.

Diotima and I walked about for a while under the glorious trees, until we came upon a bright open expanse.

Here we sat down. There was a blissful silence between us. My spirit fluttered about the maiden's divine form like a butterfly about a flower, and my whole being was eased and brought to harmony in the joy of inspiring contemplation.

"Are you so soon comforted, confused one?" said Diotima.

"Yes, yes, I am!" I answered. "What I thought was lost, I have; what I pined for as if it had vanished from the world, is here before me. No, Diotima! the spring of eternal Beauty has not yet dried up.

"I have said it to you before: I need gods and men no longer. I know that Heaven is desolate, depopulated, and that Earth, which once overflowed with beautiful human life, is become almost like an anthill. But there is still a place where the old Heaven and the old earth smile for me. For the gods of Heaven and the godlike men of the Earth—I forget them all in you.

"What care I for the shipwreck of the world; I know nothing but my blessed island."

"There is a time for love," said Diotima with gentle seriousness, "as there is a time to live in the happy cradle. But life itself drives us forth.

"Hyperion!"—here she ardently grasped my hand, and her voice rose grandly—"Hyperion! I think you are born for higher things. Do not misjudge yourself! it was lack of material that held you back. Things went too slowly. That cast you down. Like young fencers, you attacked too soon, before your aim was certain and your hand skilled; and because, as was bound to happen, you took more thrusts than you gave, you became timid and doubted yourself and everything else; for you are as sensitive as you are impetuous. But that has lost you nothing. Had your heart and your capacity for action matured so early, your spirit would not be what it is; you would not be the thinking man, would not be the suffering, turbulent man. Believe me, you would never have known the equipoise of beautiful humanity so purely if you had not lost it so completely. Your heart has at last found peace. I believe it. I understand it. But do you truly think that you have reached the end? Do you mean to shut yourself up in the heaven of your love, and let the world, which needs you, wither and grow cold before you? You must shoot down like the beam of light, you must descend like the all-refreshing rain, into the land of mortal men, you must illuminate like Apollo, shake and animate like Jupiter, or you are not worthy of your heaven. I beg you: go back into Athens *once* again, and look not only at the ruins but also at the men who walk among them, the wild Albanians and the other good-hearted, childlike Greeks, who console themselves with a merry dance and a pious tale for the infamous oppression that weighs upon them—can you say, 'I am ashamed to work with this material?' I think it can still be fashioned. Can you turn your heart from those who are in need? They are not evil, they have done you no harm!"

"What can I do for them?" I cried.

"Give them what you have within you," answered Diotima, "give—"

"Not another word, noble soul!" I cried, "else you will bend me, else it will be as if you had brought me to it by force—

"They will not be happier, but nobler—no! they will be happier too. They must arise, they must come forth, like young mountains out of the ocean when their underground fire drives them.

"It is true that I stand alone, and appear among them without a name. But cannot *one* alone, if he is a man, do more than hundreds who are but fragments of men?

"Sacred Nature, thou art the same within me and without. It cannot be so hard to unite what is outside of me and the divine within me. If the bee can make her little kingdom flourish, why should not I be able to plant and cultivate what is needful?

"What! the Arabian merchant sowed his Koran abroad, and a people of scholars grew up for him like an endless forest, and shall the field not thrive to which ancient truth returns in new, living youth?

"All shall be changed! From the root of humanity the new world shall spring! A new divinity shall rule over them, a new future brighten before them.

"In the workshop, in houses, in gatherings, in temples—there will be a change everywhere!

"But I must still go away and learn. I am an artist, and I am unskilled. I fashion in thought, but I do not yet know how to direct my hand—"

"You shall go to Italy," said Diotima, "to Germany, France—how many years do you need? three? four?—I think three are enough; you are not the phlegmatic sort, and you seek only what is noblest and most beautiful—"

"And then?"

"You will be the teacher of our people, you will be a great man, I hope. And when then, as now, I embrace you, I shall dream, as if I were a part of a glorious man, I shall rejoice, as if you had given me half of your immortality, even as Castor did to Pollux, oh! I shall be a proud girl, Hyperion!"

I remained silent for a while. I was filled with inexpressible joy.

"Is it possible that there is content between the decision and the act, is there rest before the victory?"

"It is the rest of the hero," said Diotima, "there are decisions that, like the words of gods, are at once command and fulfillment, and such is yours."

We returned, as after our first embrace. Everything had become strange and new for us.

Now I stood above the ruins of Athens like the farmer on the fallow field. "Only lie still," I thought, as we returned to our ship, "only lie still, sleeping land! Soon will the young life sprout green from thee and grow toward the blessings of Heaven! Soon will the clouds never rain in vain, soon will the Sun find his old nurslings once more.

"You ask for men, Nature? You complain, like a lyre on which only that brother of chance, the wind, plays because the artist who imposed order on it has died? They will come, your men, O Nature! A rejuvenated people will rejuvenate you, too, and you will be as its bride, and the old union of spirits will renew itself in you.

"There will be but *one* Beauty; and man and Nature will be united in *one* all-embracing divinity."

Volume Two

μη φυναι, τον απαντα νιχα λογον. το δ'επει φανη βηναι
χειθεν, οθεν περ ηχει, πολυ δευτερον ως ταγιστα.

Sophocles

(Not to be born is, past all prizing, best; but, when a man has
seen the light, this is next best by far, that with all speed he
should go thither, whence he hath come.)

Book One

Hyperion to Bellarmin

We were experiencing the last beautiful moments of the year,
after our return from Attica.

Autumn was a brother of spring for us, full of mild fire, a festival time for memories of sorrows and past joys of love. The fading leaves bore the rosy hue of sunset; only the spruce and the laurel stood in eternal green. Migrating birds lingered in the clear air, others swarmed in vineyard and garden, joyously reaping what men had left. And the heavenly light ran pure from the cloudless sky, the sacred sun smiled through every twig—the kindly one, never named by me but with joy and gratitude, the sun that with a look has often healed me in deep sorrow, and cleansed my soul of discontent and cares.

We visited all our best loved paths once more, Diotima and I; vanished blissful hours met us everywhere.

We remembered the past May; never, we said, had we seen the Earth as it was then; it had been transformed, a silver cloud of flowers, a joyous flame of life, purified of all crude matter.

"Oh! all was so full of pleasure and hope," cried Diotima, "so full of unceasing growth and yet so effortless, so blessedly quiet, like a child playing on and on without another thought."

"In that," I cried, "I recognize the soul of Nature—in that still fire, in that lingering in its mighty haste."

"And how dear it is to the happy, that lingering," cried Diotima; "do you remember? once at twilight we stood together on the bridge, after a hard storm, and the red mountain stream shot away under us like an arrow, but there beside it the forest stood in green peace and the bright leaves scarcely stirred. We felt so glad then that the living green did not flee from us too, like the brook, and that the beautiful spring stayed for us like a tame bird; yet now spring, too, is over the hills and away."

We smiled at that, although sorrow was closer to us.

So was our own bliss to depart, and we foresaw it.

O Bellarmin! who shall dare to say that he stands fast, when even the beautiful thus ripens to its doom, when even the divine must humble itself and share mortality with all that is mortal!

Hyperion to Bellarmin

I had lingered before her house with the lovely maid, until the lamp of night shone into the peaceful twilight; then I returned to Notara's dwelling, full of thoughts, full of seething, heroic life, as always when I left her embraces. A letter had come from Alabanda.

"Things are stirring, Hyperion," he wrote to me, "Russia has declared war on the Porte; they are bringing a fleet into the Archipelago;* the Greeks are to be free if they rise and help drive the Sultan to the Euphrates. The Greeks will do their share, the Greeks will be free, and I am heartily glad that at last there is something to do again. I took no pleasure in the light of day, so long as this remained undone.

"If you are still what you were, come! You will find me in the village before Coron as you come by the road from Mistra. I live beside the hill, in the white house at the edge of the woods.

"I have broken with the men whom you met through me in Smyrna. You were right, with your finer sensitivity, not to enter their sphere.

"I long for us to see each other again in the new life. Until now, you have seen the world as too evil for you to let it know you. Because you refused to perform servile tasks, you did nothing, and doing nothing made you morose and dreamy.

"You refused to swim in the swamp. Come now, come and let us bathe in the open sea!

"It will do us good, O you who alone I love!"

So he wrote. For a moment I was aghast. My face burned with shame, my heart seethed like hot springs, and I could not stand still, such anguish did I feel at being outdistanced by Alabanda, outdone forever. But then I all the more eagerly embraced the work before us.

"I have grown too idle," I cried, "too fond of my ease, too remote, too inactive!—Alabanda looks into the world like a noble pilot; Alabanda is diligent and searches the waves for booty, and your hands sleep on your lap? would you make do with words, and exorcise the world with magic spells? But your words are like snowflakes, useless, they only make the air darker, and your magic formulas are for believers, but the unbelievers do not hear you.— Yes! to be mild at the right time is a fine thing, but to be mild at the wrong time is ugly, for it is cowardly!—But, Harmodius! I will match your myrtle, your myrtle, in which the sword lay hidden. I will not have been idle for nothing, and my sleep shall be like oil

*In the year 1770 (Hölderlin's note).

when flame touches it. I will not look on when the time is at hand, and will not go about asking for news while Alabanda earns the laurel."

Hyperion to Bellarmin

Diotima's increasing pallor as she read Alabanda's letter pierced my soul. She then began, calmly and earnestly, to advise me against the step, and we said many things for and against it. "O men of violence!" she cried at last, "who so quickly go to extremes, think of Nemesis!"

"He who suffers extremes," I said, "is right to go to extremes."

"Even if it is right," she said, "you were not born for it."

"So it seems," I said; "but I have dallied long enough. Oh, would that I could load an Atlas upon me, to make good the sins of my youth. Is there consciousness in me? is there endurance? Oh, let me, Diotima! Here, in just such work, must I gain it."

"This is vain pride!" cried Diotima; "not long ago you were more modest, not long ago when you said, 'I must still go away and learn.'"

"Dear sophist!" I cried; "then we were talking of something entirely different. To lead my people to the Olympus of divine Beauty, where Truth and all Goodness gushes from springs forever young—I am not yet fit to do that. But I have learned to use a sword, and for the moment that is all that is needed. The new union of spirits cannot live in the air, the sacred theocracy of the Beautiful must dwell in a free state, and that state must have a place on earth, and that place we shall surely conquer."

"You will conquer," cried Diotima, "and forget what for; you will, at the most, force the establishment of a free state, and then ask yourself, 'What have I been building for?' Ah! it will be consumed, all the beautiful life that was to have being there, it will be exhausted even in you! The savage fight will tear you to pieces, beautiful soul, you will grow old, blissful spirit! and, weary unto death, you will ask in the end: 'Where are you now, you ideals of youth?'"

"It is cruel, Diotima," I cried, "thus to reach into my very heart, thus to hold me fast by my own fear of death, by my highest joy in life, but no! no! no! Servitude kills, but just war brings every soul to life. It is casting the gold into the fire that gives it the color of the sun! It is breaking fetters that first gives a man all his youth! It is arising and trampling on the adder, on the crawling century that poisons all Beauty and Nature in the bud—that alone saves a man!—I shall grow old, shall I, Diotima, setting Greece free? grow old and miserable, become a common man? Oh, then was he, too, shallow and empty and forsaken of the gods, that Athenian youth, when, bearing news of victory from Marathon, he came over the peak of Pentelicus and looked down into the valleys of Attica!"

"My love! my love!" cried Diotima, "oh, be still! I will not say another word. You shall go, shall go, proud man! Ah! when you are thus, I have no power over you, no right to you."

She wept bitterly, and I stood before her like a criminal. "Forgive me, divine maid!" I cried, kneeling at her feet, "oh, forgive me, when I am compelled! I do not choose; I do not reflect. There is a power in me, and I know not if it is myself that drives me to this step." "Your whole soul commands you to it," she answered. "Not to obey one's soul often leads to destruction, yet obeying it does too. It is best that you go, for it is nobler. Act; I will bear it."

Hyperion to Bellarmin

From then on Diotima was strangely changed.

I had seen with joy how, from the time we fell in love, her silent life had opened into looks and fond words and her inborn quietude had often met me with shining enthusiasm.

But how strange the beautiful soul becomes to us, when, after its first blossoming, after the morning of its course, it must rise to its high noon! The blessed child had grown almost unrecognizable, so sublime and so sorrowful had she become.

Oh, how often did I lie before that divine, mourning figure, and thought that I should weep my soul away in grief for her, and then myself rose up in admiration and filled with unconquerable powers! A flame had ascended into her eyes from her full heart. Her bosom, teeming with longings and sorrows, had become too confining for her; that is why her thoughts were so glorious and bold. A new greatness, a visible power over everything that could feel, ruled in her. She was a higher being. She belonged to the race of mortals no longer.

O my Diotima, if I had thought then to what this must come!

Hyperion to Bellarmin

The prudent Notara, too, was enchanted by the new projects, promised me a strong following, hoped soon to occupy the Isthmus of Corinth and there take Greece as it were by the handle. But Fate decreed otherwise, and made his work useless before it achieved its end.

He advised me not to go to Tina, but to travel directly down the Peloponnesus, escaping notice as far as possible. I was to write to my father on the way, since the cautious old man would more easily condone a step that had been taken than give permission for one that had not. This was not quite to my taste, but we are prone to sacrifice our private feelings when a great goal is before our eyes.

"I doubt," Notara continued, "if you will be able to count on your father's help in a matter of this sort. So I shall give you what you will need in order to live and work for a time, come what may. If you are ever able to, you can repay me; if not, what was mine was yours as well. Feel no embarrassment about the money," he added with a smile; "even Phoebus' horses do not live on air alone, so the poets tell us."

Hyperion to Bellarmin

And now the day of parting came.

I had spent the whole morning up in Notara's garden, in the fresh winter air, among the ever green cypresses and cedars. The great powers of youth supported me, and my premonition of suffering to come bore me higher, like a cloud.

Diotima's mother had invited Notara and our other friends and myself to pass that last day together at her house. Their kind hearts had all rejoiced over me and Diotima, and the element of the divine in our love had not been lost on them. And now they were to bless my parting too.

I went down, I found the dear girl at the hearth. She took it as a sacred, priestly duty to attend to the housekeeping that day. She had put everything to rights, had beautified everything in the house, and no one was allowed to help her with it. She had gathered all the flowers that still remained in the garden, she had brought roses and fresh bunches of grapes, even at that late time of year.

She recognized my footstep as I approached, she came softly toward me; her pale cheeks glowed from the fire of the hearth, and her eyes, larger in her new seriousness, were bright with tears. She saw how overcome I was. "Go inside, my dear," she said; "Mother is there, and I will follow at once."

I went in. There she sat, the noble woman, and held out her beautiful hand to me. "Have you come, have you come, my son?" she cried. "I ought to be angry with you, you have taken my child from me, have talked me out of all common sense, do just what you please and then go away; but forgive him, you Heavenly Powers, if what he means to do is wrong! and if it is right, then be not slow to help the dear lad!" I was going to speak, but just then Notara and our other friends came in, with Diotima behind them.

We were silent for a while. We honored the grieving love that was in us all; we feared to presume upon it with words and arrogant thoughts. Finally, after a few desultory remarks, Diotima asked me to tell them something about Agis and Cleomenes; I had often named those great souls with ardent respect and had said that they were no less demigods than Prometheus, and their battle against Sparta's fate more heroic than any in the most illustrious myths. The genius of those men, I had said, was the sunset of the Greek day, as Theseus and Homer had been its dawn.

I told their story, and at its end we all felt stronger and more exalted.

"Happy is he," cried one of our friends, "whose life alternates between joy of heart and brisk battle!"

"Yes!" cried another, "that is eternal youth, when enough powers are always in exercise and our whole selves are occupied in pleasure and work."

"Oh, that I could go with you!" Diotima cried to me.

"Yet it is fitting that you remain here, Diotima!" said I. "The priestess may not leave the temple. You guard the sacred flame, in silence you guard the Beautiful, that I may find it again in you."

"You are right of course, it is better," she said, and her voice trembled, and the ether-blue eyes hid themselves in her handkerchief, that their tears, their despair might not be seen.

O Bellarmin, my heart was near to breaking because I had made her blush so red. "Friends!" I cried, "preserve this angel for me. I know nothing more, if I know her not. O Heavens! I dare not think for what I would be fit if I lost her."

"Rest easy, Hyperion!" Notara interrupted me.

"Easy?" I cried; "O you good people! you can often give thought to how your garden will bloom and how good your harvest will be, you can pray for your grapevine—and shall I part without concern from what alone my soul serves?"

"No, my good friend!" cried Notara, deeply moved, "no! I do not ask that you part from her without concern! no, by the divine innocence of your love! you have my blessing, be sure of that!"

"You remind me," I cried quickly. "She shall bless us, this dear mother, she shall bear witness for us with you all—come, Diotima! your mother shall bless our union, until the beautiful society for which we hope joins us in marriage."

I went down on one knee; and she, wide-eyed, blushing, smiling, and festive, sank down at my side too.

"For a long time," I cried, "O Nature! has our life been at *one* with you, and the world that is ours is divinely young, like you and all your gods, through the power of love."

"In your groves we wandered," Diotima continued, "and were like you, by your springs we sat and were like you, there over the mountains we went, with your children the stars, like you.

"When we were far from each other," I cried, "when, like a whispering harp, our coming delight first sounded for us, when we found each other, when there was no more sleep for us, and all the tones in us awoke to the full harmony of life, divine Nature! then were we ever like you, and so now, too, when we part and joy dies, we are like you, full of sorrow, yet good; therefore a pure mouth shall bear witness for us that our love is holy and eternal, as are you."

"I bear witness to it," her mother said.

"We bear witness to it," cried the others.

Now there was no word left for us to speak. I felt my heart beat its highest; I felt ripe for departure. "Now I will go, my loved ones," I said, and life vanished from every face. Diotima stood like a marble statue and I felt her hand die in mine. I had killed everything around me; I was alone, and I reeled before the boundless silence in which my seething life had no holdfast.

"Ah!" I cried, "my heart is fiery hot, and you all stand so coldly, my loved ones! and do only the Gods of the household lend ear?—Diotima! you are silent, you do not see!—oh, well for you that you do not see!"

"Go now," she sighed, "It must be; go now, dear heart!"

"O sweet music from those blissful lips!" I cried, and stood like a suppliant before that lovely statue, "sweet music! drift upon me *once* more, dawn *once* more, dear eyes of light!"

"Speak not so, beloved!" she cried, "speak to me more seriously, speak to me with more heart!"

I wanted to restrain myself, but I was as in a dream.

"Alas!" I cried, "it is no parting from which there is a return."

"You will kill her," cried Notara. "See how gentle she is, and you are so beside yourself."

I looked at her, and tears poured from my burning eyes.

"Farewell, then, Diotima!" I cried, "heaven of my love, farewell!—Let us be strong, dear friends! Dear Mother, I gave you joy and sorrow. Farewell, farewell!"

I staggered away. Diotima alone followed me.

Evening had come, and the stars were rising in the sky. We stopped and stood below the house. There was an eternity within us, above us. Delicate as the ether, Diotima embraced me. "Silly! what is parting?" she whispered mysteriously, with the smile of an immortal.

"I feel differently now, too," I said, "and I do not know which of the two is a dream—my grief or my happiness."

"Both are," she answered, "and both are good."

"Perfect one!" I cried, "I speak as you do. Let us know each other by the starry sky. Let that be the sign between me and you, so long as our lips are dumb."

"So be it!" she said, with a lingering tone that I had never heard before—it was her last. Her image vanished from me in the twilight, and I do not know if it was really she when I turned back for the last time and the fading figure hovered before my eyes a moment longer and then died into the night.

Hyperion to Bellarmin

Why do I recount my grief to you, renew it, and stir up my restless youth in me again? Is it not enough to have traveled *once* through mortality? why do I not remain still in the peace of my spirit?

It is, my Bellarmin! because every living breath that we draw remains dear to our heart, because all the transformations of pure Nature are part of her beauty too. Our soul, when it puts off mortal experiences and lives only in blessed quietness—is it not like a leafless tree? like a head without hair? Dear Bellarmin! I was quiet for a while; like a child, I lived under the still knolls of Salamis, oblivious to mankind's fate and striving. Since then much has changed in my eyes, and now I have peace enough in me to remain quiet when I look at human existence. O friend! in the end the Spirit reconciles us with all things. You will not believe it, at least not of me. But I think that even my letters should suffice to show you that my soul is becoming more and more still every day. And I will continue to tell you of it hereafter, until I have said enough for you to believe me.

Here are letters of Diotima's and mine, which we wrote to each other after my departure from Calaurea. They are the most precious part of all that I entrust to you. They are the warmest picture from those days of my life. They tell you little of the clamor of war. But hence all the more of my own life, and that is what you want. Ah, and you must see, too, how greatly I was loved. That I could never tell you, that only Diotima can tell.

Hyperion to Diotima

I have awakened from the death of absence, my Diotima! my spirit arises, strengthened, as from sleep.

I write to you from a summit in the mountains of Epidaurus.

There, far in the distance, your island looms faintly, Diotima! out there, my stadium, where I must conquer or fall. O Peloponnesus! O you springs of the Eurotas and Alpheus! There we shall prove ourselves. There, from the forests of Sparta, the ancient genius of the land will plunge down like an eagle with our army, as on roaring pinions.

My soul is filled with longing for high deeds and filled with love, Diotima, and in these Greek valleys my eye looks out as if to command by magic: "Rise once more, you cities of the gods!"

There must be a god in me, for I scarcely feel our separation. Like the blessed shades of Lethe, my soul now lives with yours in heavenly freedom, and Fate has no more power over our love.

Hyperion to Diotima

I am now deep in the Peloponnesus. In the same hut where I spent last night, I once spent the night when, scarcely more than a boy, I traveled through these regions with Adamas. How happily I sat here then, on the bench in front of the house, listening to the bells of arriving caravans tinkling in the distance and the plash of the nearby spring, which poured its silver waters into the basin under flowering acacias.

Now I am no less happy. I rove through this land as through Dodona's grove, where the oaks resounded with oracles prophesying fame. I see only deeds, past and to come, even though I wander from morning to night under the open sky. Believe me, he who travels through this land and still tolerates a yoke on his neck, still becomes no Pelopidas: he is empty-hearted or without understanding.

Can this sleep have lasted so long? so long has time, dark and dumb as the River of Hell, glided on in drear sloth?

And yet all is ready. The mountain folk hereabout are full of vengeful energy; they lie like a silent storm cloud that waits only for the wind to drive it on. Diotima! let me breathe the breath of God among them; let me speak a word to them from my heart, Diotima. Fear not! They will not be so savage. I know untutored nature. It scorns reason, but it is close kin to enthusiasm. He who but works with his whole soul never goes wrong. He need not ponder, for no power is against him.

Hyperion to Diotima

Tomorrow I shall be with Alabanda. It is a delight for me to ask the way to Coron, and I ask more often than I need to. I would take the wings of the sun and be off to him, yet I find myself inclined to hang back and ask, "What will he be like?"

The kingly youth! why was I born after him? why did I not spring from *one* cradle with him? I cannot bear the difference between us. Oh, why did I live in Tina like an idle shepherd boy, and did not even dream of such a man as he until he was already testing Nature by living work, already battling sea and air and all the elements? was not a longing for the glory of action astir in me then too?

But I will catch up with him; I will be speedy. By Heaven! I am overripe for work. My soul has only itself to be angry with if I do not soon free myself by some living action.

Noble maiden! how could you not find me wanting? How could you possibly love a being so empty of deeds?

Hyperion to Diotima

I have him, dear Diotima!

My breast is light, and swift my sinews, ha! and the future tempts me, as clear deep water tempts us to leap into it and cool our exuberant blood in that freshening bath. But this is idle chatter. We are dearer to each other than ever, my Alabanda and I. We are freer together, and yet all the fullness and depth of life is there, as it used to be.

Oh, how right the tyrants of old were to forbid such friendships as ours! Then a man is as strong as a demigod and tolerates no insolence within his sphere!—

It was evening when I entered his room. He had just laid aside his work and was sitting by the window in a moonlit corner, communing with his thoughts. I was standing in the dark, he did not recognize me, he looked toward me unconcernedly. Heaven knows who he took me to be. "Well, how goes it?" he cried. "Well enough," I said. But my dissembling availed nothing. My voice was filled with secret delight. "What is this?" he sprang up; "is it you?" "Yes, you blindman," I cried, and flew into his arms. "Oh, now," Alabanda cried at last, "now everything will be different, Hyperion!"

"So I think too," said I, and happily shook his hand.

"And do you still know me," Alabanda continued after a time, "have you still your old devout belief in Alabanda? Magnanimous Hyperion! things have not gone as well for me since, as they did when I felt the light of your love on me."

"What!" I cried, "can Alabanda ask this? There was no pride in those words, Alabanda. But it is a sign of this age that the old heroic nature goes begging for respect and the living human heart pines for a drop of love, like an orphan."

"Dear youth!" he cried; "I have grown old, that is all. The slackness of life everywhere, and that matter of the old men with whom I wanted to put you to school in Smyrna—"

"Oh, it is bitter," I cried; "the deadly Goddess, the Nameless One whom men call Fate, has not spared even this man."

Lights were brought, and again we looked at each other in cautiously loving scrutiny. My dear friend's figure had changed very much since those days of hope. His large, ever-animated eye shone upon me from his faded face like the midday sun from a pallid heaven.

"Dear youth!" cried Alabanda, lovingly vexed to find me staring at him so, "enough of these dolorous looks, dear youth! I know very well that I have sunk. O my Hyperion! I long so much for something great and true and, with you, I hope to find it. You have outgrown me, you are freer and stronger than in the past, and, believe me! it rejoices my heart. I am the parched land, and you come like a fortunate storm—oh, it is glorious that you are here!"

"Stop!" I said, "you drive me out of my senses, and we should not talk of ourselves at all until we are in the midst of life, among deeds."

"Yes, yes!" Alabanda cried joyously, "not until the horn sounds do the hunters feel like hunters."

"Will it start soon, then?" I said.

"It will," cried Alabanda, "and I tell you, dear heart! it will be quite a fire. Ha! may it reach to the tower's top and melt its vane and rage and swirl about it until it bursts and falls!—and you must not take offense at our allies. I know that the good Russians would like to use us as firearms. But let that pass! when our strong Spartans have once learned in the field who they are and of what they are capable, when once we have conquered the Peloponnesus with them, then we will laugh in the North Pole's face and make a life of our own."

"A life of our own," I cried, "a new, an honorable life. Were we born of the swamp, like a will-o'-the-wisp, or are we descended from the victors at Salamis? How is this? how, O free nature of the Greeks, have you become a maidservant? how have you so declined, ancestral race, of which the divine images of Jupiter and Apollo were once only the copy?—But hear me, sky of Ionia! hear me, my native soil, you that, half naked, dress yourself like a beggarwoman in the rags of your ancient glory; I will bear it no longer!"

"Oh Sun, who fostered us!" cried Alabanda, "you shall witness it when our courage grows under our toil, when our resolution takes shape under the blows of Fate like iron under the hammer."

Each of us enflamed the other.

"And let no spot remain, none of the abject nonsense with which this century would smear us as the rabble do the walls!"

"Oh," cried Alabanda, "that is the reason war is so good—"

"Yes, yes, Alabanda," I cried, "even as are all great undertakings, in which men's strength and spirit, not crutches and wings of wax, are the means. There we take off the slaves' clothing branded with the mark which Fate would set upon us—"

"There all that is frivolous, all that is forced, has no more currency," cried Alabanda, "we go stripped of ornaments as of chains, naked as in the races at Nemea, straight to the goal."

"To the goal," I cried, "where the young free state dawns and the pantheon of all Beauty arises from the soil of Greece."

Alabanda was silent for a while. A new red rose into his face and his form grew as a plant refreshed.

"O Youth, Youth!" he cried, "then will I drink from your spring; then will I live and love. I am very joyful, Sky of Night," he went on as if intoxicated, walking to the window, "your vault is over me like the foliage of a vine, and your stars hang down like clusters of grapes."

Hyperion to Diotima

It is my good fortune that my life is completely occupied with work. I should fall into one folly after another, so full is my soul, so am I intoxicated by the proud, the wonderful man who loves nothing but me and heaps all the humility that is in him upon me alone. O Diotima! this Alabanda has wept before me, has begged me like a child to forgive him for what he did to me in Smyrna.

Who am I, you loved ones, that I call you mine, that I dare to say, "They are my own," that, like a conqueror, I stand between you and hold you as my treasure?

O Diotima! O Alabanda! noble, calmly great beings! how much there is for me to accomplish, if I am not to flee from my happiness, from you?

Just now, while I was writing, I received your letter, dear one.

Grieve not, lovely being, grieve not! Preserve yourself unwithered by sorrow, for the future festivals of our country! Diotima, preserve yourself for the shining celebration of Nature and for all the serene days set aside to honor the gods!

Do you not see Greece already?

Oh, do you not see how, rejoicing in their new neighbor, the eternal stars smile over our towns and groves, how the ancient ocean, when it sees our people wandering happily along the shore, remembers the beautiful Athenians and speeds good fortune to us again, as then it did to its favorites, on rejoicing waves? O soulful maiden! you are so beautiful already! when the true climate nourishes you at last, in what enchanting glory will you not flower!

Diotima to Hyperion

I had shut myself up indoors most of the time since you went away, dear Hyperion! Today I went out again.

In the sweet February air I gathered life, and I bring you what I gathered. It still did me good, the fresh warming of the sky; I still felt in sympathy with the new joy of the plant world, ever pure, ever the same, where all things grieve and rejoice again in their time.

Hyperion! O my Hyperion! then why do not we too walk the quiet paths of life? They are holy names, winter and spring and summer and autumn! yet we know them not. It is not a sin to grieve in spring? Why do we, then?

Forgive me! Earth's children live through the sun alone; I live through you; I have other joys, so is it any wonder if I have other griefs? and must I grieve? must I?

Brave one! loved one! shall I wither while you shine? shall my heart grow weary when the joy of victory wakes in your every vein? Had I heard in times past that a Greek youth had risen to raise our good people out of their shame, to give them back the maternal Beauty from which they are sprung, how I should have started from the dream of childhood and thirsted for the image of one so precious! and now that he is there, now that he is mine, can I still weep? Oh, the silly girl! is it not true? is he not the glorious one, and is he not mine! O you shadows of a blessed time! you my beloved memories!

Yet it seems as if it was scarcely yesterday, that magical evening when the sacred stranger came to me for the first time, when, like a grieving genius, he shone into the shadows of the wood where the carefree maiden sat in the dream of youth—in the air of May he came, in the enchanting May air of Ionia, and it made him bloom all the more, it waved his hair, opened his lips like flowers, dissolved sorrow in smiles, and O you rays of heaven! how you shone on me from those eyes, from those intoxicating springs where in the shadow of screening brows eternal life shimmers and wells!—

Merciful Gods! how beautiful he became with his gaze upon me! how the whole youth, grown a span taller, stood there in easy strength, save that his dear, modest arms dropped down as if they were nothing! and how, then, he looked up in rapture, as if I had flown into the sky and were no longer there, ah! how, aware of me again, his eye shone bright as Phoebus through the darkening tears and, smiling, he blushed with inborn grace to ask me, "Is it you? is it you indeed?"

And why did he come to me with thoughts so devout, so full of dear superstition? why did he first stand with bowed head, why was the divine youth so full of shyness and grief? His genius was too blessed to remain alone, and the world too poor to comprehend him. Oh, it was a dear image, woven of greatness and sorrow! But now it is otherwise! the sorrowing is over! He has found work to do, he is sick no longer!—

I was full of sighs when I began to write to you, my beloved! Now I am pure joy. To talk of you has been to grow happy. And look! even so shall it remain. Farewell!

Hyperion to Diotima

We have managed to celebrate your birthday, beautiful being! before the uproar begins. It was a heavenly day. The lovely springtime wafted and shone from the East, conjured your name from us as it conjures the flowers from the trees, and all the blessed secrets of love took my breath away. My friend had never known of such a love as ours, and it was ravishing to see how attentive the proud man became and how his eye and his spirit glowed as they strove to apprehend your image, your being.

"Oh," he cried at last, "our Greece is well worth fighting for when it still bears such offspring!"

"Yes indeed, my Alabanda," said I; "then we go joyfully into battle, then a divine fire drives us on to do high deeds when our spirit is rejuvenated by the image of such natures, then we run for no petty goal, then we are not concerned for this thing and that thing, do not tinker with outsides, unheeding the spirit, nor drink the wine for the cup's sake, then we will not rest, Alabanda, until the ecstasy of the Genius is a secret no longer, when all eyes are transformed into triumphal arches from which man's spirit, long absent, shines forth out of error and sufferings and greets the paternal ether in the joy of victory.—Ha! let no one think to know our people, as they are to be, from their flag alone; everything must be rejuvenated, everything be changed from the ground up; pleasure must be full of seriousness, and all work gleeful! nothing, not even the least and most commonplace of things, must be without spirit and the gods!

Love and hate and every tone from us must make the commoner world wonder, not a *single* moment must ever dare to remind us of the lowly past!"

Hyperion to Diotima

The volcano is erupting. The Turks are besieged in Coron and Modon and we are pushing on against the Peloponnesus with our mountaineers.

Now all depression is ended, Diotima, and my spirit is firmer and swifter since I am occupied with vital work and yes! I now even have a daily schedule.

I begin with the sun. I go out to where my troops are lying in the shadow of the woods and greet the thousand clear eyes that now open to me with wild affection. An awakening army! I know of nothing like it and all the life of towns and villages is like a swarm of bees in comparison.

Man cannot hide it from himself: once he was happy, like the deer in the forest, and even now, after untold years, there rises in us a longing for the days of the primal world, when he roved over the earth like a god, before I know not what tamed man, and, instead of walls and dead wood, the soul of the World, sacred Air, still wrapped him in its universal presence.

Diotima! I am often filled with wonder when I go about among my carefree men and one after another stands up as if sprung from the earth and stretches himself toward the dawn, and among the martial groups the crackling flame rises, where the mother sits with the freezing infant, where the restoring dish is cooking, while the horses, sniffing the day, snort and whinny, and the wood resounds with shattering military music, and everywhere glitters and rings with weapons—but these are words, and the unique pleasure of such a life cannot be told.

Then my troop gathers eagerly around me, and it is wonderful how even the oldest and most recalcitrant respect me, despite my youth. We become more and more intimate, and many of them tell me what their lives have been, and my heart often swells with their so various fates. Then I begin to speak of better days, and their eyes open wide and shine when they think of the covenant that will unite us, and the proud image of the free state that is soon to be looms before them.

All for one and one for all! There is a joyous spirit in the words, and it takes possession of my men, too, like a divine decree. O Diotima! to see how their stubborn natures are softened by hopes, and all their pulses beat more strongly, and the burdened brow is smoothed and cleared by planning! to stand there in a sphere of men, surrounded by faith and joy—that is more, far more, than to behold earth and sky and sea in all their glory.

Then I drill them in weapons and marching until toward noon. The happy mood makes them eager pupils, as it makes me a teacher. Now they stand close together in the Macedonian phalanx, moving only their arms; now like rays they fly in different directions to more hazardous combat in separate squads, where their flexible strength changes with every position and each is his own general, then assemble again in a place of safety—and always, wherever they go or stand in this sort of war dance, before their eyes and mine floats the image of the tyrant's cohorts and the field of real battle.

Then, when the sun shines hotter, we hold council deep in the wood, and it is a joy thus in quiet thought to determine our great future. We strip chance of its power; we master destiny. We let resistance arise as suits our purpose; we lure the enemy into actions for which we are prepared. Or we bide our time and appear to be afraid, and let him come nearer until he exposes his head to our blow, or we utterly disconcert him with our speed, and that is my panacea. But the more experienced physicians do not hold with such a cure.

After that, how good I feel in the evening, with my Alabanda, when we rove for pleasure around the sun-red hills on our spirited horses, and on the summits where we linger, the wind plays in the manes of our mounts and the soothing rustle mingles with our talk, while we gaze into the distances of Sparta, which are the prize for which we shall fight! and then when we have returned and sit together in the pleasant cool of the night, and the winecup is sweet in our nostrils and the moon's rays light our frugal meal, and amid our smiling silence, the history of the men of old rises like a cloud from the soil that bears us, how blissful it is in such moments to grasp each other's hands!

Then perhaps Alabanda speaks of many another whom the ennui of this century torments, of so many a strangely crooked course that life takes, now that its straight path has been blocked, and then I think, too, of my Adamas, with his journeyings, his strange longing for the innermost parts of Asia—"These are but stopgaps, dear old man," I would cry to him now, "come! and build your world! with us! for our world is yours, too."

And yours, too, Diotima, for it is copied after you. O you, with your Elysian quiet, could we but create that which you are!

Hyperion to Diotima

We have now won three battles in succession—small ones, to be sure, but in them the combatants collided like thunderbolts and all was *one* consuming flame. Navarin is ours, and we are now before the fortress of Mistra, that remnant of ancient Sparta. And the flag that I wrested from an Albanian horde, I have planted on a ruin that lies before the city, and in my joy have thrown my Turkish turban into the Eurotas and since then wear the Greek casque.

And now would that I could see you, O maiden! that I could see you and take your hands and press them to my heart, whose joy will soon perhaps be too great! soon! in a week perhaps the old, noble land will be set free, the sacred Peloponnesus.

Then, O precious one, teach me to be pious! then teach my overflowing heart a prayer! I should be silent, for what have I done? and if I had done anything worth speaking of, how much is nonetheless left to do! But how can I help it if my thought is swifter than time? I wish so much that it were the other way around, that time and the deed overtook the thought, that winged victory outstripped the hope itself.

My Alabanda blooms like a bridegroom. From his every look the coming world smiles at me, and with that I still quiet my impatience somewhat.

Diotima! I would not change this budding happiness for the most beautiful life that was ever lived in ancient Greece, and the smallest of our victories is dearer to me than Marathon and Thermopylae and Plataea. Is it not true? is not life recovering health more cherished than the pure life that has not yet known sickness? Not until youth is gone do we love it, not until what has been lost returns does it rejoice all the depths of the soul.

My tent is pitched beside the Eurotas, and when I wake up after midnight the ancient River God roars past exhorting me, and, smiling, I pick the flowers on the bank and throw them into his shining waves and say to him: "Take it as a sign, thou lonely one! Soon the old life will bloom around thee again."

Diotima to Hyperion

I have received the letters, my Hyperion, that you have written me along your way. You move me powerfully by all that you say, and in the midst of my love I often shudder to see the gentle youth who wept at my feet transformed into this robust being.

Will you not forget all that you have learned of love?

But change as you will! I follow you. I believe that if you could hate me, I, too, should even come to feel as you felt, would make an effort to hate you, and so our souls would remain alike—and this that I say is no exaggeration, Hyperion.

I, too, am wholly different from what I was. I have lost my serene view of the world and my free delight in everything that has life. Only the field of the stars still draws my eyes. On the other hand, I think all the more fondly of the great spirits of the past and how they ended on earth, and the noble women of Sparta have won my heart. With all this, I do not forget the new champions, the strong whose hour has come, I often hear their shouts of victory through the Peloponnesus roar nearer and nearer to me, I often see them surging down like a cataract through the woods of Epidaurus, and their weapons glitter far off in the sunlight that guides them on like a herald, O my Hyperion! and you come swiftly across to Calaurea and greet the quiet woods of our love, greet me, and then fly back to your work;—and do you think I fear for the outcome! Dearest! often I am close to being troubled, but my nobler thoughts are like flames and hold off the chill.—

Farewell! Accomplish what the spirit bids you! and let not the war go on too long, for peace's sake, Hyperion, for the sake of the beautiful, new, golden peace, when, as you said, the laws of Nature will yet be written in our statute book, and when life itself, when divine Nature, that can be written in no book, will dwell in the hearts of the community. Farewell.

Hyperion to Diotima

You should have calmed me, my Diotima! should have said that I must not go too fast, must extort victory from Fate little by little, as what they owe is wrung from impecunious debtors. O maiden! to stand still is worse than anything. My blood dries up in my veins, I so thirst to go forward, and must stand here idle, laying siege day in and day out. Our men want to storm, but that would heat their excited spirits to frenzy, and alas! then for our hopes, if every savagery erupts and bursts the bonds of discipline and love.

I do not know, it can be but a few days longer before Mistra must surrender, but I wish we were farther forward. Here in the camp I feel as if I were in the atmosphere of a brewing storm. I am impatient, and my men are not to my liking. There is a recklessness among them that is terrifying.

But I am stupid to make so much of my state of mind. Yes, a little concern is a cheap price to pay for making ancient Lacedaemon ours.

Hyperion to Diotima

It is over, Diotima! our men have plundered, murdered, indiscriminately, even our brothers were killed, the innocent Greeks in Mistra, or they wander helplessly about, their deathly faces calling Heaven and Earth to wreak vengeance on the barbarians, whose leader I was.

Now indeed I can go forth and preach my good cause. Oh now indeed all hearts will fly to me!

How cleverly I went about it. How well I knew my men. Yes! it was indeed a remarkable undertaking, to establish my Elysium with a pack of thieves!

No! by sacred Nemesis! I have got what I deserved, and I will bear it too, bear it until the pain destroys my last consciousness.

Do you think I am raving? I have an honorable wound, which one of my faithful followers gave me while I was trying to avert the horror. If I were raving, I would tear the bandage from it, and then my blood would run where it should—into this sorrowing soil.

This sorrowing soil! whose nakedness I sought to clothe with sacred groves! this soil which I sought to adorn with all the flowers of Greek life!

Oh, it would have been beautiful, my Diotima!

Do you tell me I have lost faith? Dear girl! the evil is too great. Bands of madmen are bursting in on every side; rapacity rages like the plague in Morea, and he who does not also take the sword is hunted down and slain, and the maniacs say they are fighting for our freedom. Others of these wild men are paid by the Sultan and do the same things.

I have just heard that our dishonored army is now scattered. The cowards encountered a troop of Albanians near Tripolissa, only half as many as themselves. But since there was nothing to plunder, the wretches all ran away. Only the Russians who risked this campaign with us, forty brave men, put up a resistance, and they all found death.

So now I am again alone with my Alabanda, as before. Ever since he saw me fall and bleed in Mistra, that true-hearted friend has forgotten everything else—his hopes, his longing for victory, his despair. He who in his fury came down upon the plunderers like an avenging god, he led me out of the fight so gently, and his tears wet my clothes. He stayed with me, too, in the hut where I have lain since then, and only now am I glad that he did so. For had he gone on, he would now be lying in the dust before Tripolissa.

What is to follow I know not. Fate casts me adrift in uncertainty, and I have deserved it; my own feeling of shame banishes me from you, and who knows for how long?

Ah! I promised you a Greece, and instead you receive only an elegy. Be your own consolation!

Hyperion to Diotima

I can scarcely bring myself to speak.

To be sure, men delight in speaking, they chatter away like the birds, so long as the world breathes upon them like the air of May; but between noon and evening that can change, and what is lost in the end?

Believe me, and consider that I say it to you from the depths of my soul: speech is a great superfluity. The best is ever for itself, and rests in its own depth like the pearl at the bottom of the sea.—But what I really wanted to write to you is this: because the painting needs its frame and man his daily work, I am now going to take service for a time in the Russian fleet; for I have nothing more to do with the Greeks.

O dear girl! It has grown very dark around me!

Hyperion to Diotima

I have hesitated, I have struggled. But now at last it must be.

I see what is necessary. And since I see it, it shall come to pass. Do not misunderstand me! do not condemn me! I must advise you to give me up, my Diotima.

I am nothing more for you, lovely being! This heart has dried up toward you, and my eyes no more see what has life. Oh, my lips have withered; the sweet breath of love no longer wells up in my breast.

One day has taken all my youth from me; beside the Eurotas my life wept itself weary, ah! beside the Eurotas which, in irreparable dishonor, goes mourning with its every wave past Lacedaemon's ruins. There, there did Fate mow down my harvest.—Am I to have your love as an alms?—I am as utterly nothing, as inglorious, as the most wretched serf. I am banished, cursed, like a common rebel, and many a Greek in Morea will hereafter narrate our heroic deeds to his children's children as a tale of thieves.

And, ah! I have long kept one thing from you. My father has solemnly disowned me, banished me irrevocably from the home of my youth; he will never see me again, either in this life or the next, as he puts it. So reads the answer to the letter in which I wrote to him of my undertaking.

But let not pity, now or ever, lead you astray. Believe me, there is one joy left for us everywhere. True grief inspires. He who steps on his misery stands higher. And it is glorious that only in suffering do we truly feel freedom of soul. Freedom! if any understand the word—it is a deep word, Diotima. I am so inwardly assailed, so extraordinarily hurt, I am without hope, without a goal, utterly dishonored, and yet there is a power in me, something indomitable, that sets my frame sweetly trembling whenever it awakes in me.

And I still have my Alabanda. He has as little to gain as I have. I can keep him for myself without injuring him. Ah! the kingly youth would have deserved a better lot. He has become so gentle and so quiet. It often comes near to breaking my heart. But each of us sustains the other. We do not talk together; what should we say? but there is a blessing in many little affectionate things that we do for each other.

There he sleeps, smiling resignedly, in all our misfortune. The good soul! he does not know what I am doing. He would not tolerate it. "You must write to Diotima," he ordered me, "and tell her to be ready soon to fly with you to a more endurable country." But he does not know that a heart that has learned to despair like his and like mine is nothing more for its beloved. No! no! you would forever find no peace with Hyperion, you could not but be unfaithful, and that I shall spare you.

And so farewell, sweet maid! farewell! Would that I could say to you: "Go here, go there; there the springs of life murmur." Would that I could show you a freer country, a country filled with beauty and soul, and say: "Escape there." But, O Heaven! if I could do that, I should be other than I am, and then I should not need to take my leave—take leave? Ah, I know not what I am doing. I thought that I was so self-possessed, so cool-headed. Now my brain reels, my heart tosses like an impatient sick man. woe to me! I am destroying my last happiness. But it must be, and mortal nature's "Alas!" is unavailing here. I owe it to you, and, besides that, I was born to be homeless and without a resting place. O Earth! O you Stars! shall I find nowhere to abide, even to the end?

Could I but *once* return to your arms, no matter where! Eyes clear as the ether! could I but *once* again find myself in you! hang on those lips of yours, O lovable, inexpressible one! and drink down your ravishing, blessed sweet life—but listen not to this! I implore you, heed it not! If you listened, I should say I am a seducer. You know me, you understand me. You recognize what deep respect you pay me, if you do not pity me, do not listen to me.

I can, I may no more—how should the priest live when his God is no more? O Genius of my people! O Soul of Greece! I must descend, I must seek you in the realm of the dead.

Hyperion to Diotima

I have waited long, I will confess to you; I have hoped anxiously for a parting word from your heart, but you are silent. That, too, is a language of your beautiful soul, Diotima.

Is it not true that the more sacred harmonies do not therefore cease? is it not true, Diotima, that even when the soft moonlight of love sets, the higher stars of its heaven still shine on? Oh, that is indeed my last joy, that we are inseparable, even if no sound returns to me from you, no shadow of our fair young days.

I gaze out to the reddened sea of evening; I stretch my arms toward the far place where you live, and my soul is warmed once again by all the joys of love and youth.

O Earth! my cradle! all bliss and all sorrow is in our leave-taking from you!

You dear Ionian islands! and you, my Calaurea, and you, my Tina, you are all before my eyes, distant though you be, and my spirit flies with the breeze over the moving waters; and you that loom dimly over there, you shores of Teos and Ephesus, where once I walked with Alabanda in the days of hope, you appear to me again as in that time, and I would sail across to the mainland and kiss that soil and warm it at my breast and stammer out all sweet words of farewell to the silent Earth, before I fly up into freedom.

Alas, alas, that things are not now better among mankind! were it otherwise, I would gladly remain upon this goodly star. But I can forego this globe of the Earth, and that is more than all that it can give.

"Let us bear slavery, O child, in the light of the Sun," said her mother to Polyxena, and her love of life could find no more beautiful expression. But it is the light of the Sun that exhorts me not to bear slavery, that will not let me remain upon the degraded Earth, and his holy rays draw me on, like paths that lead home.

Long since has the majesty of the soul that is outside of Fate been more present to me than anything else; I have often lived within myself in glorious solitude; I have grown used to shaking off outside things like flakes of snow; why, then, should I be afraid to seek so-called death? have I not freed myself a thousand times in thought? why should I hesitate to do it *once* in reality? Are we like slaves, then, bound to the soil that we plow? are we like barnyard fowls, which dare not run out of the courtyard because they are fed there?

We are like young eagles whose father drives them out of the nest that they may seek their prey in the high ether.

Tomorrow our fleet goes into action, and the fight will be hot enough. I look on this battle as a bath that will wash the dust from me; and I shall doubtless find what I wish for; wishes like mine are easily granted, and on the spot. And so I should have gained something after all from my campaign, and behold! no effort that man makes is wholly in vain.

Devout soul! I would say, "Think of me when you come upon my grave." But they will doubtless throw me into the sea, and I am content to have my remains sink down where the springs and all the rivers that I loved gather together, and where the storm cloud arises to drench the mountains and the valleys that I loved. And we? O Diotima! Diotima! when shall we see each other once again?

It is impossible, and my inmost life rebels if I try to think that we are lost to each other. I would wander among the stars for millenniums, clothe myself in all forms, in all the languages of life, that I might meet you *once* again. But I think that what is alike is soon united.

Great soul! you will be able to reconcile yourself to this parting, and so let me be off on my journey! Greet your mother! greet Notara and our other friends!

And greet the trees where I found you before me for the first time and the joyous brooks where we walked and the lovely gardens of Angele, and, dear one, let my image be before you. Farewell.

Book Two

Hyperion to Bellarmin

I was in a lovely dream when I copied out for you the letters that I once exchanged. Now I write to you again, my Bellarmin! and lead you yet further down, down into the deepest depth of my sorrow, and then, you last of my loves! come out with me again, to the place where a new day shines upon us.

The battle of which I had written to Diotima began. The Turkish ships had withdrawn into the strait between the island of Chios and the Asiatic coast, and had taken up a position along the mainland near Cheshme. My admiral left the line with his ship, on which I was, and began the prelude with the first Turkish ship. The enraged pair were heated to frenzy at the very first attack; it was an intoxication of revenge, a terrible battle. The ships were soon fast together by their rigging; the furious fight was ever at closer quarters.

A profound sense of life still pervaded me. I felt warm and good in every limb. My spirit, like one taking tender leave, was aware of itself for the last time in all its senses. And now, filled with hot disgust at knowing nothing better than to let myself be slaughtered in a crush of barbarians, I rushed on, with tears of rage in my eyes, to where certain death awaited me.

I had not far to seek for the enemy, and it was not many minutes before, of the Russians who were fighting beside me, not even *one* was left. I stood there alone, filled with pride, and flung my life down before the barbarians like a beggar's penny; but they would have none of me. They looked at me as at a man whom one is afraid to offend, and Fate seemed to feel consideration for me in my despair.

In desperate self-defense, one of them at last aimed a blow at me, striking me so that I fell. After that I knew nothing, until I came to my senses again in Paros, to which I had been brought by ship.

From the servant who carried me out of the battle I later heard that the two ships that had begun the fight had blown up the moment after he and the surgeon had taken me off in a boat. The Russians had thrown fire into the Turkish ship; and since theirs was fast to the other, it had burned too.

How this terrible battle ended, you know. "Thus one poison wreaks vengeance upon the other," I cried, when I learned that the Russians had burned the entire Turkish fleet—"thus do tyrants exterminate themselves."

Hyperion to Bellarmin

Six days after the battle I lay in a tortured, deathly sleep. My life was like a night interrupted by pains as from flashing lightning. My first returning consciousness was of Alabanda. He had not—so I learned—stirred from my side for an instant, had taken care of me almost single-handed, with incredible assiduity, with a thousand tender, homely services of which he would otherwise never in his life have thought, and he had been heard to cry, on his knees beside my bed: "O live, my loved one, that I may live!"

It was a happy awakening, Bellarmin! when my eyes opened to the light again, and the glorious youth stood before me with tears of emotion at our reunion.

I held out my hand, and, proud as he was, he kissed it with all the rapture of love. "He lives," he cried, "O Nature! O kindly, all-healing savior! you do not, will not forsake your wretched pair, your wanderers without a country. O Hyperion! never will I forget seeing your ship go up in fire before my eyes and, thundering, carry the sailors with it in raging flame, and among the few who were saved there was no Hyperion. I was out of my mind, and the fierce clamor of battle did not quiet me. But I soon heard news of you and flew after you as soon as we had finished with the enemy."—

And how he watched over me now! with what loving caution he kept me imprisoned in the magic circle of his kind services! how, without a word, he taught me by his great quietude to understand the free course of the world without envy and like a man!

O you sons of the Sun! you freer souls! much has been lost in this Alabanda. I sought in vain, in vain I prayed to Life; since he is gone, such a Roman nature I have never found. Untroubled, profoundly understanding, brave, noble Alabanda! where is there a man if he was not one? And when he was friendly and simple, it was as when the light of evening plays through the darkness of the majestic oak and its leaves drip with the rainstorm of the day.

Hyperion to Bellarmin

It was in the beautiful days of autumn that, half recovered from my wound, I made my way to the window again for the first time. I returned to life with calmer senses and my soul had grown more attentive. The air of heaven breathed its most delicate magic upon me, and the serene sunbeams poured down as mildly as a rain of flowers. There was a great, quiet, tender spirit in the season, and among the rustling twigs the peace of completion, the bliss of maturity surrounded me like the renewed youth for which the Ancients hoped in their Elysium.

It had been long since I had enjoyed it in purity of soul, this childlike love of the world; now my eyes opened with all the joy of recognition and blessed Nature had remained unchanged in her beauty. My tears flowed before her like an atoning sacrifice, and a heart renewed rose tremblingly from my old discontent. "O holy world of plants!" I cried, "we struggle and take thought, and yet have you! with our mortal powers we strive to cultivate the Beautiful, yet it grows light-heartedly beside us! Is it not so, Alabanda? men are made to provide for their necessities; all else is freely given. And yet—I cannot forget how much more I wanted."

"Let it suffice you, dear one, that you exist," cried Alabanda, "and let grieving no longer hinder what is quietly at work within you."

"Yes, I will rest," said I. "Oh, I will tear up all those projects, all those claims, like promissory notes. I will keep myself pure, as an artist keeps himself; you will I love, innocent Life, Life of the grove and the spring! you will I honor, O light of the Sun! by you will I calm myself, beautiful Ether, which givest life to the stars and yet here breathest about these trees and here touchest us in the depths of our hearts! O willfulness of men! I have bowed my neck like a beggar, and the Gods of Nature watched me in silence with all their gifts!—Do you smile, Alabanda? Oh how often, in our earliest days, did you smile so when your lad chattered to you in the intoxicated pride of youth, the while you stood like a quiet temple pillar amid the rubble of the world and could not but suffer the wild tendrils of my love to grow about you—see what a blindfold falls from my eyes, and the old golden days are here and live again!"

"Ah!" he cried, "the earnestness that was ours, and the joy of life!"

"When we hunted in the forest," I cried, "when we bathed in the sea, when we sang and drank, and through the laurel shade the sun and the wine and our eyes and our lips were bright—that was a life without equal and our spirit illuminated our youthful happiness like a shining heaven." "And therefore neither of us can abandon the other," said Alabanda.

"Oh, I have a heavy confession to make to you," said I. "Will you believe that I wanted to go away? from you! that I sought my death by sheer strength? was that not heartless? madness? ah, and my Diotima! she must leave me, I wrote to her, and after that another letter, the evening before the battle—" "and you wrote in it," he cried, "that you would seek your end in the battle? O Hyperion! But she cannot yet have received that last letter. You must write to her, quickly, that you are still alive."

"Best Alabanda!" I cried. "You comfort me indeed! I will write at once and send my servant off with it. Oh, I will offer him all that I have to hurry and reach Calaurea while it is still time."—

"And the other letter, in which you wrote of renunciation—the good soul will easily understand and forgive you for that," he added.

"Does she forgive?" I cried; "O all you hopes! yes! if I could still be happy with that angel!"

"You will still be happy," cried Alabanda; "the most beautiful age of life is yet left to you. The youth is a hero, the man a god, if he can live to see it."

A wondrous light dawned in my soul as he spoke.

The tops of the trees stirred softly; like flowers from the dark earth, stars sprouted from the womb of night and the springtime of the heavens shone on me in holy joy.

Hyperion to Bellarmin

A few minutes later, just as I was about to write to Diotima, Alabanda came joyfully back into the room. "A letter, Hyperion!" he cried; I gave a start and flew to it.

"How long," wrote Diotima, "I had to live without a sign from you! You wrote me about the fatal day at Mistra, and I answered speedily; but everything would indicate that you did not receive my letter. Immediately afterward you wrote to me again, briefly and gloomily, and said you were of a mind to join the Russian fleet; I answered again; but that letter did not reach you either; now I, too, waited in vain, from May to the end of summer, until some days ago the letter arrived which tells me I should renounce you, beloved!

"You relied on me, had enough trust in me to believe that your letter could not offend me. That made me heartily glad, even in my distress.

"Unhappy, lofty spirit! I have understood you only too well. Oh, it is so completely natural that you will not love, because your greater wishes are dying a lingering death. Must you not scorn food when you are perishing of thirst?

"I soon understood; I could not be all to you. Could I loose the bonds of mortality for you? could I quiet the flame in your breast, that flame for which no spring flows and no vine bears grapes? could I offer you the joys of the world in a scallop shell?

"That is what you want. That is what you need, and you cannot do otherwise. The unbounded impotence of your contemporaries has robbed you of your life.

"*He who, like you, has been hurt to the depths of his soul can no longer find rest in an individual joy, he who, like you, has felt nothingness in all its vapidity finds exhilaration only in the highest spirit, he who has experienced death as you did recovers only among the gods.*

"They are fortunate—all those who do not understand you! He who understands you must share in your greatness and in your despair.

"I found you as you are. Life's first curiosity impelled me toward that wonderful being. Your tender soul drew me inexpressibly on, with the fearlessness of a child I played about your dangerous flame.—The beautiful joys of our love softened you; but only, wicked man! to make you the more savage. They soothed, they solaced me, too, they made me forget that you were essentially inconsolable, and that I, too, was not far from becoming so ever since I had looked into your beloved heart.

"In Athens, beside the ruins of the Olympieion, it came over me again. In carefree hours, it is true, I had been thinking: This youth's sorrow is not perhaps so deep and inexorable. It is so seldom that a man, at his first step into life, has at *once* so suddenly, so minutely, so quickly, so deeply felt the whole inevitable course of his time, and that this feeling is so ineradicably fixed in him because he is not rugged enough to cast it out and not weak enough to weep it away— that, my dear one, is so unusual that we think it almost out of the course of Nature.

"Now, in the rubble of serene Athens, it came home to me all too grievously: the leaf has been turned, the dead now walk the earth and the living, the divine men, are under it, now I saw it all too literally and all too really written on your face, now I admitted that you were eternally right. But at the same moment I saw you greater. A being filled with secret strength, filled with a deep, undeveloped significance, a youth uniquely promising—thus you appeared to me. 'He to whom Destiny speaks so loudly has the right to speak yet more loudly to Destiny,' I told myself; 'the more unfathomably he suffers, the more unfathomably strong he is.' From you, from you alone, I hoped for all restoration. I saw you traveling. I saw you working. Oh, the transformation! Established by you, the grove of Academe spread green again over listening pupils, and the plane tree of the Ilissus heard sacred conversations, as of old.

"In your school the genius of our youths soon acquired the seriousness of the Ancients, and its transitory games became more nearly immortal, for it felt ashamed, deemed its butterfly flight a prison.—

"To manage a horse would have sufficed one of them; now he is a general. Only too contentedly would another have sung an idle song; now he is an artist. For you had revealed the powers of the heroes, the powers of the world to them in open battle; you had given them the riddles of your heart to solve; so the youths learned to bring together great things, learned to understand the living play of Nature, and forgot jesting.—Hyperion! Hyperion! did you not make me, immature as I was, a Muse? So it was, too, with the others.

"Ah! now men, born to companionship, did not so easily forsake one another; no longer did they wander in mutual confusion, like sand in the desert storm, nor did youth and age mock each other, nor did the stranger lack a hospitable host, and fellow countrymen no longer stood aside, and lovers no longer tired of each other; at your springs, Nature, they refreshed themselves, ah! at the sacred joys that pour secretly from your depths and renew the spirit; and the gods restored to the souls of men the joy without which they wither away; the heart-sustaining gods were guardians of every bond of friendship. For you, Hyperion! had healed the eyes of your Greeks so that they saw the living, you had kindled the enthusiasm that slept in them like fire in wood so that they felt the still, never-failing enthusiasm of Nature and of her pure children. Ah! now men no longer took the beautiful world as the uninitiated take the artist's poem when they praise the words of it and look for profit in them. O living Nature, you became a magical example to the Greeks, and, fired by the happiness of the ever-young gods, all the activities of men were, as of old, a festival; and more beautiful than martial music, Helios' light escorted the young heroes to high deeds.

"Enough! enough! it was my most beautiful dream, my first and my last. You are too proud any longer to concern yourself with this villainous race. And you are right. You led them to freedom, and they thought of robbery. You led them victoriously into their ancient Lacedaemon, and these monsters fall to plundering and you are cursed by your father, great son! and no wilderness, no cave is safe enough for you on this Greek soil that you revered as a sacred shrine, that you loved more than you loved me.

"O my Hyperion! I am no longer the gentle maiden, since I have learned all this. Indignation bears me upward so that I can hardly see down to the Earth, and my offended heart trembles incessantly.

"We will part. You are right. And I want no children; for I will not bestow them on this world of slaves, and besides, the poor plants would wither away before my eyes in this drought.

"Farewell, dear youth! go wherever you think it worth going to yield up your soul. The world must yet have *one* battlefield, *one* place of sacrifice, where you can free yourself. It would be a shame if all these goodly powers but vanished like a dream. But however you find your end, you return to the gods, return into the sacred, free, youthful life of Nature, whence you came, and that is your desire as it is mine."

So she wrote to me. I was stricken to the core, filled with terror and joy, but I tried to control myself and find words in which to answer.

"You assent, Diotima?" I wrote, "you approve of my renunciation? you could understand it?—Loyal soul! you could reconcile yourself to it? could reconcile yourself even to my dark wanderings, in your heavenly patience? you submitted, eclipsed yourself for love, happy child of Nature? became like me and by your concurrence sanctified my grief? Beautiful heroine! what crown did you not earn?

"But now let there be enough of grieving, O loved one! You have followed me into my darkness, now come! and let me follow you to your light, let us return to your graces, beautiful heart! oh, let me look upon your calm once again, blessed nature! let me lull my discontent to sleep forever before you, image of peace!

"Is it not true, dear one! it is not too late for me to return even now? and you will take me back and can love me again, as before? is it not true that the happiness of past days is not lost to us?

"I have behaved unconscionably. I have dealt most ungratefully with Mother Earth; my blood and all the gifts of love that she gave me, I have thrown away like the base wage of a serf, and ah! how many thousand times more ungrateful have I been to you, O sacred maiden! who once received me into her peace, me, a shy, lacerated being from whose sorely oppressed heart scarcely a glimmer of youth stole forth, as here and there a grass blade steals up from trodden paths. Had you not called me to life? was I not yours? then how could I—oh, you know not yet, I hope, it has not reached your hands, the unhappy letter that I wrote to you before the last battle? I wanted to die then, Diotima, and I thought thus to perform a sacred act. But how can that be sacred which parts lovers? how can that be sacred which destroys the innocent happiness of our lives?—O Diotima! O life born in beauty! now I have become all the more like you in what is most uniquely yourself, I have at last learned to value, I have learned to guard, what is good and intrinsic on earth. Oh, even if I could land up there, on the shining islands of the sky, should I find more than I find in Diotima?

"Hear me now, beloved!

"In Greece I can remain no longer. That you know. When he dismissed me my father sent me enough out of what he could spare to enable us to flee to some blessed valley in the Alps or the Pyrenees and there to buy a pleasant house and with it as much green ground as life's golden mean requires.

"If you are willing, I will come at once and conduct you and your mother with a loyal arm, we will kiss the shore of Calaurea and dry our tears and hasten across the Isthmus to the Adriatic Sea, where a safe ship will take us farther.

"Oh come! in the depths of the mountain world the secret of our hearts will rest like the precious stone in the mine; in the bosom of woods that tower to the sky we shall be as among the pillars of the inmost temple, where the godless draw not near, and we shall sit by the spring, and behold our world in it—sky and house and garden and ourselves. On a clear night we shall often wander in our orchard's shade and listen for the loving god in us, while the plant raises its bowed head from its midday sleep, and the still life of your flowers is refreshed when they bathe their tender arms in the dew and the night air breathes its penetrating coolness around them, and above us the meadow of the sky blooms with all its twinkling flowers, and to one side the moon behind westerly clouds shyly imitates the setting of the youthful sun as if for love of him—and then in the morning when our valley is like a riverbed filled with warm light, and the golden stream runs silently through our trees and flows around our house and makes the lovely room that is your handiwork more beautiful for you, and you move through its sunny brightness and, in your grace, bless the day for me, beloved! then, as we thus celebrate the delight of morning, when the busy life of Earth is kindled before our eyes like a burnt sacrifice and we go forth to our day's work, to cast our share, too, into the rising flame, will you not say then, 'We are happy, we are again like the ancient priests of Nature, who, sacred and free, were already pious before ever a temple stood'?

"Have I said enough? now decide my fate, dear maid, and soon!— It is fortunate that I am still half an invalid, as I have been since the last battle, and that I have not yet been released from service; otherwise I could not remain here, I could not but go myself, ask you myself, and that would not be right, for it would be to besiege you.—

"Ah, Diotima! anxious, foolish thoughts assail my heart, and yet—I cannot think that this hope, too, will founder.

"Have you perhaps become too great to return now to earthly happiness? does the mighty flame of spirit that was kindled at your sorrow, does it perhaps consume all that is mortal in you?

"I know well that he who lightly quarrels with the world is reconciled with it even more lightly. But you, who have the quiet of a child, you, once so happy in your high humility, Diotima! who shall reconcile you when your quarrel is with destiny?

"Dear life! is there then no more power of healing for you in me? of all the notes of the heart, does none any longer call you back to the life of men, where once you lingered so beautifully in descended flight? oh, come! oh, remain in this twilight! This shadow-land is surely love's element, only here does the quiet dew of melancholy run from the heaven of your eyes.

"And do you no longer remember our golden days, those enchanting, divinely melodious days? do they not rustle to you from all the groves of Calaurea?

"And see! so much has perished in me, and I have few hopes left. Your image with its heavenly awareness—that I still have, like a household god saved from the conflagration. Our life, ours, is still inviolate in me. Should I now arise and bury this too! Shall I go forth, with no rest and no goal, from one homelessness to another? Is it for this that I learned to love?

"No, no! you my first and my last! You were mine, and mine you shall remain."

Hyperion to Bellarmin

I was sitting with Alabanda on a hill near where we were staying, in the kindly warmth of the sun, and around us the wind played with fallen leaves. The countryside was quiet; only here and there, a tree felled by the farmer crashed far away in the woods and, close by, the intermittent rain-fed stream murmured down to the peaceful sea.

I was almost carefree; I hoped to see my Diotima soon now, soon now to live with her in quiet happiness. Alabanda had talked me out of all my doubts; he was so certain of it himself. He, too, was serene, but in another sense. The future had no more power over him. Oh, I did not know it: he was at the end of his joys; with all his claims on the world, all his conquering nature, he saw himself useless, ineffectual, and alone, and he accepted it as if he had lost some game played but to while away the time.

A messenger arrived. He brought us the discharge from military service for which we had both petitioned the command of the Russian fleet because there was nothing left for us to do that seemed worth the effort. I could now leave Paros whenever I pleased. And I was now well enough to travel. I did not want to wait for Diotima's answer; I wanted to be off to her, it was as if a god were driving me to Calaurea. When Alabanda heard me say this, his color changed and he looked at me sorrowfully. "Is it so easy for my Hyperion," he cried, "to forsake his Alabanda?"

"Forsake?" I said. "What do you mean?"

"Oh, you dreamers!" he cried. "Do you not see that we must part?"

"How should I see it?" I answered; "you have not said a word about it; and what I have seen in you now and again that seemed to point to a separation I took in good part as a momentary mood, as coming from a heart too full—"

"Oh, I know it well," he cried, "that divine game when love in its wealth pretends to be in need, so that it can shower its plenty on itself, and I would that it were thus with me, good heart! but in this case I am in earnest!"

"In earnest?" I cried. "But why?"

"Why, my Hyperion," he said gently. "Because I would not wish to trouble your future happiness, because I cannot but fear to be close to Diotima. Believe me, it is risky to live with lovers, and a heart with nothing to do, as mine now is, can scarcely bear it."

"Ah, my good Alabanda," I said with a smile, "how little you know yourself! You are not such a thing of wax, and your steadfast soul is not so easily carried out of its domain. For the first time in your life you give in to groundless fancies. You played nurse for me here, and it is plain to see how little your nature is suited to it. This sitting about doing nothing has made you timorous—"

"There you are!" he cried, "that is it exactly. Living with you and Diotima, should I be any more active? If it were some other woman! but this Diotima! can I help it? can I feel her with half my soul? she, who is so utterly at one with herself, *one* divinely undivided life? Believe me, it is childishness to undertake to see such a being and not love her. You look at me as if you did not know me, do you? But I have grown a stranger to myself these last days, since her being has become so living a presence in me."

"Oh, why cannot I give her to you?" I cried.

"Enough!" he said. "Do not try to console me, for here there is no place for consolation, I am alone, alone, and my life is running out like an hourglass."

"Great soul!" I cried, "must it come to this for you?"

"Accept what is!" he said. "I was already beginning to wither when we found each other in Smyrna. Yes! in the days when I was still a ship's boy and my spirit and all my limbs were strong and swift on coarse food and daring work! In those days, when in the clear air after a stormy night I clung to the top of the mast under the billowing flag and gazed after the seabird over the shining deep, when in frequent battle our raging ships tore up the sea as the boar's tusk tears the earth and I stood at my captain's side clear-eyed—in those days I lived, oh, then I lived! And long after that, when the young Tiniote met me on the Smyrnean shore, with his earnestness, and his love, and my hardened soul was bedewed again by the youth's gaze and learned to love and to hold sacred all that is too good to be subdued, when I began a new life with him, and new, more spiritual powers germinated in me to make me better able to delight in the world and to struggle with it, then I hoped again—ah! and all that I hoped and had was inseparably linked with you; I took you to me, sought to drag you into my destiny by force, lost you, found you again; our friendship alone was my world, my value, my fame; now that is over too, forever, and my whole existence is in vain."

"But is that true?" I answered, sighing.

"True as the sun," he cried, "but let it be! Everything is provided for."

"What do you mean, my Alabanda?" said I.

"Let me tell you," he said. "I have never yet spoken to you fully about a certain matter. And then—it quiets both you and me a little when we talk of the past.

"Once long ago, helpless and desperate, I was wandering about the waterfront of Trieste. The privateer on which I was serving had been shipwrecked some years earlier, and I had barely managed to save myself, with a few others, on the shore near Seville. My captain was drowned and my life and my dripping garments were all that remained to me. I undressed and rested in the sunshine and dried my clothes on the bushes. Then I resumed my journey along the road to the city. Before I came to the gates, I saw people making merry in the gardens; I entered and sang a happy Greek song. I did not know a sad one. All the while I was hot with the shame and pain of exhibiting my misfortune in this way. I was an eighteen-year-old boy, wild and proud, and I hated like death to be the object of people's attention. 'Forgive me,' I said, when I had finished my song; 'I have just escaped from a shipwreck and at present know no better way to do the world a service than to sing to it.' I had said this in such Spanish as I could manage. A man with a fine face came up to me, gave me money, and, speaking our language, said with a smile: 'There! buy yourself a grindstone with that and learn to sharpen knives, and you can resume your travels, but on dry land!' The advice pleased me. 'Sir! I will do just that,' I answered. All the others rewarded me liberally too, and I left them and did as the man had advised me, and so wandered for a time through Spain and France.

"What I experienced during that time, how the thousand forms that servitude assumes intensified my love of freedom and many a hard hour of need increased my courage to live and sharpened my wits, I have often delighted in telling you.

"I practiced my innocent, wandering trade with pleasure, but finally it was spoiled for me.

"People took it to be a mask, probably because I did not look mean enough for such an occupation; they imagined I was covertly engaged in some dangerous undertaking, and in fact I was twice arrested. All this decided me to give it up, and with the little money I had earned I set out to make my way back to the home from which I had run away. I was soon in Trieste and about to start down through Dalmatia. Just then the accumulated hardships of my journey laid me low with an illness that made my small capital vanish. Only half recovered, I was wandering sadly along the waterfront at Trieste. Suddenly, there stood the man who had once befriended me when I was cast ashore at Seville. He was wonderfully glad to see me, told me that he often thought of me, and asked how things had gone with me meanwhile. I told him all. 'I see,' he cried, 'that it was no bad thing to send you to the school of Fate for a while. You have learned endurance, now you shall go to work whenever you please.'

"The words, his tone, his handclasp, his manner, his look, all went like some divine force to my inmost being, which much suffering had now made even more inflammable than before, and I surrendered.

"The man of whom I speak, Hyperion, was one of those whom you saw with me in Smyrna. The very next night he introduced me to the members of a solemn society. A shudder ran through me as I entered the room and my companion, pointing to the earnest group of men, said: 'This is the League of Nemesis.' Intoxicated by the immense sphere of action that opened before me, I solemnly made over my blood and my soul to these men. Soon afterward the meeting was adjourned, to be reconvened in some other place years later, and each set out on the appointed path that he was to follow through the world. I was made an associate of those whom you found with me some years afterward in Smyrna.

"The constraint under which I lived often tortured me; then too, I saw little of the great accomplishments of the League and my hunger for action found little nourishment. But all this was not enough to enable me to desert. My love for you finally led me away. I have often told you that I was as if without air and sun when you were absent; and I had no other choice: I must give up either you or my League. What I chose, you see.

"But every human act finds its punishment at last; only gods and children are not smitten by Nemesis.

"I put the divine right of the heart first. For my dear one's sake I broke my oath. Was not that right? must not the noblest longing be the freest?—My heart took me at my word; I gave it freedom, and you see it uses it.

"*Once* do homage to the Genius and he will heed no mortal hindrance thereafter, he will tear all the bonds of life in two for you.

"I broke my obligation for my friend's sake; I would break friendship for the sake of love. For Diotima's sake I would betray you, and finally kill Diotima and myself because, even so, we should not be *one*. But it shall stop here; if I must pay for what I did, I will do it freely; I choose my own judge; those whom I failed shall have me."

"Do you speak of your fellows in the League?" I cried; "O my Alabanda! do it not!"

"What can they take from me but my blood?" he answered. Then he gently clasped my hand. "Hyperion!" he cried, "my time has run out, and all that remains to me is a noble end. Leave me! do not make me less than I am, have faith in my word! I know as well as you do that I could still trump up some kind of existence for myself, could, now that life's meal is eaten, still sit playing with the crumbs; but that is not for me, nor for you. Need I say more? Do I not speak to you from your own soul? I thirst for air, for coolness, Hyperion! My soul seethes over of itself and will no longer be confined to the old circle. Soon the beautiful days of winter will be here, when the dark earth is but the foil to the shining heavens—that would be the right time, then the isles of light glimmer the more hospitably!— You are amazed by what I say? Dearest one! all who are departing talk like drunken men and delight to behave as at a feast. When the tree begins to wither, do not all its leaves bear the red of morning?"

"Great soul," I cried, "must I bear to pity you?"

I sensed from his exaltation how deeply he was suffering. I had never felt such grief in my life. And yet, O Bellarmin, yet I felt the greatness of all joys, to hold such a godlike figure in my eyes and arms. "Yes! die," I cried, "die! Your heart is glorious enough, your life is ripe, like grapes in autumn. Go, perfected one! I would go with you, if there were no Diotima."

"Have I convinced you now?" answered Alabanda, "are these your words? how deep, how full of soul does all become when once my Hyperion comprehends it!" "He flatters," I cried, "to wheedle the unconsidered word from me a second time! good gods! to wrest leave from me for his journey to the tribunal of blood!"

"I do not flatter," he answered gravely, "I have a right to do what you would prevent, and no common right! Honor it!"

There was a fire in his eyes that struck me down like a divine command, and I felt ashamed to say another word in opposition to him.

"They will not," I thought meanwhile, "they cannot do it. It is too senseless to slaughter such a glorious life, like a sacrificial animal," and this conviction calmed me.

It was strangely profitable still to hear him the following night, when each of us had made ready for his separate journey and, just before daybreak, we had gone out again to be alone together once more.

"Do you know," he said, among other things, "why I have never thought anything but lightly of death? I feel a life in me which no god created and no mortal begot. I believe that our existence is from ourselves and that it is only of our own free pleasure that we are so intimately connected with all that is."

"I have never heard you say such a thing before," I replied.

"And what," he went on, "what would this world itself be, if it were not a harmony of free beings? if from the beginning the living did not work together, of their own free impulse, in *one* full-voiced life, how wooden would it not be? how cold? what a heartless assemblage of forms?"

"So it would be true here in the highest sense," I answered, "that without freedom all is dead."

"Yes, yes," he cried, "why! not a blade of grass sprouts up if it has not its own seed of life within it! And how much more in me! and therefore, dear lad, because I feel that I am free in the highest sense, that I have no beginning, therefore I believe that I shall have no end, that I am indestructible. If a potter's hand made me, he may smash his vessel whenever he pleases. But what lives must be unbegotten, must be of divine nature in its seed, raised above all force and all art, and therefore inviolable, eternal.

"Every man has his mysteries, dear Hyperion! his more secret thoughts; these were mine—ever since I have thought.

"What lives is ineradicable, remains free in its deepest form of servitude, remains one even if you split it to the base, remains unwounded even if you pierce it to the marrow and its being flies victorious from your hands.—But the morning wind freshens; our ships are awake. O my Hyperion! I have won through; I have had the strength to pronounce the death sentence on my heart and to divide you and me, beloved of my life! be tender to me now! spare me your leave-taking! let us be quick! come!—"

A chill ran through my every bone, as I heard him begin thus.

"Oh, by your loyalty, Alabanda!" I cried, prostrate before him, "must it be, must it be indeed? You shouted me down unfairly, you dragged me along in a frenzy. Brother! you did not leave me sense enough even to ask: 'Where are you going?' "

"I may not name the place, dear heart!" he answered; "yet perhaps we shall see each other once again."

"See each other again?" I answered; "then I am the richer by one belief! and so I shall become richer and richer in belief and in the end all will be but belief for me."

"Dear one!" he cried, "let us be still when words do not help! let us end like men! You are spoiling these last moments for yourself."

Meanwhile, we had come to the harbor.

"One thing more!" he said, when we were beside his ship. "Greet your Diotima! Love each other! be happy, beautiful souls!"

"O my Alabanda," I cried, "why can I not go in your stead?"

"What you are called to is more beautiful," he answered; "hold to it! you belong to her, that fair being is henceforth your world—ah! since there is no happiness without sacrifice, accept me as the sacrifice, O Fate, and leave the lovers in their joy!—"

His heart began to overpower him, and he tore himself from me and leaped into the ship, to shorten the parting for himself and for me. I felt the moment like a thunderclap, on which night and deathly silence followed, but in the midst of this annihilation my soul recovered to hold him back, the dear one who was departing, and my arms sprang out toward him of themselves. "Alas! Alabanda! Alabanda!" I cried, and heard a muffled "Farewell" from the ship.

Hyperion to Bellarmin

As it happened, the vessel that was to take me to Calaurea delayed until late in the day on which Alabanda had gone his way in the morning.

I stayed by the shore and, wearied by the pains of parting, gazed silently at the sea, hour after hour. My spirit told over the sorrowful days of my slowly dying youth and waveringly, like the beautiful dove, flitted over the time to come. I wanted to strengthen myself, I took out my long forgotten lute to sing a Song of Fate that once in happy, heedless youth I had repeated after my Adamas.

> You move up there in the light
>   On easeful ground, blessed Geniuses!
>   Bright divine airs
>   Touch you lightly,
>   As the player's fingers
>   Her holy strings.
>
> Outside of Fate, like the sleeping
>   Babe, the Heavenly Ones breathe;
>   Chastely guarded
>   In modest bud,
>   Ever for them
>   The spirit blooms,
>   And their blessed eyes
>   Gaze in still,
>   Eternal light.
>
> But to us it is given
>   Nowhere to rest,
>   Suffering men
>   Falter and fall
>   Blindly from one
>   Hour to the next,
>   Like water flung down
>   From cliff to cliff,
>   Yearlong into uncertainty.

So I sang to the strings. I had scarcely finished when a boat arrived; in it I immediately recognized my servant, who brought me a letter from Diotima.

"So you are still on earth?" she wrote, "and still see the light of day? I thought I should find you elsewhere, my love! Sooner than you afterward wished, I received the letter that you wrote before the battle at Cheshme, and so for a whole week I lived believing that you had thrown yourself into the arms of death, before your servant arrived with the joyful news that you are still alive. Moreover, I had heard only a few days after the battle that the ship on which I knew you to be had blown up with all hands.

"But O sweet voice! again I heard you, once again the speech of the beloved touched me like the air of May, and your beautiful, hopeful joy, the lovely phantom of our future happiness, for a moment deceived me too.

"Dear dreamer, why must I wake you? why can I not say, 'Come, and make them true, the beautiful days that you promised me!' But it is too late, Hyperion, it is too late. Your maiden has withered since you have been gone; a fire in me has slowly consumed me, and there is only a little left. Do not be dismayed! Everything in Nature purifies itself, and everywhere the flower of life frees itself more and more from coarser stuff.

"Dearest Hyperion! little did you think to hear my swan song this year.

Continuation

"Almost as soon as you had gone—nay, even in the days of our parting—it began. A strength in my spirit that made me afraid, an inner life before which the life of earth paled and faltered, like night lights in the red of morning—Shall I say it? I could have wished to go to Delphi and build a temple to the God of Inspiration under the cliffs of ancient Parnassus, and, a new Pythia, fire the indolent peoples with divine oracles; and my soul knows that my maidenly mouth would have opened the eyes and unknit the brows of all those godforsaken dullards, so powerful was the spirit of life in me! But my mortal limbs grew wearier and wearier and my tormenting melancholy bore me inexorably down. Ah! often in my quiet arbor I wept over the roses of youth! they faded and faded, and your maiden's cheeks were red from tears. The trees of old were still there, and the bower of old—there once your Diotima stood, your child, Hyperion, before your happy eyes, a blossom among the blossoms, and the powers of Earth and Heaven met peacefully in her; now she walked a stranger among the buds of May, and her trusted confidants, the lovely plants, nodded to her as to a friend, but she could only mourn; yet I passed none of them by; yet, one after one, I took leave of all the companions of my youth, the groves and springs and rustling hillocks.

"Ah! as long as I could, I went with sweet effort up to the height where you lived with Notara, and talked of you with our friend, as cheerfully as possible, so that he should not write to you of me; but soon, when her heart grew too loud, the dissembler slipped out into the garden, and now there I was at the railing, above the cliff from which I once looked down with you and out into untrammeled Nature; ah! where once I stood, held by your hands, guarded round by your eyes, in the first trembling warmth of love and would fain have poured my overflowing soul, like sacrificial wine, into the abyss of life, there now I staggered about and bewailed my grief to the wind, and my gaze flitted like a shy bird and scarcely dared to look at the beautiful Earth from which I was to depart.

Continuation

"Thus has it befallen your maiden, Hyperion. Ask not how; seek not to explain this death to yourself! He who thinks to fathom such a fate ends by cursing himself and all things, and yet not a soul is to blame.

"Am I to tell you that grief for you has killed me? oh no! oh no! it was welcome to me, that grief, it gave the death that I carried within me form and grace; 'You die to honor your beloved,' I could tell myself now.—

"Or did my soul grow overripe in all the enchantments of our love, and is that why, like a restive youth, it will no longer stay in its humble home? speak! was it my heart's exuberance that divorced me from mortal life? did my nature, having known your glorious self, become too proud to be content on this mediocre star? But if you taught it to fly, why do you not also teach my soul to return to you? If you kindled the ether-loving fire, why did you not guard it for me?—Hear me, beloved! for your fair soul's sake! do not accuse yourself of my death!

"Could you hold me back, when your destiny showed you the same road? and if, amid the heroic struggle of your heart, you had preached to me: 'Be satisfied, child! and adapt yourself to the times!' would you not have been the most futile of all the futile?

Continuation

"I will tell you exactly what I believe. Your fire lived in me, your spirit had passed into me; but that could hardly have harmed me, and only your destiny made my new life deadly to me. My soul had grown too strong for me through you, yet through you it would have grown quiet again. You drew my life away from the Earth, but you would also have had power to bind me to the Earth; you would have conjured my soul into your embracing arms as into a magic circle; ah! *one* of your loving looks would have held me fast, *one* of your loving speeches would have made me a happy, healthy child again; but when a unique destiny bore you away to solitude of spirit as waters are borne to mountain peaks, oh then, when at last I believed that the storm of battle had burst open your prison and my Hyperion had soared up into his old freedom again, only then was all decided for me, and now must soon end.

"I have used many words, yet the great Roman heroine died silent when her Brutus and her country were struggling in the throes of death. What better could I do in the best of my last days of life?—Yet still I feel an urgency to say many things. My life was silent; my death is loquacious. Enough!

Continuation

"I must tell you but *one* thing more.

"You would have to perish, you would be bound to despair, but the spirit will save you. No laurel will comfort you and no crown of myrtle; Olympus will be your comfort, the living, present Olympus that blooms ever young about all your senses. The beautiful world is my Olympus; in it you will live; and with the holy beings of the world, with the Gods of Nature, with them you will be happy.

"O be you welcome, you good and true! you deeply missed, you unrecognized! children and eldest of all! Sun and Earth and Ether, with all living souls that play about you, about whom you play, in eternal love! oh, take all-endeavoring mankind, take the fugitives back into the family of the gods, receive them into the home of Nature, from which they fled!—

"You know this word, Hyperion! You began it in me. You will fulfill it in yourself, and then rest.

"I have enough of it to die happily, a Grecian maiden.

"The poor creatures who know nothing but to toil at their petty labors, who serve only necessity and scorn the Genius and pay you no honor, childlike life of Nature! let them fear death. Their yoke has become their world; they know nothing better than their servitude; they shrink from the divine freedom that death gives us!

"But not I! I have risen above the piecework that human hands have made. I have felt the life of Nature, which is higher than all thought—if I become a plant, would that be so great a loss?—I shall be. How should I be lost from the sphere of life, in which eternal love, common to all, holds all natures together? how should I escape from the union that binds all beings together? It does not break as easily as the loose bonds of this age. It is not like a market day, when the people run together and make a hubbub and part. No! by the spirit that makes us one, by the divine spirit that is each man's own and is common to all! no! no! in the union of Nature fidelity is no dream! We part only to be more intimately one, more divinely at peace with all, with each other. We die that we may live.

"I shall be; I ask not what I shall be. To be, to live—that is enough, that is the honor of the gods; and therefore all things that but have life are equal in the divine world, and in it there are no masters and servants. Natures live together, like lovers; they hold all in common, spirit, joy, and eternal youth.

"The stars have chosen permanence; they float forever in quiet fullness of life and know not age. We represent perfection in mutability; we divide the great harmonies of joy into changing melodies.

Like harp players about the thrones of the eldest of all, we live, ourselves divine, among the quiet Gods of the World; with our fleeting lovesong we temper the blissful seriousness of the Sun God and the rest.

"Look up into the world! Is it not like an advancing triumphal procession by which Nature celebrates her eternal victory over all corruption? and does not life lead death with it to glorification, as the general once led captive kings with him? and we, we are the virgins and the youths, who accompany the majestic procession with dance and song in changing shapes and tones.

"Now let me be silent. To say more would be too much. We shall, I must believe, meet again.—

"Sorrowing youth! soon, soon will you be happier. Your laurel did not ripen, and your myrtles faded, for you shall be the priest of divine Nature, and your days of poetry are already germinating."

"Oh, could I but see you in your future beauty! Farewell."

At the same time I received a letter from Notara, in which he wrote:

"The day after she wrote to you for the last time, she became very quiet, spoke a few words more, and then said that she would rather leave the earth in fire than be buried, and that we should collect her ashes in an urn and put them in the forest, in the place where you, dear one! first met her. Soon afterward, as it began to grow dark, she bade us good night, as if she wanted to sleep, and put her arms around her beautiful head; we heard her breathing until nearly morning. As it became perfectly still then and I heard nothing more, I went in to her and listened.

"O Hyperion! what else shall I say? It was over, and our lamenting wakened her no more.

"It is a terrible mystery that such a life must die, and I will confess to you that I myself have neither mind nor belief since I saw this happen.

"But a beautiful death is always better, Hyperion! than such a somnolent life as ours now is.

"To brush away flies is our work in the future; and to gnaw on the things of the world as children gnaw on the hard iris-root—that, in the end, is our pleasure. To grow old among young peoples seems to me a delight, but to grow old where all is old seems to me worse than anything.—

"I would advise you, my Hyperion! not to come here. I know you. It would drive you out of your mind. Then too, you are not safe here. My dear friend! think of Diotima's mother, think of me, and preserve yourself!

"I will confess to you that I shudder when I consider your fate. But I believe, too, that the burning summer does not dry up the deep springs, but only the shallow rain-fed stream. I have seen you at moments, Hyperion, when you seemed to me a higher being. You are now put to the test, and you must show who you are. Farewell."

So Notara wrote; and you ask, my Bellarmin! how it is with me now, while I tell you of this.

Best of friends! I am at peace, for I want nothing better than the gods. Must not all things suffer? And the more excellent, the more deeply! Does not sacred Nature suffer? O my Divinity! that you could mourn as you are blissful—that was long beyond my understanding. But the bliss that does not suffer is sleep, and without death there is no life. Should you be eternally like a child, and sleep like that which is nothing? forego victory? not run through all perfections? Yes! yes! sorrow is worthy to lie at man's heart and to be your intimate, O Nature! For it but leads from one bliss to another, and there is no other companion on the way.—

I wrote to Notara, when I began to revive again, from Sicily, to which a ship from Paros first brought me:

"I have obeyed you, my dear Notara! I am already far from my friends in Calaurea and now wish to send you news; but words are hard for me, I must confess. The blessed, among whom Diotima now is, do not speak much; in my night, in the abyss of the mourner, there is an end to speech too.

"My Diotima died a beautiful death; in that you are right; and it is that, too, which awakens me, and gives me back my soul.

"But it is not to the world as it was that I return. I am a stranger, like the unburied when they come up from Acheron, and if I were on my native island, in the gardens of my youth, which my father bars to me, ah! even then, even then I should be a stranger on earth, and no god would join me to the past again.

"Yes! all is over. I must only say that to myself again and again, must bind my soul with it, so that it shall remain quiet and not fire up in senseless, childish efforts.

"All is over; and even if I could weep, beautiful Divinity, as once you wept for Adonis, my Diotima will not come back to me and the word of my heart has lost its power, for only the winds hear me.

"God! that I myself am nothing, and that the meanest workman can say he has done more than I! that they are free to solace themselves, the shallow of mind, and smile and mockingly call me dreamer, because my deeds did not ripen for me, because my arms are not free, because the time in which I live is like the raging Procrustes who, capturing men, put them in a child's cradle and, to make them fit into that little bed, hacked off their limbs!

"If only it were not too utterly desperate to fling myself among the crowd of fools and be torn to pieces! or if only noble blood need not be ashamed to mix with the blood of serfs! oh, if there were a banner, you Gods! under which my Alabanda might serve, a Thermopylae where I could honorably let it bleed to death, all the lonely love for which I never find a use! To be sure, it would be better if I could live, could live, and quiet great woe with great joy in the new temples, in the newly assembled Agora of our people; yet I speak not of that, for I but weep my strength wholly away when I think of it all.

"Ah! Notara! it is over with me too; I am weary of my own soul because I reproach it with Diotima's death, and the thoughts of my youth, which I prized so greatly, mean nothing to me now. Did they not poison my Diotima!

"And now tell me, what refuge remains?—Yesterday I went to the summit of Aetna. There I remembered the great Sicilian who, weary of counting the hours, knowing the soul of the World, in his bold joy in life there flung himself down into the glorious flames, for 'the cold poet had to warm himself at the fire,' said someone later, to mock him.

"O how gladly would I have taken such mockery upon myself! but one must think more highly of oneself than I do before, thus unbidden, one can flee to Nature's heart, or whatever else you may be pleased to call it, for, believe me! as I am now I have no names for things and all before me is uncertainty.

"And now, Notara! tell me what refuge remains?

"In Calaurea's woods?—Yes! in the green darkness there where our trees, the faithful witnesses of our love, still stand, where, like the red of evening, their dying foliage falls on Diotima's urn and their beautiful crowns, gradually growing old, bend over Diotima's urn, until they, too, fall upon the beloved ashes—there, there, I could perhaps live as I wished.

"But you advise me to stay away, you think that I am not safe in Calaurea, and it may be so.

"I know very well you will tell me to go to Alabanda. But listen! he is destroyed! even that firm, slender tree is mouldering, too, and boys will gather up the chips and make themselves a merry fire with them. He has gone; he has certain good friends who will make things easy for him, who are peculiarly skilled in helping out anyone who finds life something of a burden; he has gone to visit them, and why? because there is nothing else for him to do, or, if you would know all, because a passion is eating out his heart, and do you know for whom? for Diotima, whom he believes to be still alive and married to me and happy—poor Alabanda! now she belongs to us both!

"He traveled into the east, and I am taking a ship northwestward, because chance will have it so.—

"And now farewell to all of you! all you dear ones who have been close to my heart, friends of my youth and you my parents, and all you dear Greeks, you sufferers!

"You airs that nourished me in tender childhood, and you dark laurel woods and you cliffs by the shore and you majestic waters that taught my soul to surmise your greatness—and ah! you monuments of sorrow, where my melancholy began, you sacred walls with which the heroic cities girdle themselves, and you ancient gates through which many a beautiful traveler passed, you temple pillars and you rubble of the gods! and you, O Diotima! and you valleys of my love, and you brooks that once saw her blessed form, you trees where she rejoiced, you springtimes in which she lived, lovely with her flowers, depart not, depart not from me! yet if it must be, you sweet memories! grow dim you too and leave me, for man can change nothing and the light of life comes and departs as it will."

Hyperion to Bellarmin

So I arrived among the Germans. I did not demand much and was prepared to find even less. I came there humbly, like homeless, blind

Oedipus to the gates of Athens, where the sacred grove received him; and fair souls came to greet him—

How different my experience!

Barbarians from the remotest past, whom industry and science and even religion have made yet more barbarous, profoundly incapable of any divine emotion, spoiled to the core for the delights of the sacred Graces, offensive to every well-conditioned soul through the whole range from pretense to pettiness, hollow and tuneless, like the shards of a discarded pot—such, my Bellarmin! were my comforters.

It is a hard saying, and yet I speak it because it is the truth: I can think of no people more at odds with themselves than the Germans. You see artisans, but no men, thinkers, but no men, priests, but no men, masters and servants, but no men, minors and adults, but no men—is this not like a battlefield on which hacked-off hands and arms and every other member are scattered about, while the life-blood flows from them to vanish in the sand?

Everyone follows his own trade, you will tell me, and I say the same. Only, he must follow it with his whole soul, must not stifle every power in him that does not precisely accord with his official designation, must not, with this niggardly anxiety, literally and hypocritically be only what he is called; let him be what he is, earnestly, lovingly, then a spirit lives in all that he does; and if he is forced into an occupation in which the spirit may not live, let him cast it off with scorn and learn to plow! But your Germans choose not to go beyond the barest necessities, which is the reason why there is so much botched work among them and so little that is free, that gives any genuine pleasure. Yet that could be overlooked, were not such men of necessity insensitive to what is beautiful in life, did not the curse of godforsaken unnature everywhere lie upon such a people.—

"The virtues of the Ancients were but glittering vices," was once said by some malicious tongue (I forget whose); and yet their vices themselves are virtues, for a childlike, beautiful spirit still lived in them, and of all that they did nothing was done without soul. But the virtues of the Germans are glittering vices and nothing more; for they are but forced labor, wrung from the sterile heart in craven fear, with the toil of slaves, and they impart no comfort to any pure soul that would draw its sustenance from Beauty, that, ah! made fastidious by the sacred harmony in noble natures, cannot bear the discord that cries out in all the dead order of these men.

I tell you: there is nothing sacred that is not desecrated, is not debased to a miserable expedient among this people; and what even among savages is usually preserved in sacred purity, these all-calculating barbarians pursue as one pursues any trade, and cannot do otherwise; for where a human being is once conditioned to look, there it serves its ends, seeks its profit, it dreams no more—God forbid!—it remains sedate; and when it makes holiday and when it loves and when it prays, and even when spring's lovely festival, when the season of reconciliation for the world dissolves all cares and conjures innocence into a guilty heart, when, intoxicated by the sun's warm rays, the slave in his joy forgets his chains, and the enemies of mankind, softened by the divinely living air, are as peaceable as children—when the caterpillar itself grows wings and the bees swarm, even then the German sticks to his petty tasks and scarcely deigns to notice the weather!

But you will sit in judgment, sacred Nature! For were they but modest, these people, did they but not make themselves a law unto the better among them! did they but revile not what they are not, yet even that could be condoned in them, did they but not mock the divine!—

Or is not that divine which you Germans mock and call soulless? Is not the air that you drink in better than your chatter? are not the sun's rays nobler than all of you in your cleverness? the earth's springs and the morning dew refresh your forests; can you too do as much? ah! you can kill, but you cannot bring to life, unless it is done by love, which proceeds not from you, which you did not invent. You worry and contrive, that you may escape Fate, and cannot understand it when your childish arts are unavailing; and meanwhile the stars move innocently on above you. Where she tolerates you, you degrade and mangle patient Nature, yet she lives on, in eternal youth, and you cannot drive away her autumn and her spring, you corrupt not her ether.

Oh, she must indeed be divine, since you are permitted to destroy and she grows not old and despite you Beauty remains beautiful!—

It is heart-rending, too, to see your poets, your artists, and all those who still honor the Genius, who love and cultivate Beauty. The poor good creatures live in the world like strangers in their own house, they are exactly like long-suffering Ulysses when he sat at his door disguised as a beggar while the shameless suitors rioted in the hall and asked "Who sent us this vagabond?"

Their Muse-inspired youths grow up for the German people full of love and spirit and hope; see them seven years later, and they are wandering about like shades, silent and cold, they are like a soil that the enemy has sown with salt so that it shall never put forth a blade of grass, and when they speak, alas for him who understands them! for him who in their raging Titan strength, as in their protean arts, can see the desperate battle that their beautiful, troubled spirit wages against the barbarians with whom it is forced to deal!

"Everything on earth is imperfect," is the Germans' old refrain. If only someone would once tell these people whom God has forsaken that everything is so imperfect among them only because they leave nothing pure uncorrupted, nothing sacred untouched by their coarse hands, that nothing thrives among them because they do not respect the root of all thriving, divine Nature, that life with them is stale and burdened with cares and full of cold, silent discord, because they scorn the Genius, which brings power and nobility into human endeavor, and serenity into suffering, and love and brotherhood to towns and houses.

And that too is why they are so afraid of death and, for the sake of their molluscan existence, bear every indignity, for they know nothing higher than the bungling job that they have made of things.

O Bellarmin, where a people loves Beauty, where it honors the Genius in its own artists, there a common spirit is astir like the breath of life, there the shy mind opens, self-conceit melts away, and all hearts are reverent and great and enthusiasm brings forth heroes. The home of all men is with such a people and gladly can the stranger linger there. But where divine Nature and her artists are so insulted, ah! there life's greatest joy is gone, and any other star is better than earth. There men grow ever more sterile, ever more empty, who yet were all born beautiful; servility increases and with its insolence, intoxication grows with troubles and, with luxury, hunger and dread of starvation; the blessing of each year becomes a curse, and all gods flee.

And woe for the stranger who journeys in love and comes to such a people and three times woe for him who comes to such a people as I came, driven by great grief, a beggar as I was a beggar!—

Enough! you know me, and will take this in good part, Bellarmin! I spoke in your name too, I spoke for all who are in that country and who suffer as I suffered there.

Hyperion to Bellarmin

I now wanted to leave Germany. I looked for nothing more among these people, I had been sufficiently offended by relentless affronts, I was unwilling to let my soul bleed to death among such men.

But the heavenly spring detained me; it was the only pleasure that remained to me, it was indeed my last love, how could I think of other things and leave the country where spring too was?

Bellarmin! never had I so fully experienced the old unchanging decree of Fate that a new bliss rises in the heart when it perseveres and suffers through the midnight of anguish, and that, like nightingale voices in the dark, the world's song of life first sounds divinely for us in deep affliction. For I now lived with the blooming trees as with geniuses, and the clear brooks that flowed under them whispered the care from my breast like divine voices. And so it befell me everywhere, dear friend!—when I lay in the grass and tender life grew green around me, when I climbed the warm hill on which the rose grew wild about the stone path, and when I rowed along the gay river shore and among all the islands that the river tenderly protects.

And when on many a morning, as the sick to medicinal springs, I climbed to the mountain's summit through the sleeping flowers, but all about me, sated with sweet sleep, the dear birds flew out of the foliage, reeling in the half-light and craving the day, and the more active air now carried up the prayers of the valleys, the voices of the flocks, and the notes of the morning bells, and now the high light, divinely serene, followed its accustomed path, enchanting the Earth with immortal life, so that her heart grew warm and all her children felt their existence again—oh! like the moon, which still waited in the sky to share the joy of the day, I stood lonely too above the plains and wept loving tears down to the shores and the shining waters and for a long time could not turn away my eyes.

Or at evening, when I wandered far into the valley, to the cradle of the spring, where the dark oak tops rustled around me and Nature buried me in her peace like one who dies a blessed death, when the earth was a shadow, and invisible life whispered among the branches, among the summits, and over the summits hung the still evening cloud, a shining mountain from which heaven's rays flowed down to me, like brooks to quench the traveler's thirst—

"O Sun, O you breezes," I cried, "by you alone my heart still lives, as among brothers!"

Thus more and more I surrendered myself to blessed Nature, and almost too endlessly. How gladly would I have become a child again to be nearer to her, how gladly would I have known less and become like the pure ray of light to be nearer to her! oh, one moment in her peace, to feel her beauty, oh, how much more it meant to me than years full of thought, than all the endeavors of all-endeavoring mankind! What I had learned, what I had done in my life, dissolved like ice, and all the projects of youth died away in me; O you loved ones far away, you dead and you living, how intimately at *one* we were!

Once I sat far in the fields, by a spring, in the shadow of ivy-green cliffs and overhanging shrubs in flower. It was the fairest noonday I have known. Sweet breezes blew and the land still shone in morning freshness and the light smiled silently from its native ether. The laborers had all gone home to eat and rest from their work; my love was alone with the springtime and in me was an inconceivable longing. "Diotima," I cried, "where are you, oh, where are you?" And it seemed to me that I heard Diotima's voice, the voice that cheered me in the days of happiness—

"I am with my kindred," she cried, "with your kindred, whom the erring minds of men know not."

A gentle terror seized me and my thought fell asleep.

"O dear word from holy mouth," I cried when again I awakened, "dear riddle, do I understand you?"

And *once* more I looked back into the cold night of men, and shuddered and wept for joy that I was so blessed, and I uttered words, I think, but they were like the roar of fire when it flies up and leave the ashes behind—

"O you," so I thought, "with your gods, Nature! I have dreamed it out, the dream of human things, and I say, Only you live, and what they who know no peace have attempted and conceived melts away from your flame like beads of wax!

"How long have they done without you? oh, how long have their tribe abused you, called you and your gods common, your living gods, your silent, blissful gods!

"Men fall from you like rotten fruits, oh, let them perish, for thus they return to your root; so may I, too, O tree of life, that I may grow green again with you and breathe your crown about me with all your budding twigs! peacefully and devoutly, for we are all sprung from the same golden seed!

"You springs of earth! you flowers! and you woods and you eagles and you brotherly light! how old and new is our love!—We are free, we are not narrowly alike in outward semblance; how should the mode of Life not vary? yet we love the ether, all of us, and in the inmost of our inmost selves we are alike.

"We too, we too, are not parted, Diotima, and tears for you understand it not. Living tones are we, we sound together in thy harmony, Nature! which who can undo? who can part lovers?—

"O Soul! Soul! Beauty of the World! indestructible, ravishing one! with your eternal youth! you are; what, then, is death and all the woe of men?—Ah! those strange creatures have spoken many empty words. Yet from delight all comes, and all ends in peace.

"Like lovers' quarrels are the dissonances of the world. Reconciliation is there, even in the midst of strife, and all things that are parted find one another again.

"The arteries separate and return to the heart and all is one eternal glowing life."

So I thought. More soon.

Translated by Willard R. Trask
Adapted by David Schwarz

Poems

Da ich ein Knabe war ...

Da ich ein Knabe war,
  Rettet' ein Gott mich oft
    Vom Geschrei und der Ruthe der Menschen,
     Da spielt' ich sicher und gut
      Mit den Blumen des Hains,
       Und die Lüftchen des Himmels
        Spielten mit mir.

Und wie du das Herz
Der Pflanzen erfreust,
Wenn sie entgegen dir
Die zarten Arme streken,

So hast du mein Herz erfreut
Vater Helios! und, wie Endymion,
War ich dein Leibling,
Heilige Luna!

O all ihr treuen
Freundlichen Götter!
Daß ihr wüßtet,
Wie euch meine Seele geliebt!

Zwar damals rieff ich noch nicht
Euch mit Nahmen, auch ihr
Nanntet mich nie, wie die Menschen sich nennen
Als kennten sie sich.

Doch kannt' ich euch besser,
Als ich je die Menschen gekannt,
Ich verstand die Stille des Aethers
Der Menschen Worte verstand ich nie.

Mich erzog der Wohllaut
Des säuselnden Hains
Und lieben lernt' ich
Unter den Blumen.

Im Arme der Götter wuchs ich groß.

When I was a boy . . .

When I was a boy
  A god rescued me often
    From shouts and whips of men,
      It was then that I played
        Safely and well with woodland flowers
       And the winds of heaven
        Played with me.

And as you delight
The hearts of plants,
When to you they extend
Their delicate arms,

So you delighted my heart,
Father Helios, and like Endymion
I was your darling,
Sacred Moon!

O all you faithful
Friendly gods!
If only you knew
How my soul loved you.

True, in those days I did not
Call you by name, and you
Never called me as men do, as if
They knew one another, with names.

Yet I knew you better
Than I ever knew men,
I understood air, its stillness,
Never the language of men.

The whispering woodland's
Harmony taught me,
And I learned to love
Among the flowers.

I grew tall in the arms of the gods.

Christopher Middleton

Empedokles

Das Leben suchst du, suchst, und es quillt und glänzt
  Ein göttlich Feuer tief aus der Erde dir,
    Und du in schauderndem Verlangen
      Wiftst dich hinab, in des Aetna Flammen.

So schmelzt' im Weine Perlen der Übermuth
  Der Königin; und mochte sie doch! hättst du
    Nur deinen Reichtum nicht, o Dichter
      Hin in den gährenden Kelch geopfert!

Doch heilig bist du mir, wie der Erde Macht,
  Die dich hinwegnahm, kühner Getödteter!
    Und folgen möcht' ich in die Tiefe,
      Hielte die Liebe mich nicht, dem Helden.

Sophokles

Viele versuchten umsonst das Freudigste freudig zu sagen
  Hier spricht endlich es mir, hier in der Trauer sich aus.

Wurzel alles Übels

Einig zu seyn, ist göttlich und gut; woher ist die Sucht denn
  Unter den Menschen, daß nur Einer und Eines nur sie?

Empedocles

You look for life, you look and from deeps of Earth
  A fire, divinely gleaming wells up for you,
    And quick, aquiver with desire, you
      Hurl yourself down into Etna's furnace.

So did the Queen's exuberance once dissolve
  Rare pearls in wine, and why should she not? But you,
    If only you, O poet, had not
      Offered your wealth to the seething chalice!

Yet you are holy to me as is the power
  Of Earth that took you from us, the boldly killed!
    And gladly, did not love restrain me,
      Deep as the hero plunged down I'd follow.

Michael Hamburger

Sophocles

Many have tried, but in vain, with joy to express the most joyful;
  Here at last, in grave sadness, wholly I find it expressed.

Michael Hamburger

The Root of All Evil

Being at one is god-like and good, but human, too human, the
    mania
  Which insists there is only the One, one country, one truth and
    one way.

Michael Hamburger

Mein Eigentum

In seiner Fülle ruhet der Herbsttag nun,
  Geläutert ist die Traub und der Hain ist roth
    Vom Obst, wenn schon der holden Blüthen
      Manche der Erde zum Danke fielen.

Und rings im Felde, wo ich den Pfad hinaus
  Den stillen wandle, ist den Zufriedenen
    Ihr Gut gereift und viel der frohen
      Mühe gewähret der Reichtum ihnen.

Vom Himmel bliket zu den Geschäfftigen
  Durch ihre Bäume milde das Licht herab,
    Die Freude theilend, denn es wuchs durch
      Hände der Menschen allein die Frucht nicht.

Und leuchtest du, o Goldnes, auch mir, und wehst
  Auch du mir wieder, Lüftchen, als seegnetest
    Du eine Freude mir, wie einst, und
      Irrst, wie um Glükliche, mir am Busen?

Einst war ichs, doch wie Rosen, vergänglich war
  Das fromme Leben, ach! und es mahnen noch,
    Die blühend mir geblieben sind, die
      Holden Gestirne zu oft mich dessen.

Beglükt, wer, ruhig liebend ein frommes Weib,
  Am eignen Heerd in rühmlicher Heimath lebt,
    Es leuchtet über vestem Boden
      Schöner dem sicheren Mann sein Himmel.

Denn, wie die Pflanze, wurzelt auf eignem Grund
  Sie nicht, verglüht die Seele des Sterblichen,
    Der mit dem Tageslichte nur, ein
      Armer, auf heiliger Erde wandelt.

My Possessions

At rest in fulness, calm lies the autumn day,
    The mellow grape is clear and the orchard red
        With fruit, though many treasured blossoms
            Long ago fell to the Earth in tribute.

And all around where now by the quiet path
    I cross the field, for satisfied men their crops
        Have ripened, and their riches grant them
            Hour after hour of rewarding labor.

From heaven through leafy boughs on the busy ones
    A light subdued and temperate glances down
        To share their pleasure; for not human
            Hands by themselves made the cornfield prosper.

And, golden light, for me will you also shine,
    And, breeze, once more for me will you waft, as though
        To bless a joy, and still around me
            Flutter and play, as for happy mortals?

I too was one, but brief as the full-blown rose
    My good life passed, and they that alone are left
        In flower for me, the constellations,
            Often, too often, remind me of it.

Blessed he who calmly loving a gentle wife
    Can call a worthy homeland and hearth his own;
        Above firm ground more brightly to the
            Settled, secure man his heaven glitters.

For like the plant that fails to take root within
    Its native ground, the soul of that mortal wilts
        Who with the daylight only roams, a
            Pauper astray on our Earth, the hallowed.

Zu mächtig ach! ihr himmlischen Höhen zieht
  Ihr mich empor, bei Stürmen, am heitern Tag
    Fühl ich verzehrend euch im Busen
      Wechseln, ihr wandelnden Götterkräfte.

Doch heute laß mich stille den trauten Pfad
  Zum Haine gehn, dem golden die Wipfel schmükt
    Sein sterbend Laub, und kränzt auch mir die
      Stirne, ihr holden Erinnerungen!

Und daß mir auch zu retten mein sterblich Herz,
  Wie andern eine bleibende Stätte sei,
    Und heimathlos die Seele mir nicht
      Über das Leben hinweg sich sehne,

Sei du, Gesang, mein freundlich Asyl! sei du
  Beglükender! mit sorgender Liebe mir
    Gepflegt, der Garten, wo ich, wandelnd
      Unter den Blüthen, den immerjungen,

In sichrer Einfalt wohne, wenn draußen mir
  Mit ihren Wellen allen die mächtge Zeit
    Die Wandelbare fern rauscht und die
      Stillere Sonne mein Wirken fördert.

Ihr seegnet gütig über den Sterblichen
  Ihr Himmelskräfte! jedem sein Eigentum,
    O seegnet meines auch und daß zu
      Frühe die Parze den Traum nicht ende.

Too strongly always, heavenly heights, you pull
   Me upward; gales that rage on a sunny day
      Bring home to me your clashing powers,
         Mutable gods, and they rend, destroy me.

Today, though, let me walk the familiar path
   In silence to the copse that is crowned with gold
      Of dying leaves; and my brow also
         Garland with gold now, dear recollections!

And that my mortal heart nonetheless may last,
   A quiet, sure retreat, as are other men's,
      And that my soul may not outfly this
         Life in its longing, for ever homeless,

You be my gracious refuge now, song, and you,
   Joy-giver, now be tended with loving care,
      The garden where intently walking
         Under the blossoms that do not wither,

I live in safe ingenuousness while outside
   With all its waves the changeable, mighty time,
      Roars far away, and to my labors
         Only the quieter sun contributes.

Above us mortals, heavenly powers, you bless
   Each man's possessions, kindly disposed to all;
      O bless mine also, lest too soon the
         Fate put an end to my earthly dreaming.

                        Michael Hamburger

Heidelberg

Lange lieb' ich dich schon, möchte dich, mir zur Lust,
    Mutter nennen, und dir schenken ein kunstlos Lied,
        Du, der Vaterlandsstädte
            Ländlichschönste, so viel ich sah.

Wie der Vogel des Walds über die Gipfel fliegt,
    Schwingt sich über den Strom, wo er vorbei dir glänzt,
        Leicht und kräftig die Brüke,
            Die von Wagen und Menschen tönt.

Wie von Göttern gesandt, fesselt' ein Zauber einst
    Auf die Brüke mich an, da ich vorüber gieng,
        Und herein in die Berge
            Mir die reizende Ferne schien,

Und der Jüngling, der Strom, fort in die Ebne zog,
    Traurigfroh, wie das Herz, wenn es, sich selbst zu schön,
        Liebend unterzugehen,
            In die Fluthen der Zeit sich wirft.

Quellen hattest du ihm, hattest dem Flüchtigen
    Kühle Schatten geschenkt, und die Gestade sahn
        All' ihm nach, und es bebte
            Aus den Wellen ihr lieblich Bild.

Aber schwer in das Thal hieng die gigantische,
    Schiksaalskundige Burg nieder bis auf den Grund,
        Von den Wettern zerrissen;
            Doch die ewige Sonne goß

Ihr verjüngendes Licht über das alternde
    Riesenbild, und umher grünte lebendiger
        Epheu; freundliche Wälder
            Rauschten über die Burg herab.

Sträuche blühten herab, bis wo im heitern Thal,
    An den Hügel gelehnt, oder dem Ufer hold,
        Deine fröhlichen Gassen
            Unter duftenden Gärten ruhn.

Heidelberg

Long have I loved you and for my own delight
   Would call you mother, give you an artless song,
      You, of all the towns in our country
        The loveliest that ever I saw.

As the forest bird crosses the peaks in flight,
   Over the river shimmering past you floats
      Airy and strong the bridge,
        Humming with sounds of traffic and people.

Once, as if it were sent by gods, enchantment
   Seized me as I was passing over the bridge
      And the distance with its allure
        Shone into the mountainscape,

And that strong youth, the river, was rushing on down
   To the plain, sorrowing-glad, like the heart that overflows
      With beauty and hurls itself,
        To die of love, into the floods of time.

You had fed him with streams, the fugitive, given him
   Cool shadow, and all the shores looked on
      As he followed his way, their image
        Sweetly jockeying over the waves.

But into the valley hung heavy the vast
   And fate-acquainted fort, by lightnings torn
      To the ground it stood on; yet
        Eternal sun still poured

Its freshening light across the giant and aging
   Thing, and all around was green with ivy,
      Living; friendly woodlands ran
        Murmurous down across the fort.

Bushes flowered all down the slope to where,
   In the vale serene, with hills to prop them, shores
      For them to cling to, your small streets
        Mid fragrant garden bowers repose.

Christopher Middleton

Lebenslauf

Größers wolltest auch du, aber die Liebe zwingt
  All uns nieder, das Laid beuget gewaltiger,
    Doch es kehret umsonst nicht
      Unser Bogen, woher er kommt.

Aufwärts oder hinab! herrschet in heil'ger Nacht,
  Wo die stumme Natur werdende Tage sinnt,
    Herrscht im schiefesten Orkus
      Nicht ein Grades, ein Recht noch auch?

Diß erfuhr ich. Denn nie, sterblichen Meistern gleich,
  Habt ihr Himmlischen, ihr Alleserhaltenden,
    Daß ich wüßte, mit Vorsicht
      Mich des ebenen Pfads geführt.

Alles prüfe der Mensch, sagen die Himmlischen,
  Daß er, kräftig genährt, danken für Alles lern',
    Und verstehe die Freiheit,
      Aufzubrechen, wohin er will.

Der Abschied
Zweite Fassung

Trennen wollten wir uns? wähnten es gut und klug?
  Da wirs thaten, warum schrökte, wie Mord, die That?
    Ach! wir kennen uns wenig,
      Denn es waltet ein Gott in uns.

Den verrathen? ach ihn, welcher uns alles erst,
  Sinn und Leben erschuff, ihn, den beseelenden
    Schuzgott unserer Liebe,
      Diß, diß Eine vermag ich nicht.

The Course of Life

More you also desired, but every one of us
   Love draws earthward, and grief bends with still greater power;
     Yet our arc not for nothing
       Brings us back to our starting place.

Whether upward or down—does not in holy night
   Where mute Nature thinks out days that are still to come,
     Though in crookedest Orcus,
       Yet a straightness, a law prevail?

This I learned. For not once, as mortal masters do,
   Did you heavenly ones, wise preservers of all,
     To my knowledge, with foresight
       Lead me on by a level path.

All a man shall try out, thus say the heavenly,
   So that strongly sustained he shall give thanks for all,
     Learn to grasp his own freedom
       To be gone where he's moved to go.

Michael Hamburger

The Farewell
Second Version

So we wanted to part? Thought it both good and wise?
   Why, then, why did the act shock us as murder would?
     Ah, ourselves we know little,
       For within us a god commands.

Wrong that god? And betray him who created for us
   Meaning, life, all we had, him who inspired and moved,
     Who protected our loving,
       This, this one thing I cannot do.

Aber anderen Fehl denket der Weltsinn sich,
  Andern ehernen Dienst übt er und anders Recht,
    Und es listet die Seele
      Tag für Tag der Gebrauch uns ab.

Wohl! ich wußt' es zuvor. Seit die gewurzelte
  Ungestalte die Furcht Götter und Menschen trennt,
    Muß, mit Blut sie zu sühnen,
      Muß der Liebenden Herz vergehn.

Laß mich schweigen! o laß nimmer von nun an mich
  Dieses Tödtliche sehn, daß ich im Frieden doch
    Hin ins Einsame ziehe,
      Und noch unser der Abschied sei!

Reich die Schaale mir selbst, daß ich des rettenden
  Heilgen Giftes genug, daß ich des Lethetranks
    Mit dir trinke, daß alles
      Haß und Liebe vergessen sei!

Hingehn will ich. Vieleicht seh' ich in langer Zeit
  Diotima! dich hier. Aber verblutet ist
    Dann das Wünschen und friedlich
      Gleich den Seeligen, fremde gehn

Wir umher, ein Gespräch führet uns ab und auf,
  Sinnend, zögernd, doch izt mahnt die Vergessenen
    Hier die Stelle des Abschieds,
      Es erwarmet ein Herz in uns,

Staunend seh' ich dich an, Stimmen und süßen Sang,
  Wie aus voriger Zeit hör' ich und Saitenspiel,
    Und die Lilie duftet
      Golden über dem Bach uns auf.

But a different wrong, different slavery
   Now the world's mind invents, threatens with other laws,
      And, by cunning, convention
         Day by day steals away our souls.

Oh, I knew it before. Ever since deep-rooted Fear,
   Ugly, crippled, estranged mortals from heaven's gods
      To appease them with bloodshed
         Lovers' hearts must be sacrificed.

Silent now let me be! Never henceforth let me know
   This, my deadly disgrace, so that in peace I may
      Hide myself where it's lonely
         And the parting at least be ours.

Pass the cup, then, yourself, that of the rescuing,
   Holy poison enough, that of the lethal draught
      I may drink with you, all things,
         Hate and love be forgotten then.

To be gone is my wish. Later perhaps one day,
   Diotima, we'll meet—here, but desire by then
      Will have bled away, peaceful
         Like the blessed, and like strangers we'll

Walk about, as our talk leads us now here, now there,
   Musing, hesitant, but then the oblivious ones
      See the place where they parted,
         And a heart newly warms in us,

Wondering I look at you, voices and lovely song
   As from distant times, music of strings, I hear
      And the lily unfolds her
         Fragrance, golden above the brook.

                                        Michael Hamburger

Natur und Kunst oder Saturn und Jupiter

Du waltest hoch am Tag' und es blühet dein
  Gesez, du hälst die Waage, Saturnus Sohn!
    Und theilst die Loos' und ruhest froh im
      Ruhm der unsterblichen Herrscherkünste.

Doch in den Abgrund, sagen die Sänger sich,
  Habst du den hiel'gen Vater, den eignen, einst
    Verwiesen und es jammre drunten,
      Da, wo die Wilden vor dir mit Recht sind,

Schuldlos der Gott der goldenen Zeit schon längst:
  Einst mühelos, und größer, wie du, wenn schon
    Er kein Gebot aussprach und ihn der
      Sterblichen keiner mit Nahmen nannte.

Herab denn! oder schäme des Danks dich nicht!
  Und willst du bleiben, diene dem Älteren,
    Und gönn' es ihm, daß ihn vor Allen,
      Göttern und Menschen, der Sänger nenne!

Denn, wie aus dem Gewölke dein Bliz, so kömmt
  Von ihm, was dein ist, siehe! so zeugt von ihm,
    Was du gebeutst, und aus Saturnus
      Frieden ist jegliche Macht erwachsen.

Und hab' ich erst am Herzen Lebendeiges
  Gefühlt und dämmert, was du gestaltetest,
    Und war in ihrer Wiege mir in
      Wonne die wechselnde Zeit entschlummert:

Dann kenn' ich dich, Kronion! dann hör' ich dich,
  Den weisen Meister, welcher, wie wir, ein Sohn
    Der Zeit, Geseze giebt und, was die
      Heilige Dämmerung birgt, verkündet.

Nature and Art or Saturn and Jupiter

High up in day you govern, your law prevails,
   You hold the scales of judgement, O Saturn's son,
      Hand out our lots and well-contented
         Rest on the fame of immortal kingship.

Yet, singers know it, down the abyss you hurled
   The holy father once, your own parent, who
      Long now has lain lamenting where the
         Wild ones before you more justly languish,

Quite guiltless he, the god of the golden age:
   Once effortless and greater than you, although
      He uttered no commandment, and no
         Mortal on earth ever named his presence.

So down with you! Or cease to withhold your thanks!
   And if you'll stay, defer to the older god
      And grant him that above all others,
         Gods and great mortals, the singer name him!

For as from clouds your lightning, from him has come
   What you call yours. And, look, the commands you speak
      To him bear witness, and from Saturn's
         Primitive peace every power developed.

And once my heart can feel and contain that life
   Most living, his, and things that you shaped grow dim,
      And in his cradle changing Time has
         Fallen asleep and sweet quiet lulls me—

I'll know you then, Kronion, and hear you then,
   The one wise master who, like ourselves, a son
      Of Time, gives laws to us, uncovers
         That which lies hidden in holy twilight.

Michael Hamburger

Dichterberuf

Des Ganges Ufer hörten des Freudengotts
   Triumph, als allerobernd vom Indus her
     Der junge Bacchus kam, mit heilgem
       Weine vom Schlafe die Völker wekend.

Und du, des Tages Engel! erwekst sie nicht,
   Die jezt noch schlafen? gieb die Geseze, gieb
     Uns Leben, siege, Meister, du nur
       Hast der Eroberung Recht, wie Bacchus.

Nicht, was wohl sonst des Menschen Geschik und Sorg'
   Im Haus und unter offenem Himmel ist,
     Wenn edler, denn das Wild, der Mann sich
       Wehret und nährt! denn es gilt ein anders,

Zu Sorg' und Dienst den Dichtenden anvertraut!
   Der Höchste, der ists, dem wir geeignet sind,
     Daß näher, immerneu besungen
       Ihn die befreundete Brust vernehme.

Und dennoch, o ihr Himmlischen all, und all
   Ihr Quellen und ihr Ufer und Hain' und Höhn,
     Wo wunderbar zuerst, als du die
       Loken ergriffen, und unvergeßlich

Der unverhoffte Genius über uns
   Der schöpferische, göttliche kam, daß stumm
     Der Sinn uns ward und, wie vom
       Strale gerührt das Gebein erbebte,

Ihr ruhelosen Thaten in weiter Welt!
   Ihr Schiksaalstag', ihr reißenden, wenn der Gott
     Stillsinnend lenkt, wohin zorntrunken
       Ihn die gigantischen Rosse bringen,

The Poet's Vocation

Shores of Ganges heard the paean for the god
    Of joy when Bacchus came, conquering all,
        Young, from the Indus, with holy wine
            Rousing the people from their slumber.

And you, angel of our time, shall you arouse them too,
    The peoples unawakened? Give the laws,
        Give life to us, conquer, you alone,
            As Bacchus once, have right of conquest.

Not the thing that is man's care and skill,
    Inside a house or underneath the sky,
        Though a man fends and feeds more nobly
            Than animals do. Something else

Is put in the poet's trust and care to serve.
    To the highest lord, to him it is, we own,
        That, being sung ever anew, him
            Friendly hearts may sense more clearly.

Nevertheless, O all you heavenly gods
    And all you streams and shores, hilltops and woods,
        Where first, when by the hair one of you
            Seized us and the unhoped-for spirit

Unforgettably came, astonishing, down
    Upon us, godlike and creative, dumbfounding
        The mind, every bone shook
            As if struck by lightning—should we not,

You deeds rampaging out in the wide world,
    You days of destiny, fast and furious, when the god goes,
        Keeping his counsel, wherever the rage-drunk
            Gigantic horses happen to take him—

Euch sollten wir verschweigen, und wenn in uns
  Vom stetigstillen Jahre der Wohllaut tönt,
    So sollt'es klingen, gleich als hätte
      Muthig und müßig ein Kind des Meisters

Geweihte, reine Saiten im Scherz gerührt?
  Und darum hast du, Dichter! des Orients
    Propheten und den Griechensang und
      Neulich die Donner gehört, damit du

Den Geist zu Diensten brauchst und die Gegenwart
  Des Guten übereilest, in Spott, und den Albernen
    Verläugnest, herzlos, und zum Spiele
      Feil, wie gefangenes Wild, ihn treibest?

Bis aufgereizt vom Stachel im Grimme der
  Des Ursprungs sich erinnert und ruft, daß selbst
    Der Meister kommt, dann unter heißen
      Todesgeschossen entseelt dich lässet.

Zu lang is alles Göttliche dienstbar schon
  Und alle Himmelskräfte verscherzt, verbraucht
    Die Gütigen, zur Lust, danklos, ein
      Schlaues Geschlecht und zu kennen wähnt es,

Wenn ihnen der Erhabne den Aker baut,
  Das Tagslicht und den Donnerer, und es späht
    Das Sehrohr wohl sie all und zählt und
      Nennet mit Nahmen des Himmels Sterne.

Der Vater aber deket mit heilger Nacht,
  Damit wir bleiben mögen, die Augen zu.
    Nicht liebt er Wildes! Doch es zwinget
      Nimmer die weite Gewalt den Himmel.

Noch ists auch gut, zu weise zu seyn. Ihn kennt
  Der Dank. Doch nicht behält er es leicht allein,
    Und gern gesellt, damit verstehn sie
      Helfen, zu anderen sich ein Dichter.

Should we not speak of you? And when from the calm
   And constant year harmony sounds in us, should
      It ring as if in idle caprice
         Some child had dared to touch for fun

The master's consecrated and pure strings?
   Was it for this you heard the prophets of the East
      And Greek song and lately, poet,
         Voices of thunder? Was it for this—

To press the spirit into service, burst in upon
   The presence of the good, deriding it, heartless
      Disavow simplicity itself and make it
         Play for a fee like a beast captive?

Until the selfsame spirit, goaded to a rage,
   Cries out, remembering its source, and the master
      Hurling his hot darts comes
         And leaves you flat, a soul extinguished.

Too long all things divine have been put to use,
   Heavenly powers trifled away, mercies
      Squandered for sport, thankless, a
         Generation of schemers, and it presumes,

When the most sublime lord tills their fields,
   To know daylight and the thunderer, all these
      The telescope scans and quantifies
         And names with names the heaven's stars.

And yet with holy night the father will veil
   Our eyes, that still we may not perish. Untamed
      Excess he loves not. Power
         Expands but cannot suborn heaven.

Nor is it good to be too knowing. Gratitude
   Knows him. Yet to keep and contain it alone
      Is a hard burden, others the poet
         Gladly joins who help understanding.

Furchtlos bleibt aber, so er es muß, der Mann
Einsam vor Gott, es schüzet die Einfalt ihn,
   Und keiner Waffen brauchts und keiner
      Listen, so lange, bis Gottes Fehl hilft.

Stimme des Volks
Zweite Fassung

Du seiest Gottes Stimme, so glaubt' ich sonst
In heil'ger Jugend; ja, und ich sag' es noch!
   Um unsre Weisheit unbekümmert
      Rauschen die Ströme doch auch, und dennoch,

Wer liebt sie nicht? und immer bewegen sie
Das Herz mir, hör' ich ferne die Schwindenden,
   Die Ahnungsvollen meine Bahn nicht,
      Aber gewisser ins Meer hin eilen.

Denn selbstvergessen, allzubereit den Wunsch
Der Götter zu erfüllen, ergreift zu gern
   Was sterblich ist, wenn offnen Augs auf
      Eigenen Pfaden es einmal wandelt,

Ins All zurük die kürzeste Bahn; so stürzt
Der Strom hinab, er suchet die Ruh, es reißt,
   Es ziehet wider Willen ihn, von
      Klippe zu Kippe den Steuerlosen

Das wunderbare Sehnen dem Abgrund zu;
Das Ungebundne reizet und Völker auch
   Ergreifft die Todeslust und kühne
      Städte, nachdem sie versucht das Beste,

Fearless yet, if he must, man stands, and lonely
  Before God, simplicity protects him, no
    Weapon he needs, nor subterfuge
      Till God's being not there helps him.

Christopher Middleton

Voice of the People
Second Version

The voice of God I called you and thought you once,
  In holy youth; and still I do not recant!
    No less indifferent to our wisdom
      Likewise the rivers rush on, but who does

Not love them? Always too my own heart is moved
  When far away I hear those foreknowing ones,
    The fleeting, by a route not mine but
      Surer than mine, and more swift, roar seaward,

For once they travel down their allotted paths
  With open eyes, self-oblivious, too ready to
    Comply with what the gods have wished them,
      Only too gladly will mortal beings

Speed back into the All by the shortest way;
  So rivers plunge—not movement, but rest they seek—
    Drawn on, pulled down against their will from
      Boulder to boulder—abandoned, helmless—

By that mysterious yearning toward the chasm;
  Chaotic deeps attract, and whole peoples too
    May come to long for death, and valiant
      Towns that have striven to do the best thing,

Von Jahr zu Jahr forttreibend das Werk, sie hat
  Ein heilig Ende troffen; die Erde grünt
    Und stille vor den Sternen liegt, den
      Betenden gleich, in den Sand geworfen

Freiwillig überwunden die lange Kunst
  Vor jenen Unnachahmbaren da; er selbst,
    Der Mensch, mit eigner Hand zerbrach, die
      Hohen zu ehren, sien Werk der Künstler.

Doch minder nicht sind jene den Menschen hold,
  Sie lieben wieder, so wie geliebt sie sind,
    Und hemmen öfters, daß er lang im
      Lichte sich freue, die Bahn des Menschen.

Und, nicht des Adlers Jungen allein, sie wirft
  Der Vater aus dem Neste, damit sie nicht
    Zu lang' ihm bleiben, uns auch treibt mit
      Richtigem Stachel hinaus der Herrscher.

Wohl jenen, die zur Ruhe gegangen sind,
  Und vor der Zeit gefallen, auch die, auch die
    Geopfert, gleich den Erstlingen der
      Erndte, sie haben ein Theil gefunden.

Am Xanthos lag, in griechischer Zeit, die Stadt,
  Jezt aber, gleich den größeren die dort ruhn
    Ist durch ein Schiksaal sie dem heilgen
      Lichte des Tages hinweggekommen.

Sie kamen aber nicht in der offnen Schlacht
  Durch eigne Hand um. Fürchterlich ist davon,
    Was dort geschehn, die wunderbare
      Sage von Osten zu uns gelanget.

Es reizte sie die Güte von Brutus. Denn
  Als Feuer ausgegangen, so bot er sich
    Zu helfen ihnen, ob er gleich, als Feldherr,
      Stand in Belagerung vor den Thoren.

Year in, year out pursuing their task—these too
   A holy end has stricken; the earth grows green,
      And there beneath the stars, like mortals
         Deep in their prayers, quite still, prostrated

On sand, outgrown, and willingly, lies long art
   Flung down before the Matchless; and he himself,
      The man, the artist with his own two
         Hands broke his work for their sake, in homage.

Yet they, the Heavenly, to men remain well-disposed,
   As we love them so they will return our love
      And lest too briefly he enjoy the
         Light, will obstruct a man's course to ruin.

And not the eagle's fledglings alone their sire
   Throws out of eyries, knowing that else too long
      They'd idle—us the Ruler also
         Goads into flight with a prong that's fitting.

Those men I praise who early lay down to rest,
   Who fell before their time, and those also, those
      Like firstfruits of the harvest offered
         Up—they were granted a part, a portion.

By Xanthos once, in Grecian times, there stood
   The town, but how, like greater ones resting there,
      Because a destiny ordained it
         Xanthos is lost to our holy daylight.

But not in open battle, by their own hands
   Her people perished. Dreadful and marvelous
      The legend of that town's destruction,
         Traveling on from the East, has reached us.

The kindliness of Brutus provoked them. For
   When fire broke out, most nobly he offered them
      His help, although he led those troops which
         Stood at their gates to besiege the township.

Doch von den Mauren warfen die Diener sie
Die er gesandt. Lebendiger ward darauf
   Das Feuer und sie freuten sich und ihnen
     Streket' entgegen die Hände Brutus

Und alle waren außer sich selbst. Geschrei
   Entstand und Jauchzen. Drauf in die Flamme warf
   Sich Mann und Weib, von Knaben stürzt' auch
     Der von dem Dach, in der Väter Schwerdt der.

Nich räthlich ist es, Helden zu trozen. Längst
   Wars aber vorbereitet. Die Väter auch
   Da sie ergriffen waren, einst, und
     Heftig die persischen Feinde drängten,

Entzündeten, ergreiffend des Stromes Rohr,
   Daß sie das Freie fänden, die Stadt. Und Haus
   Und Tempel nahm, zum heilgen Aether
     Fliegend, und Menschen hinweg die Flamme.

So hatten es die Kinder gehört, und wohl
   Sind gut die Sagen, denn ein Gedächtniß sind
   Dem Höchsten sie, doch auch bedarf es
     Eines, die heiligen auszulegen.

Chiron

Wo bist du, Nachdenkliches! das immer muß
   Zur Seite gehn, zu Zeiten, wo bist du, Licht?
   Wohl ist das Herz wach, doch mir zürnt, mich
     Hemmt die erstaunende Nacht nun immer.

Yet from the walls they threw all the servants down
   Whom he had sent. Much livelier then at once
      The fire flared up, and they rejoiced, and
         Brutus extended his arms towards them,

All were beside themselves. And great crying there,
   Great jubilation sounded. Then into flames
      Leapt man and woman; boys came hurtling
         Down from the roofs or their fathers stabbed them.

It is not wise to fight against heroes. But
   Events long past prepared it. Their ancestors
      When they were quite encircled once and
         Strongly the Persian forces pressed them,

Took rushes from the rivers and, that their foes
   Might find a desert there, set ablaze their town;
      And house and temple—breathed to holy
         Aether—and men did the flame carry off there.

So their descendants heard, and no doubt such lore
   Is good, because it serves to remind us of
      The Highest; yet there's also need of
         One to interpret these holy legends.

                       Michael Hamburger

Chiron

Where are you, thought-infusing, which at this time
   Must always move beside me, where are you, light?
      Indeed the heart's awake, but, wrathful,
         Always astonishing Night constricts me.

Sonst nemlich folgt' ich Kräutern des Walds und lauscht'
   Ein waiches Wild am Hügel; und nie umsonst.
      Nie täuschten, auch nicht einmal deine
         Vögel; denn allzubereit fast kamst du,

So Füllen oder Garten dir labend ward,
   Rathschlagend, Herzens wegen; wo bist du, Licht?
      Das Herz ist wieder wach, doch herzlos
         Zieht die gewaltige Nacht mich immer.

Ich war's wohl. Und von Krokus und Thymian
   Und Korn gab mir die Erde den ersten Straus.
      Und bei der Sterne Kühle lernt' ich,
         Aber das Nennbare nur. Und bei mir

Das wilde Feld entzaubernd, das traur'ge, zog
   Der Halbgott, Zevs Knecht, ein, der gerade Mann;
      Nun siz' ich still allein, von einer
         Stunde zur anderen, und Gestalten

Aus frischer Erd' und Wolken der Liebe schafft,
   Weil Gift ist zwischen uns, mein Gedanke nun;
      Und ferne lausch' ich hin, ob nicht ein
         Freundlicher Retter vieleicht mir komme.

Dann hör' ich oft den Wagen des Donnerers
   Am Mittag, wenn er naht, der bekannteste,
      Wenn ihm das Haus bebt und der Boden
         Reiniget sich, und die Quaal Echo wird.

Den Retter hör' ich dann in der Nacht, ich hör'
   Ihn tödtend, den Befreier, und drunten voll
      Von üpp'gem Kraut, als in Gesichten
         Schau ich die Erd', ein gewaltig Feuer;

Die Tage aber wechseln, wenn einer dann
   Zusiehet denen, lieblich und bös', ein Schmerz,
      Wenn einer zweigestalt ist, und es
         Kennet kein einziger nicht das Beste;

For then I'd look for herbs of the wood, and on
   The hillside hear soft game; and never in vain.
     And never once your birds deceived me,
       Never; but almost too promptly then you

Would come, when foal or garden contented you,
   Advising, for the heart's sake; where are you, light?
     The heart's awake once more, but, heartless,
       Always most powerful Night allures me.

That one was I, it seems. And of crocus, thyme
   And corn then Earth would pick the first bunch for me.
     And in the cool of stars I learned, but
       Only the nameable. Disenchanting

That wild, sad open meadow the demigod,
   Zeus' servant came, the straight man, to lodge with me;
     Now here I sit alone in silence
       Hour after hour, and my mind devises

Shapes for itself—since poison divides us now—
   Made up of love's new earth and the clouds of love;
     And far I strain my hearing lest a
       Kindly deliverer perhaps is coming.

Then often I can hear the great Thunderer's voice
   At noon when he, the best-known of all, draws near,
     When his own house quakes, the foundations,
       Shaken, are cleansed and my torment echoes.

The Savior then I hear in the night, I hear
   Him kill, the liberator, and down below,
     As if in visions, full of luscious
       Weeds I see Earth, a tremendous fire;

But days go by, both lovely and bad, when one
   Observes their changes, suffering pain because
     Of twofold nature, and when none can
       Ever be sure what is best and fittest;

Das aber ist der Stachel des Gottes; nie
Kann einer lieben göttliches Unrecht sonst.
    Einheimisch aber ist der Gott dann
        Angesichts da, und die Erd' ist anders.

Tag! Tag! Nun wieder athmet ihr recht; nun trinkt,
Ihr meiner Bäche Weiden! ein Augenlicht,
    Und rechte Stapfen gehn, und als ein
        Herrscher, mit Sporen, und bei dir selber

Örtlich, Irrstern des Tages, erscheinest du,
Du auch, o Erde, friedliche Wieg', und du,
    Haus meiner Väter, die unstädtisch
        Sind, in den Wolken des Wilds, gegangen.

Nimm nun ein Roß, und harnische dich und nimm
Den leichten Speer, o Knabe! Die Wahrsagung
    Zerreißt nicht, und umsonst nicht wartet,
        Bis sie erscheinet, Herakles Rükkehr.

Blödigkeit

Sind denn dir nicht bekannt viele Lebendigen?
    Geht auf Wahrem dein Fuß nicht, wie auf Teppichen?
        Drum, mein Genius! tritt nur
            Baar in's Leben, und sorge nicht!

Was geschiehet, es sei alles gelegen dir!
    Sei zur Freude gereimt, oder was könnte denn
        Dich belaidigen, Herz, was
            Da begegnen, wohin du sollst?

But that's the very sting of the god; and else
    Divine injustice never could claim men's love.
        But native then, at home, the god is
            Visibly present, and Earth is different.

Day! Day! Once more you can breathe, now drink,
    You willows of my streams, an illumined sight,
        And sure, true footsteps go, and as a
            Ruler, with spurs, and located in your

Own orbit you, the planet of day, appear,
    And you, O Earth, our cradle of peace, and you,
        House of my forbears who unurban
            Traveled in clouds with the woodland creatures.

Now take a horse and armour and lastly, boy,
    Take up the slender spear! For the prophecy
        Will not be torn, and not for nothing
            Heralces' promised return awaits it.

Michael Hamburger

Timidness

Of the living are not many well-known to you?
    On the truth don't your feet walk as they would on rugs?
        Boldly, therefore, my genius,
            Step right into the thick of life!

All that happens there be welcome, a boon to you!
    Be disposed to feel joy, or is there anything
        That could harm you there, heart, that
            Could affront you, where you must go?

Denn, seit Himmlischen gleich Menschen, ein einsam Wild
  Und die Himmlischen selbst führet, der Einkehr zu,
    Der Gesang und der Fürsten
      Chor, nach Arten, so waren auch

Wir, die Zungen des Volks, gerne bei Lebenden,
  Wo sich vieles gesellt, freudig und jedem gleich,
    Jedem offen, so ist ja
      Unser Vater, des Himmels Gott,

Der den denkenden Tag Armen und Reichen gönnt,
  Der, zur Wende der Zeit, uns die Entschlafenden
    Aufgerichtet an goldnen
      Gängelbanden, wie Kinder, hält.

Gut auch sind und geschikt einem zu etwas wir,
  Wenn wir kommen, mit Kinst, und von den Himmlischen
    Einen bringen. Doch selber
      Bringen schikliche Hände wir.

Ganymed

Was schläfst du, Bergsohn, liegest in Unmuth, schief,
  Und frierst am kahlen Ufer, Gedultiger!
    Denkst nicht der Gnade du, wenn's an den
      Tischen die Himmlischen sonst gedürstet?

Kennst drunten du vom Vater die Boten nicht,
  Nicht in der Kluft der Lüfte geschärfter Spiel?
    Trift nicht das Wort dich, das voll alten
      Geists ein gewanderter Mann dir sendet?

For since gods grew like men, lonely as woodland beasts,
   And since, each in its way, song and the princely choir
      Brought the Heavenly in person
         Back to earth, so we too, the tongues

Of the people, have liked living men's company,
   Where all kinds are conjoined, equal and open to
      Everyone, full of joy—for
         So our Father is, Heaven's God,

Who to rich men and poor offers the thinking day,
   At the turning of Time hold us, the sleepy ones,
      Upright still with his golden
         Leading-strings, as one holds a child.

Someone, some way, we too serve, are of use, are sent
   When we come, with our art, and of the heavenly powers
      Bring one with us. But fitting,
         Skilful hands we ourselves provide.

                                  Michael Hamburger

Ganymede

Why sleep, mountain son, lying askew, despondent,
   Shivering on the bare streambank, all patience?
      Not a thought for grace now, when once
         Was thirst at the tables, among gods?

The father's heralds, is there nothing of them you see
   Down there? Sharper winds in the gully at play?
      Or hear what he says, the much-traveled
         Man filled with old spirit?

Schon tönet's aber ihm in der Brust. Tief quillt's,
   Wie damals, als hoch oben im Fels er schlief,
      Ihm auf. Im Zorne reinigt aber
         Sich der Gefesselte nun, nun eilt er

Der Linkische; der spottet der Schlaken nun,
   Und nimmt und bricht und wirft die Zerbrochenen
      Zorntrunken, spielend, dort und da zum
         Schauenden Ufer und bei des Fremdlings

Besondrer Stimme stehen die Heerden auf,
   Es regen sich die Wälder, es hört tief Land
      Den Stromgeist fern, und schaudernd regt im
         Nabel der Erde der Geist sich wieder.

Der Frühling kömmt. Und jedes, in seiner Art,
   Blüht. Der ist aber ferne; nicht mehr dabei.
      Irr gieng er nun; denn allzugut sind
         Genien; himmlisch Gespräch ist sein nun.

Menons Klagen um Diotima

1

Täglich geh' ich heraus, und such' ein Anderes immer,
   Habe längst sie befragt alle die Pfade des Lands;
Droben die kühlenden Höhn, die Schatten alle besuch' ich,
   Und die Quellen; hinauf irret der Geist und hinab,
Ruh' erbittend; so flieht das getroffene Wild in die Wälder,
   Wo es um Mittag sonst sicher im Dunkel geruht;
Aber nimmer erquikt sein grünes Lager das Herz ihm,
   Jammernd und schlummerlos treibt es der Stachel umher.
Nicht die Wärme des Lichts, und nicht die Kühle der Nacht hilft,

Nevertheless the music sounds in his heart. As then,
   When high in the hills he slept, there is a gushing up,
      But now the prisoner washes himself
         Clean of his bonds, now he hurries,

Gauche, mocking the slag, seizes and breaks
   And hurls the splinters now, drunk with wrath,
      In play, hither and thither against
         The watchful streamback, and the flocks

Rise to their feet at the special voice of the stranger,
   Forests thrill, the plain below can hear
      The far spirit of streams and the shuddering
         Spirit thrills in earth's navel again.

Spring comes. And each thing in its fashion
   Breaks into flower. But he is gone, out of it,
      He went awry; they are too generous,
         The elementals; it is with gods now he speaks.

Christopher Middleton

Menon's Lament for Diotima

1

Daily I search, now here, now there my wandering takes me
   Countless times I have probed every highway and path;
Coolness I seek on those hilltops, all the shades I revisit,
   Then the wellsprings again; up my mind roves and down
Begging for rest; so a wounded deer will flee to the forests
   Where he used to lie low, safe in the dark towards noon;
Yet his green lair no longer now can refresh him or soothe him,
   Crying and sleepless he roams, cruelly pricked by the thorn,
Neither the warmth of the daylight nor the cool darkness of night
      helps,

Und in Woogen des Stroms taucht es die Wunden umsonst.
Und wie ihm vergebens die Erd' ihr fröhliches Heilkraut
    Reicht, und das gährende Blut keiner der Zephyre stillt,
So, ihr Lieben! auch mir, so will es scheinen, und niemand
    Kann von der Stirne mir nehmen den traurigen Traum?

2

Ja! es frommet auch nicht, ihr Todesgötter! wenn einmal
    Ihr ihn haltet, und fest habt den bezwungenen Mann,
Wenn ihr Bösen hinab in die schaurige Nacht ihn genommen,
    Dann zu suchen, zu flehn, oder zu zürnen mit euch,
Oder geduldig auch wohl im furchtsamen Banne zu wohnen,
    Und mit Lächeln von euch hören das nüchterne Lied.
Soll es seyn, so vergiß dein Heil, und schlummere klanglos!
    Aber doch quillt ein Laut hoffend im Busen dir auf,
Immer kannst du noch nicht, o meine Seele! noch kannst du's
    Nicht gewohnen, und träumst mitten im eisernen Schlaf!
Festzeit hab' ich nicht, doch möcht' ich die Loke bekränzen;
    Bin ich allein denn nicht? aber ein Freundliches muß
Fernher nahe mir seyn, und lächeln muß ich und staunen.
    Wie so seelig doch auch mitten im Leide mir ist.

3

Licht der Liebe! scheinest du denn auch Todten, du goldnes!
    Bilder aus hellerer Zeit leuchtet ihr mir in die Nacht?
Liebliche Gärten seid, ihr abendröthlichen Berge,
    Seid willkommen und ihr, schweigende Pfade des Hains,
Zeugen himmlischen Glüks, und ihr, hochschauende Sterne,
    Die mir damals so oft seegnende Blike gegönnt!
Euch, ihr Liebenden auch, ihr schönen Kinder des Maitags,
    Stille Rosen und euch, Lilien, nenn' ich noch oft!
Wohl gehn Frühlinge fort, ein Jahr verdränget das andre,
    Wechselnd und streitend, so tost droben vorüber die Zeit
Über sterblichem Haupt, doch nicht vor seeligen Augen,
    Und den Liebenden ist anderes Leben geschenkt.
Denn sie alle die Tag' und Jahre der Sterne, sie waren
    Diotima! um uns innig und ewig vereint;

In the river's waves too vainly he washes his wounds.
And as vainly to him now Earth offers herbs that might heal them,
   Cheer him, and none of the winds quiets his feverish blood,
So, beloved ones, it seems, with me it is too, and can no one
   Lift this dead weight from my brow, break the all-saddening
      dream?

2

And indeed, gods of death, when once you have utterly caught him
   Seized and fettered the man, so that he cringes, subdued,
When you evil ones down into horrible night have conveyed him
   Useless it is to implore, then to be angry with you,
Useless even to bear that grim coercion with patience,
   Smiling to hear you each day chant him the sobering song.
If you must, then forget your welfare and drowse away tuneless!
   Yet in your heart even now, hoping, a sound rises up,
Still, my soul, even now you cling to your habit of music
   Will not give in yet, and dream deep in the lead of dull sleep!
Cause I have none to be festive, but long to put on a green garland;
   Am I not quite alone? Yet something kind now must be
Close to me from afar, so that I smile as I wonder
   How in the midst of my grief I can feel happy and blessed.

3

Golden light of love, for dead men, for shades, do you shine then?
   Radiant visions recalled, even this night, then, you pierce?
Pleasant gardens, and mountains tinged with crimson at sunset,
   Welcome I call you, and you, murmurless path of the grove,
Witness to heavenly joy, and stars more loftily gazing,
   Who so freely would grant looks that were blessings to me!
And you lovers, you too, the May-day's beautiful children,
   Quiet roses, and you, lilies, I often invoke!
Springs, it is true, go by, one year still supplanting the other,
   Changing and warring, so Time over us mortal men's heads
Rushes past up above, but not in the eyes of the blessed ones,
   Nor of lovers, to whom different life is vouchsafed.
For all these, all the days and years of the heavenly planets,
   Diotima, round us closely, for ever conjoined;

4

Aber wir, zufrieden gesellt, wie die liebenden Schwäne,
    Wenn sie ruhen am See, oder, auf Wellen gewiegt,
Niedersehn in die Wasser, wo silberne Wolken sich spiegeln,
    Und ätherisches Blau unter den Schiffenden wallt,
So auf Erden wandelten wir. Und drohte der Nord auch,
    Er, der Liebenden Feind, klagenbereitend, und fiel
Von den Ästen das Laub, und flog im Winde der Reegen,
    Ruhig lächelten wir, fühlten den eigenen Gott
Unter trautem Gespräch; in Einem Seelengesange,
    Ganz in Frieden mit uns kindlich und freudig allein.
Aber das Haus its öde mir nun, und sie haben mein Auge
    Mir genommen, auch mich hab' ich verloren mit ihr.
Darum irr' ich umher, und wohl, wie die Schatten, so muß ich
    Leben, und sinnlos dünkt lange das Übrige mir.

5

Feiern möcht' ich; aber wofür? und singen mit Andern,
    Aber so einsam fehlt jegliches Göttliche mir.
Diß ist's, diß mein Gebrechen, ich weiß, es lähmet ein Fluch mir
    Darum die Sehnen, und wirft, wo ich beginne, mich hin,
Daß ich fühllos size den Tag, und stumm wie die Kinder,
    Nur vom Auge mir kalt öfters die Thräne noch schleicht,
Und die Pflanze des Felds, und der Vögel Singen mich trüb macht,
    Weil mit Freuden auch sie Boten des Himmlischen sind,
Aber mir in schaudernder Brust die beseelende Sonne,
    Kühl und fruchtlos mir dämmert, wie Stralen der Nacht,
Ach! und nichtig und leer, wie Gefängnißwände, der Himmel
    Eine beugende Last über dem Haupte mir hängt!

6

Sonst mir anders bekannt! o Jugend, und bringen Gebete
    Dich nicht wieder, dich nie? führet kein Pfad mich zurük?
Soll es werden auch mir, wie den Götterlosen, die vormals
    Glänzenden Auges doch auch saßen an seeligem Tisch',
Aber übersättiget bald, die schwärmenden Gäste,
    Nun verstummet, und nun, unter der Lüfte Gesang,

4

Meanwhile we—like the mated swans in their summer contentment
   When by the lake they rest or on the waves, lightly rocked,
Down they look, at the water, and silvery clouds through that mirror
   Drift, and ethereal blue flows where the voyagers pass—
Moved and dwelled on this earth. And though the North Wind was
     threatening
   Hostile to lovers, he, gathering sorrows, and down
Came dead leaves from the boughs, and rain filled the spluttering
     storm-gusts
   Calmly we smiled, aware, sure of the tutelar god
Present in talk only ours, one song that our two souls were singing,
   Wholly at peace with ourselves, childishly, raptly alone.
Desolate now is my house, and not only her they have taken,
   No, but my own two eyes, myself I have lost, losing her.
That is why, astray, like wandering phantoms I live now
   Must live, I fear, and the rest long has seemed senseless to me.

5

Celebrate—yes, but what! And gladly with others I'd sing now,
   Yet alone as I am nothing that's godlike rings true,
This, I know, is it, my failing, a curse maims my sinews
   Only because of this, making me flag from the start,
So that numb all day long I sit like a child that is moping
   Dumb, though at times a tear coldly creeps out of my eyes,
And the flowers of the field, the singing of birds makes me sad now,
   Being heralds of heaven, bearers of heavenly joy,
But to me, in my heart's dank vault, now the soul-giving sun dawns
   Cool, infertile, in vain, feeble as rays of the night,
Oh, and futile and empty, walls of a prison, the heavens
   Press, a smothering load heaped on my head from above!

6

Once, how different it was! O youth, will no prayer bring you
     back, then,
   Never again? And no path ever again lead me back?
Shall it be my fate, as once it was that of the godless,
   Bright-eyed to sit for a time feasting at heavenly boards

Unter blühender Erd' entschlafen sind, bis dereinst sie
Eines Wunders Gewalt sie, die Versunkenen, zwingt,
Wiederzukehren, und neu auf grünendem Boden zu wandeln.—
Heiliger Othem durchströmt göttlich die lichte Gestalt,
Wenn das Fest sich beseelt, und Fluthen der Liebe sich regen,
Und vom Himmel getränkt, rauscht der lebendige Strom,
Wenn es drunten ertönt, und ihre Schäze die Nacht zollt,
Und aus Bächen herauf glänzt das begrabene Gold.—

7

Aber o du, die schon am Scheidewege mir damals,
Da ich versank vor dir, tröstend ein Schöneres wies,
Du, die Großes zu sehn, und froher die Götter zu singen,
Schweigend, wie sie, mich einst stille begeisternd gelehrt;
Götterkind! erscheinest du mir, und grüßest, wie einst, mich,
Redest wieder, wie einst, höhere Dinge mir zu?
Siehe! weinen vor dir, und klagen muß ich, wenn schon noch,
Denkend edlerer Zeit, dessen die Seele sich schämt.
Denn so lange, so lang auf matten Pfaden der Erde
Hab' ich, deiner gewohnt, dich in der Irre gesucht,
Freudiger Schuzgeist! aber umsonst, und Jahre zerrannen,
Seit wir ahnend um uns glänzen die Abende sahn.

8

Dich nur, dich erhält dein Licht, o Heldinn! im Lichte,
Und dein Dulden erhält liebend, o Gütige, dich;
Und nicht einmal bist du allein; Gespielen genug sind,
Wo du blühest und ruhst unter den Rosen des Jahrs;
Und der Vater, er selbst, durch sanftumathmende Musen
Sendet die zärtlichen Wiegengesänge dir zu.
Ja! noch ist sie es ganz! noch schwebt vom Haupte zur Sohle,
Stillherwandelnd, wie sonst, mir die Athenerinn vor.
Und wie, freundlicher Geist! von heitersinnender Stirne
Seegnend und sicher dein Stral unter die Sterblichen fällt;
So bezeugest du mir's, und sagst mir's, daß ich es andern
Wiedersage, denn auch Andere glauben es nicht,
Daß unsterblicher doch, denn Sorg' und Zürnen, die Freude
Und ein goldener Tag täglich am Ende noch ist.

But to be cloyed with that food, all those fantastical guests now
　　Fallen silent, and now, deaf to the music of winds,
Under the flowering earth asleep, till a miracle's power shall
　　Force them one day to return, deep though they lie now, at rest,
Force them to walk anew the soil that is sprouting new verdure—
　　Holy breath, then, divine, through their bright bodies will flow
While the feast is inspired and love like great flood waters gathers,
　　Fed by the heavens themselves, on sweeps the river, alive,
When the deep places boom, Night pays her tribute of riches
　　And from the beds of streams up glitters gold long submerged.—

7

You, though, who even then, already then at the crossroads
　　When I fell at your feet, comforting showed me the way,
Taught me to see what is great, to sing with a beauty more mellow,
　　Joy more serene, the gods, silent as gods are yourself,
Child of the gods, will you appear to me, greet me once more now,
　　Quietly raising me up, speak to me now of those things?
Look, in your presence I weep, lament, though remembering always
　　Worthier times that are past, deep in my soul I feel shame.
For so very long on weary paths of the earth now,
　　Still accustomed to you, you I have sought in the wilds,
Tutelar spirit, but all in vain, and whole years have gone by since
　　Late in the evenings we walked, bathed in that ominous glow.

8

You, only you, your own light, O heroine, keeps in the light still,
　　And your patience still keeps you both loving and kind;
Nor indeed are you lonely; playmates enough are provided
　　Where amid roses you bloom, rest with the flowers of the year;
And the Father himself by means of the balm-breathing Muses
　　Sends you those cradle-songs warm as a southerly breeze.
Yes, she is quite the same! From her head to her heels the Athenian,
　　Quiet and poised as before hovers in front of my eyes.
And as blessing and sure your radiance falls upon mortals,
　　Tender soul, from your brow wrapt in deep thought, yet serene,
So you prove it to me, and tell me, that also to others
　　Then I may pass it on, others who doubt as I doubt,
That more enduring than care and anger is holy rejoicing
　　And that golden the day daily still shines in the end.

9

So will ich, ihr Himmlischen! denn auch danken, und endlich
  Athmet aus leichter Brust wieder des Sängers Gebet.
Und wie, wenn ich mit ihr, auf sonniger Höhe mit ihr stand,
  Spricht belebend ein Gott innen vom Tempel mich an.
Leben will ich denn auch! schon grünt's! wie von heiliger Leier
  Ruft es von silbernen Bergen Apollons voran!
Komm! es war wie ein Traum! Die blutenden Fittige sind ja
  Schon genesen, verjüngt leben die Hoffnungen all.
Großes zu finden, ist viel, ist viel noch übrig, und wer so
  Liebte, gehet, er muß, gehet zu Göttern die Bahn.
Und geleitet ihr uns, ihr Weihestunden! ihr ernsten,
  Jugendlichen! o bleibt, heilige Ahnungen, ihr
Fromme Bitten! und ihr Begeisterungen und all ihr
  Guten Genien, die gerne bei Liebenden sind;
Bleibt so lange mit uns, bis wir auf gemeinsamem Boden
  Dort, wo die Seeligen all niederzukehren bereit,
Dort, wo die Adler sind, die Gestirne, die Boten des Vaters,
  Dort, wo die Musen, woher Helden und Liebende sind,
Dort uns, oder auch hier, auf thauender Insel begegnen,
  Wo die Unsrigen erst, blühend in Gärten gesellt,
Wo die Gesänge wahr, und länger die Frühlinge schön sind,
  Und von neuem ein Jahr unserer Seele beginnt.

9

Thanks, once more, then, I'll give to you up in heaven; once more
    now
  Freely at last can my prayer rise from a heart unoppressed.
And, as before, when with her I stood on a sun-gilded hilltop,
  Quickening, to me now a god speaks from the temple within.
I will live, then! New verdure! As though from a lyre that is
    hallowed
  Onward! from silvery peaks, Apollo's mountains ring out.
Come, it was all like a dream, the wounds in your wings have already
  Healed, and restored to youth all your old hopes leap alive.
Knowledge of greatness is much, yet much still remains to be done,
    and
  One who loved as you loved only to gods can move on.
You conduct us, then, you solemn ones, Hours of Communion,
  Youthful ones, stay with us, holy Presentiments also,
Pious prayers, and you, Inspirations, and all of you kindly
  Spirits who like to attend lovers, to be where they are.
Stay with us two until on communal ground, reunited
  Where, when their coming is due, all the blessed souls will return,
Where the eagles are, the planets, the Father's own heralds,
  Where the Muses are still, heroes and lovers began,
There we shall meet again, or here, on a dew-covered island
  Where what is ours for once, blooms that a garden conjoins,
All our poems are true and springs remain beautiful longer
  And another, a new year of our souls can begin.

Michael Hamburger

Brod und Wein
An Heinze

1

Rings um ruhet die Stadt; still wird die erleuchtete Gasse,
    Und, mit Fakeln geschmükt, rauschen die Wagen hinweg.
Satt gehn heim von Freuden des Tags zu ruhen die Menschen,
    Und Gewinn und Verlust wäget ein sinniges Haupt
Wohlzufrieden zu Haus; leer steht von Trauben und Blumen,
    Und von Werken der Hand ruht der geschäfftige Markt.
Aber das Saitenspiel tönt fern aus Gärten; vieleicht, daß
    Dort ein Liebendes spielt oder ein einsamer Mann
Ferner Freunde gedenkt und der Jugendzeit; und die Brunnen
    Immerquillend und frisch rauschen an duftendem Beet.
Still in dämmriger Luft ertönen geläutete Gloken,
    Und der Stunden gedenk rufet ein Wächter die Zahl.
Jezt auch kommet ein Wehn und regt die Gipfel des Hains auf,
    Sieh! und das Schattenbild unserer Erde, der Mond
Kommet geheim nun auch; die Schwärmerische, die Nacht kommt,
    Voll mit Sternen und wohl wenig bekümmert um uns,
Glänzt die Erstaunende dort, die Fremdlingin unter den Menschen
    Über Gebirgeshöhn traurig und prächtig herauf.

2

Wunderbar ist die Gunst der Hocherhabnen und niemand
    Weiß von wannen und was einem geschiehet von ihr.
So bewegt sie die Welt und die hoffende Seele der Menschen,
    Selbst kein Weiser versteht, was sie bereitet, denn so
Will es der oberste Gott, der sehr dich liebet, und darum
    Ist noch lieber, wie sie, dir der besonnene Tag.
Aber zuweilen liebt auch klares Auge den Schatten
    Und versuchet zu Lust, eh' es die Noth ist, den Schlaf,

Bread and Wine
To Heinse

1

Round us the town is at rest; the street, in pale lamplight, grows
    quiet
  And, their torches ablaze, coaches rush through and away.
People go home to rest, replete with the day and its pleasures,
  There to weigh up in their heads, pensive, the gain and the loss,
Finding the balance good; stripped bare now of grapes and of
    flowers,
  As of their hand-made goods, quiet the market stalls lie.
But faint music of strings comes drifting from gardens; it could be
  Someone in love who plays there, could be a man all alone
Thinking of distant friends, the days of his youth; and the
    fountains,
  Ever welling and new, plash amid fragrance from beds.
Church-bells ring; every stroke hangs still in the quivering half-
    light
  And the watchman calls out, mindful, no less, of the hour.
Now a breeze rises too and ruffles the crests of the coppice,
  Look, and in secret our globe's shadowy image, the moon,
Slowly is rising too; and Night, the fantastical, comes now
  Full of stars and, I think, little concerned about us,
Night, the astonishing, there, the stranger to all that is human,
  Over the mountain-tops mournful and gleaming draws on.

2

Marvelous is her favor, Night's, the exalted, and no one
  Knows what it is or whence comes all she does and bestows.
So she works on the world and works on our souls ever hoping,
  Not even wise men can tell what is her purpose, for so
God, the Highest, has willed, who very much loves you, and
    therefore
  Dearer even than Night reasoning Day is to you.
Nonetheless there are times when clear eyes too love the shadows,
  Tasting sleep uncompelled, trying the pleasure it gives,

Oder es blikt auch gern ein treuer Mann in die Nacht hin,
    Ja, es ziemet sich ihr Kränze zu weihn und Gesang,
Weil den Irrenden sie geheiliget ist und den Todten,
    Selber aber besteht, ewig, in freiestem Geist.
Aber sie muß uns auch, daß in der zaudernden Weile,
    Daß im Finstern für uns einiges Haltbare sei,
Uns die Vergessenheit und das Heiligtrunkene gönnen,
    Gönnen das strömende Wort, das, wie die Liebenden, sei,
Schlummerlos und vollern Pokal und Kühneres Leben,
    Heilig Gedächtniß auch, wachend zu bleiben bei Nacht.

3

Auch verbergen umsonst das Herz im Busen, umsonst nur
    Halten den Muth noch wir, Meister und Knaben, denn wer
Möcht' es hindern und wer möcht' uns die Freude verbieten?
    Göttliches Feuer auch treibet, bei Tag und bei Nacht,
Aufzubrechen. So komm! daß wir das Offene schauen,
    Daß ein Eigenes wir suchen, so weit es auch ist.
Fest bleibt Eins; es sei um Mittag oder es gehe
    Bis in die Mitternacht, immer bestehet ein Maas,
Allen gemein, doch jeglichem auch ist eignes beschieden,
    Dahin gehet und kommt jeder, wohin er es kann.
Drum! und spotten des Spotts mag gern frohlokkender Wahnsinn,
    Wenn er in heiliger Nacht plözlich die Sänger ergreift.
Drum an den Isthmos komm! dorthin, wo das offene Meer rauscht
    Am Parnaß und der Schnee delphische Felsen umglänzt,
Dort ins Land des Olymps, dort auf die Höhe Cithärons,
    Unter die Fichten dort, unter die Trauben, von wo
Thebe drunten und Ismenos rauscht im Lande des Kadmos,
    Dorther kommt und zurük deutet der kommende Gott.

4

Seeliges Griechenland! du Haus der Himmlischen alle,
    Also ist wahr, was einst wir in der Jugend gehört?
Festlicher Saal! der Boden ist Meer! und Tische die Berge,
    Wahrlich zu einzigem Brauche vor Alters gebaut!
Aber die Thronen, wo? die Tempel, und wo die Gefäße,

Or a loyal man too will gaze into Night and enjoy it,
    Yes, and rightly to her garlands we dedicate, hymns,
Since to all those astray, the mad and the dead she is sacred,
    Yet herself remains firm, always, her spirit most free.
But to us in her turn, so that in the wavering moment,
    Deep in the dark there shall be something at least that endures,
Holy drunkenness she must grant and frenzied oblivion,
    Grant the on-rushing word, sleepless as lovers are too,
And a wine-cup more full, a life more intense and more daring,
    Holy remembrance too, keeping us wakeful at night.

3

And in vain we conceal our hearts deep within us, in vain we,
    Master and novice alike, still keep our courage in check.
For who now would stop us, who would forbid us rejoicing?
    Daylong, nightlong we're urged on by a fire that's divine.
      Urged to be gone. Let us go, then! Off to see open spaces,
    Where we may seek what is ours, distant, remote though it be!
One thing is sure even now: at noon or just before midnight,
    Whether it's early or late, always a measure exists,
Common to all, though his own to each one is also allotted,
    Each of us makes for the place, reaches the place that he can.
Well, then, may jubilant madness laugh at those who deride it,
    When in hallowed Night poets are seized by its power;
Off to the Isthmus, then! To land where wide open the sea roars
    Near Parnassus and snow glistens on Delphian rocks;
Off to Olympian regions, up to the heights of Cithaeron,
    Up to the pine trees there, up to the grapes, from which rush
Thebe down there and Ismenos, loud in the country of Cadmus:
    Thence has come and back there points the god who's to come.

4

Happy land of the Greeks, you house of them all, of the Heavenly,
    So it is true what we heard then, in the days of our youth?
Festive hall, whose floor is ocean, whose tables are mountains,
    Truly, in time out of mind built for a purpose unique!
But the thrones, where are they? Where are the temples, the
    vessels,

Wo mit Nectar gefüllt, Göttern zu Lust der Gesang?
Wo, wo leuchten sie denn, die fernhintreffenden Sprüche?
  Delphi schlummert und wo tönet das große Geschik?
Wo is das schnelle? wo brichts, allgegenwärtigen Glüks voll
  Donnernd aus heiterer Luft über die Augen herein?
Vater Aether! so riefs und flog von Zunge zu Zunge
  Tausendfach, es ertrug keiner das Leben allein;
Ausgetheilet erfreut solch Gut und getauschet, mit Fremden,
  Wirds ein Jubel, es wächst schlafend des Wortes Gewalt
Vater! hieter! und hallt, so weit es gehet, das uralt
  Zeichen, von Eltern geerbt, treffend und schaffend hinab.
Denn so kehren die Himmlischen ein, tiefschütternd gelangt so
  Aus den Schatten herab unter die Menschen ihr Tag.

5

Unempfunden kommen sie erst, es streben entgegen
  Ihnen die Kinder, zu hell kommet, zu blendend das Glük,
Und es scheut sie der Mensch, kaum weiß zu sagen ein Halbgott,
  Wer mit Nahmen sie sind, die mit den Gaaben ihm nahn.
Aber der Muth von ihnen ist groß, es füllen das Herz ihm
  Ihre Freuden und kaum weiß er zu brauchen das Gut,
Schafft, verschwendet und fast ward ihm Unheiliges heilig,
  Das er mit seegnender Hand thörig und gütig berührt.
Möglichst dulden die Himmlischen diß; dann aber in Wahrheit
  Kommen sie selbst und gewohnt werden die Menschen des Glüks
Und des Tags und zu schaun die Offenbaren, das Antliz
  Derer, welche, schon längst Eines und Alles genannt,
Tief die verschwiegene Brust mit freier Genüge gefüllet,
  Und zuerst und allein alles Verlangen beglükt;
So ist der Mensch; wenn da ist das Gut, und es sorget mit Gaaben
  Selber ein Gott für ihn, kennet und sieht er es nicht.
Tragen muß er, zuvor; nun aber nennt er sein Liebstes,
  Nun, nun müssen dafür Worte, wie Blumen, entstehn.

Where, to delight the gods, brim-full with nectar, the songs?
Where, then, where do they shine, the oracles winged for far
    targets?
  Delphi's asleep, and where now is great fate to be heard?
Where is the swift? And full of joy omnipresent, where does it
  Flash upon dazzled eyes, thundering fall from clear skies?
Father Aether! one cried, and tongue after tongue took it up then,
  Thousands, no man could bear life so intense on his own;
Shared, such wealth gives delight and later, when bartered with
    strangers,
  Turns to rapture; the word gathers new strength when asleep:
Father! Clear light! and long resounding it travels, the ancient
  Sign handed down, and far, striking, creating, rings out.
So do the Heavenly enter, shaking the deepest foundations,
  Only so from the gloom down to mankind comes their Day.

5

Unperceived at first they come, and only the children
  Surge towards them, too bright, dazzling, this joy enters in,
So that men are afraid, a demigod hardly can tell yet
  Who they are, and name those who approach him with gifts.
Yet their courage is great, his heart soon is full of their gladness
  And he hardly knows what's to be done with such wealth,
Busily runs and wastes it, almost regarding as sacred
  Trash which his blessing hand foolishly, kindly has touched.
This, while they can, the Heavenly bear with; but then they appear
    in
  Truth, in person, and now men grow accustomed to joy,
And to Day, and the sight of godhead revealed, and their faces—
  One and All long ago, once and for all, they were named—
Who with free self-content had deeply suffused silent bosoms,
  From the first and alone satisfied every desire.
Such is man; when the wealth is there, and no less than a god in
  Person tends him with gifts, blind he remains, unaware.
First he must suffer; but now he names his most treasured
    possession,
  Now for it words like flowers leaping alive he must find.

6

Und nun denkt er zu ehren in Ernst die seeligen Götter,
　　Wirklich und wahrhaft muß alles verkünden ihr Lob.
Nichts darf schauen das Licht, was nicht den Hohen gefället,
　　Vor den Aether gebührt müßigversuchendes nicht.
Drum in der Gegenwart der Himmlischen würdig zu stehen,
　　Richten in herrlichen Ordnungen Völker sich auf
Untereinander und baun die schönen Tempel und Städte
　　Vest und edel, sie gehn über Gestaden empor—
Aber wo sind sie? wo blühn die Bekannten, die Kronen des Festes?
　　Thebe welkt und Athen; rauschen die Waffen nicht mehr
In Olympia, nicht die goldnen Wagen des Kampfspiels,
　　Und bekränzen sich denn nimmer die Schiffe Korinths?
Warum schweigen auch sie, die alten heilgen Theater?
　　Warum freuet sich denn nicht der geweihete Tanz?
Warum zeichnet, wie sonst, die Stirne des Mannes ein Gott nicht,
　　Drükt den Stempel, wie sonst, nicht dem Getroffenen auf?
Oder er kam auch selbst und nahm des Menschen Gestalt an
　　Und vollendet'und schloß tröstend das himmlische Fest.

7

Aber Freund! wir kommen zu spät. Zwar leben die Götter,
　　Aber über dem Haupt droben in anderer Welt.
Endlos wirken sie da und scheinens wenig zu achten,
　　Ob wir leben, so sehr schonen die Himmlischen uns.
Denn nicht immer vermag ein schwaches Gefäß sie zu fassen,
　　Nur zu Zeiten erträgt göttliche Fülle der Mensch.
Traum von ihnen ist drauf das Leben. Aber das Irrsaal
　　Hilft, wie Schlummer und stark machet die Noth und die Nacht,
Biß daß Helden genug in der ehernen Wiege gewachsen,
　　Herzen an Kraft, wie sonst, ähnlich den Himmlischen sind.
Donnernd Kommen sie drauf. Indessen dünket mir öfters
　　Besser zu schlafen, wie so ohne Genossen zu seyn,
So zu harren und was zu thun indeß und zu sagen,
　　Weiß ich nicht und wozu Dichter in dürftiger Zeit?
Aber sie sind, sagst due, wie des Weingotts heilige Priester,
　　Welche von Lande zu Land zogen in heiliger Nacht.

6

Now in earnest he means to honor the gods who have blessed
    him,
    Now in truth and in deed all must re-echo their praise.
Nothing must see the light but what to those high ones is pleasing,
    Idle and bungled work never for Aether was fit.
So, to be worthy and stand unashamed in the heavenly presence,
    Nations rise up and soon, gloriously ordered, compete
One with the other in building beautiful temples and cities,
    Noble and firm they tower high above river and sea—
Only, where are they? Where thrive those famed ones, the festival's
    garlands?
    Athens is withered, and Thebes; now do no weapons ring out
In Olympia, nor now those chariots, all golden, in games there,
    And no longer are wreaths hung on Corinthian ships?
Why are they silent too, the theaters, ancient and hallowed?
    Why not now does the dance celebrate, consecrate joy?
Why no more does a god imprint on the brow of a mortal
    Struck, as by lightning, the mark, brand him, as once he would
    do?
Else he would come himself, assuming a shape that was human,
    And, consoling the guests, crowned and concluded the feast.

7

But, my friend, we have come too late. Though the gods are living,
    Over our heads they live, up in a different world.
Endlessly there they act and, such is their kind wish to spare us,
    Little they seem to care whether we live or do not.
For not always a frail, a delicate vessel can hold them,
    Only at times can our kind bear the full impact of gods.
Ever after our life is dream about them. But frenzy,
    Wandering, helps, like sleep; Night and distress make us strong
Till in that cradle of steel heroes enough have been fostered,
    Hearts in strength can match heavenly strength as before.
Thundering then they come. But meanwhile too often I think it's
    Better to sleep than to be friendless as we are, alone,
Always waiting, and what to do or to say in the meantime
    I don't know, and who wants poets at all in lean years?
But they are, you say, like those holy ones, priests of the wine-god
    Who in holy Night roamed from one place to the next.

8

Nemlich, als vor einiger Zeit, uns dünket sie lange,
　　Aufwärts stiegen sie all, welche das Leben beglükt,
Als der Vater gewandt sein Angesicht von den Menschen,
　　Und das Trauern mit Recht über der Erde begann,
Als erschienen zu lezt ein stiller Genius, himmlisch
　　Tröstend, welcher des Tags Ende verkündet' und schwand,
Ließ zum Zeichen, daß einst er da gewesen und wieder
　　Käme, der himmlische Chor einige Gaaben zurük,
Derer menschlich, wie sonst, wir uns zu freuen vermöchten,
　　Denn zur Freude, mit Geist, wurde das Größre zu groß
Unter den Menschen und noch, noch fehlen die Starken zu höchsten
　　Freuden, aber es lebt stille noch einiger Dank.
Brod ist der Erde Frucht, doch ists vom Lichte geseegnet,
　　Und vom donnernden Gott kommet die Freude des Weins.
Darum denken wir auch dabei der Himmlischen, die sonst
　　Da gewesen und die kehren in richtiger Zeit,
Darum singen sie auch mit Ernst die Sänger den Weingott
　　Und nicht eitel erdacht tönet dem Alten das Lob.

9

Ja! sie sagen mit Recht, er söhne den Tag mit der Nacht aus,
　　Führe des Himmels Gestirn ewig hinunter, hinauf,
Allzeit froh, wie das Laub der immergrünenden Fichte,
　　Das er liebt, und der Kranz, den er von Epheu gewählt,
Weil er bleibet und selbst die Spur der entflohenen Götter
　　Götterlosen hinab unter das Finstere bringt.
Was der Alten Gesang von Kindern Gottes geweissagt,
　　Sieh! wir sind es, wir; Frucht von Hesperien ists!
Wunderbar und genau ists als an Menschen erfüllet,
　　Glaube, wer es geprüft! aber so vieles geschieht,
Keines wirket, denn wir sind herzlos, Schatten, bis unser
　　Vater Aether erkannt jeden und allen gehört.
Aber indessen kommt als Fakelschwinger des Höchsten

8

For, when some time ago now—to us it seems ages—
   Up rose all those by whom life had been brightened, made glad,
When the Father had turned his face from the sight of us mortals
   And all over the earth, rightly, they started to mourn,
Lastly a Genius had come, dispensing heavenly comfort,
   He who proclaimed the Day's end, then himself went away,
Then, as a token that once they had been down here and once
     more would
   Come, the heavenly choir left a few presents behind,
Gifts in which now as ever humanly men might take pleasure,
   Since for spiritual joy great things had now grown too great
Here, among men, and even now there's a lack of those strong for
   Joy's extremity, but silent some thanks do live on.
Bread is a fruit of Earth, yet touched by the blessing of sunlight,
   From the thundering god issues the gladness of wine.
Therefore in tasting them we think of the Heavenly who once were
   Here and shall come again, come when their advent is due;
Therefore also the poets in serious hymns to the wine-god,
   Never idly devised, sound that most ancient one's praise.

9

Yes, and rightly they say he reconciles Day with our Nighttime,
   Leads the stars of the sky upward and down without end,
Always glad, like the living boughs of the evergreen pinetree
   Which he loves, and the wreath wound out of ivy for choice
Since it lasts and conveys the trace of the gods now departed
   Down to the godless below, into the midst of their gloom.
What of the children of God was foretold in the songs of the
     ancients,
   Look, we are it, ourselves; fruit of Hesperia it is!
Strictly it has come true, fulfilled as in men by a marvel,
   Let those who have seen it believe! Much, however, occurs,
Nothing succeeds, because we are heartless, mere shadows until
     our
   Father Aether, made known, recognized, fathers us all.
Meanwhile, though, to us shadows comes the Son of the Highest,

Sohn, der Syrier, unter die Schatten herab.
Seelige Weise sehns; ein Lächeln aus der gefangnen
   Seele leuchtet, dem Licht thauet ihr Auge noch auf.
Sanfter träumet und schläft in Armen der Erde der Titan,
   Selbst der neidische, selbst Cerberus trinket und schläft.

Hälfte des Lebens

Mit gelben Birnen hänget
Und voll mit wilden Rosen
Das Land in den See,
Ihr holden Schwäne,
Und trunken von Küssen
Tunkt ihr das Haupt
Ins heilignüchterne Wasser.

Weh mir, wo nehm' ich, wenn
Es Winter ist, die Blumen, und wo
Den Sonnenschein,
Und Schatten der Erde?
Die Mauern stehn
Sprachlos und kalt, im Winde
Klirren die Fahnen.

Comes the Syrian and down into our gloom bears his torch.
Blissful, the wise men see it; in souls that were captive there
    gleams a
  Smile, and their eyes shall yet thaw in response to the light.
Dreams more gentle and sleep in the arms of Earth lull the Titan.
  Even that envious one, Cerberus, drinks and lies down.

Michael Hamburger

Half of Life

With its yellow pears
And wild roses everywhere
The shore hangs in the lake,
O gracious swans,
And drunk with kisses
You dip your heads
In the sobering holy water.

Ah, where will I find
Flowers, come winter,
And where the sunshine
And shade of the earth?
Walls stand cold
And speechless, in the wind
The weathervanes creak.

Richard Sieburth

Der Winkel von Hahrdt

Hinunter sinket der Wald,
Und Knospen ähnlich, hängen
Einwärts die Blätter, denen
Blüht unten auf ein Grund,
Nicht gar unmündig.
Da nemlich ist Ulrich
Gegangen; oft sinnt, über den Fußtritt,
Ein groß Schiksaal
Bereit, an übrigem Orte.

Lebensalter

Ihr Städte des Euphraths!
Ihr Gassen von Palmyra!
Ihr Säulenwälder in der Ebne der Wüste,
Was seid ihr?
Euch hat die Kronen,
Dieweil ihr über die Gränze
Der Othmenden seid gegangen,
Von Himmlischen der Rauchdampf und
Hinweg das Feuer genommen;
Jezt aber siz ich unter Wolken, darin
Ein jedes eine Ruh hat eigen, unter
Wohleingerichteten Eichen, auf
Der Haide des Rehs, und fremd
Erscheinen und gestorben mir
Der Seeligen Geister.

The Shelter at Hahrdt

The forest sinks off
And like buds, the leaves
Hang inward, to which
The valley floor below
Flowers up, far from mute,
For Ulrich passed through
These parts; a great destiny
Often broods over his footprint,
Ready, among the remains.

Richard Sieburth

Ages of Life

Cities of the Euphrates,
Streets of Palmyra,
Columns wooding the desert plain,
What are you?
You were stripped of your crowns,
As you crossed beyond
The bounds of breath,
By the smoke
And fire of the gods;
But now I sit under clouds, in which
Each thing finds its peace, under
A fine stand of oaks, by
The deer meadow, and strange
And dead, they appear to me,
The spirits of the blest.

Richard Sieburth

Wie wenn am Feiertage ...

Wie wenn am Feiertage, das Feld zu sehn
Ein Landmann geht, des Morgens, wenn
Aus hießer Nacht die kühlenden Blize fielen
Die ganze Zeit und fern noch tönet der Donner,
In sein Gestade wieder tritt der Strom,
Und frisch der Boden grünt
Und von des Himmels erfreuendem Reegen
Der Weinstok trauft und glänzend
In stiller Sonne stehn die Bäume des Haines:

So stehn sie unter günstiger Witterung
Sie die kein Meister allein, die wunderbar
Allgegenwärtig erzieht in leichtem Umfangen
Die mächtige, die göttlichschöne Natur.
Drum wenn zu schlafen sie scheint zu Zeiten des Jahrs
Am Himmel oder unter den Pflanzen oder den Völkern
So trauert der Dichter Angesicht auch,
Sie scheinen allein zu seyn, doch ahnen sie immer.
Denn ahnend ruhet sie selbst auch.

Jezt aber tagts! Ich harrt und sah es kommen,
Und was ich sah, das Heilige sei mein Wort.
Denn sie, sie selbst, die älter denn die Zeiten
Und über die Götter des Abends und Orients ist,
Die Natur ist jezt mit Waffenklang erwacht,
Und hoch vom Aether bis zum Abgrund nieder
Nach vestem Geseze, wie einst, aus heiligem Chaos gezeugt,
Fühlt neu die Begeisterung sich,
Die Allerschaffende wieder.

Und wie im Aug' ein Feuer dem Manne glänzt,
Wenn hohes er entwarf; so ist
Von neuem an den Zeichen, den Thaten der Welt jezt
Ein Feuer angezündet in Seelen der Dichter.
Und was zuvor geschah, doch kaum gefühlt,
Ist offenbar erst jezt,
Und die uns lächelnd den Aker gebauet,
In Knechtsgestalt, sie sind erkannt,
Die Allebendigen, die Kräfte der Götter.

As on a holiday . . .

As on a holiday, to see the field
A countryman goes out, at morning, when
Out of hot night the cooling flashes had fallen
For hours on end, and thunder still rumbles afar,
The river enters its banks once more,
New verdure sprouts from the soil,
And with the gladdening rain of heaven
The grapevine drips, and gleaming
In tranquil sunlight stand the trees of the grove:

So now in favorable weather they stand
Whom no mere master teaches, but in
A light embrace, miraculously omnipresent,
Godlike in power and beauty, Nature brings up.
So when she seems to be sleeping at times of the year
Up in the sky or among plants or the peoples,
The poets' faces likewise are sad,
They seem to be alone, but are always divining,
For divining too she herself is at rest.

But now day breaks! I waited and saw it come,
And what I saw, the hallowed, my word shall convey,
For she, she herself, who is older than the ages
And higher than the gods of Orient and Occident,
Nature has now awoken amid the clang of arms,
And from high Aether down to the low abyss,
According to fixed law, begotten, as in the past, on holy Chaos,
Delight, the all-creative,
Delights in self-renewal.

And as a fire gleams in the eye of that man
Who has conceived a lofty design,
Once more by the tokens, the deeds of the world now
A fire has been lit in the souls of the poets.
And that which happened before, but hardly was felt,
Only now is manifest,
And they who smiling worked our fields for us,
Assuming the shape of laborers, now are known,
The all-alive, all-animating powers of the gods.

Erfrägst du sie? im Liede wehet ihr Geist
Wenn es der Sonne des Tags und warmer Erd
Entwächst, und Wettern, die in der Luft, und andern
Die vorbereiteter in Tiefen der Zeit,
Und deutungsvoller, und vernehmlicher uns
Hinwandeln zwischen Himmel und Erd und unter den Völkern.
Des gemeinsamen Geistes Gedanken sind,
Still endend in der Seele des Dichters,

Daß schnellbetroffen sie, Unendlichem
Bekannt seit langer Zeit, von Erinnerung
Erbebt, und ihr, von heilgem Stral entzündet,
Die Frucht in Liebe geboren, der Götter und Menschen Werk
Der Gesang, damit er beiden zeuge, glükt.
So fiel, wie Dichter sagen, da sie sichtbar
Den Gott zu sehen begehrte, sein Bliz auf Semeles Haus
Und die göttlichgetroffne gebahr,
Die Frucht des Gewitters, den heiligen Bacchus.

Und daher trinken himmlisches Feuer jezt
Die Erdensöhne ohne Gefahr.
Doch uns gebührt es, unter Gottes Gewittern,
Ihr Dichter! mit entblößtem Haupte zu stehen,
Des Vaters Stral, ihn selbst, mit eigner Hand
Zu fassen und dem Volk ins Lied
Gehüllt die himmlische Gaabe zu reichen.
Denn sind nur reinen Herzens,
Wie Kinder, wir, sind schuldlos unsere Hände,

Des Vaters Stral, der reine versengt es nicht
Und tieferschüttert, die Leiden des Stärkeren
Mitleidend, bleibt in den hochherstürzenden Stürmen
Des Gottes, wenn er nahet, das Herz doch fest.
Doch weh mir! wenn von

Weh mir!

Und sag ich gleich,

Do you ask where they are? In song their spirit wafts
When from the sun of day and from warm soil
It grows, and storms that are in the air, and others
That, more prepared in the depths of time,
More full of meaning and more audible to us,
Drift on between Heaven and Earth and amid the peoples.
The thoughts of the communal spirit they are,
And quietly come to rest in the poet's soul,

So that quickly struck and long familiar
To infinite powers, it shakes
With recollections and kindled by
The holy ray, that fruit conceived in love, the work of gods and
    men,
To bear witness to both, the song succeeds.
So once, the poets tell, when she desired to see
The god in person, visible, did his lightning fall
On Semele's house, and the divinely struck gave birth to
The thunderstorm's fruit, to holy Bacchus.

And hence it is that without danger now
The sons of Earth drink heavenly fire.
Yet, fellow poets, us it behoves to stand
Bare-headed beneath God's thunderstorms,
To grasp the Father's ray, no less, with our own two hands
And, wrapping in song the heavenly gift,
To offer it to the people.
For if only we are pure in heart,
Like children, and our hands are guiltless,

The Father's ray, the pure, will not sear our hearts
And, deeply convulsed, and sharing his sufferings
Who is stronger than we are, yet in the far-flung down-rushing
    storms of
The God, when he draws near, will the heart stand fast.
But, oh, my shame! when of

My shame!

And let me say at once

Ich sei genaht, die Himmlischen zu schauen,
Sie selbst, sie werfen mich tief unter die Lebenden
Den falschen Priester, ins Dunkel, daß ich
Das warnende Lied den Gelehrigen singe.
Dort

Am Quell der Donau

* * *

Denn, wie wenn hoch von der herrlichgestimmten, der Orgel
Im heiligen Saal,
Reinquillend aus den unerschöpflichen Röhren,
Das Vorspiel, wekend, des Morgens beginnt
Und weitumher, von Halle zu Halle,
Der erfrischende nun, der melodische Strom rinnt,
Bis in den kalten Schatten das Haus
Von Begeisterungen erfüllt,
Nun aber erwacht ist, nun, aufsteigend ihr,
Der Sonne des Fests, antwortet
Der Chor der Gemeinde; so kam
Das Wort aus Osten zu uns,
Und an Parnassos Felsen und am Kithäron hör' ich
O Asia, das Echo von dir und es bricht sich
Am Kapitol und jählings herab von den Alpen

Kommt eine Fremdlingin sie
Zu uns, die Erwekerin,
Die menschenbildende Stimme.
Da faßt' ein Staunen die Seele
Der Getroffenen all und Nacht
War über den Augen der Besten.

That I approached to see the Heavenly,
And they themselves cast me down, deep down
Below the living, into the dark cast down
The false priest that I am, to sing,
For those who have ears to hear, the warning song.
There

Michael Hamburger

At the Source of the Danube

* * *

For as when high from the gloriously voiced, the organ
Within a holy hall
Untainted welling from inexhaustible pipes,
The prelude, awakening men, rings out in the morning
And far and wide, from mansion to mansion,
Now pours the refreshing, the melodious current,
Down to the chilly shadows even filling
The house with inspirations,
But now awake and rising to it, to
The sun of celebration, responds the
Community's choir—so the word
Came down to us from the East,
And by the rocks of Parnassus and by Cithaeron,
O Asia, I hear the echo of you, and it breaks
Upon the Capitol and sudden down from the Alps

A stranger it comes
To us, that quickening word,
The voice that moulds and makes human.
Amazement then took hold of
The souls of all who were struck, and night
Obscured the eyes of the best men.

Denn vieles vermag
Und die Fluth und den Fels und Feuersgewalt auch
Bezwinget mit Kunst der Mensch
Und achtet, der Hochgesinnte, das Schwerdt
Nicht, aber es steht
Vor Göttlichem der Starke neidergeschlagen,

    Und gleichet dem Wild fast; das,
Von süßer Jugend getrieben,
Schweift rastlos über die Berg'
Und fühlet die eigene Kraft
In der Mittagshizze. Wenn aber
Herabgeführt, in spielenden Lüften,
Das heilige Licht, und mit dem kühleren Stral
Der freudige Geist kommt zu
Der seeligen Erde, dann erliegt es, ungewohnt
Des Schönsten und schlummert wachenden Schlaf,
Noch ehe Gestirn naht. So auch wir. Denn manchen erlosch
Das Augenlicht schon vor den göttlichgesendeten Gaben,

    Den freundlichen die aus Ionien uns,
Auch aus Arabia kamen, und froh ward
Der theuern Lehr' und auch der holden Gesänge
Die Seele jener Entschlafenen nie,
Doch einige wachten. Und sie wandelten oft
Zufrieden unter euch, ihr Bürger schöner Städte,
Beim Kampfspiel, wo sonst unsichtbar der Heros
Geheim bei Dichtern saß, die Ringer schaut und lächelnd
Pries, der gepriesene, die müßigernsten Kinder.
Ein unaufhörlich Lieben wars und ists.
Und wohlgeschieden, aber darum denken
Wir aneinander doch, ihr Fröhlichen am Isthmos,
Und am Cephyß und am Taygetos,
Auch eurer denken wir, ihr Thale des Kaukasos,
So alt ihr seid, ihr Paradiese dort
Und deiner Patriarchen und deiner Propheten,

For much can our kind
Accomplish, and flood and rock and even the might of fire
With art can subdue,
Nor, noble in mind, recoils from
The sword blade, but faced with powers divine
The strong will stand abashed

　　And almost are like the beast of the wilds; which
Impelled by sweet youth
Roams restless over the hills
And feels its own strength in
The noonday heat. But when,
Led down, in frolicking breezes,
The holy light, and with its cool beam
The joyful spirit descend
To blessèd Earth, it succumbs, unfamiliar
With utmost beauty, and drowses in waking sleep,
Though stars are not rising yet. So it is with us. For many's
The man whose vision went out in face of those god-sent gifts,

　　The kindly, that from Ionia came
To us, from Arabia too, and never
The souls of these now gone to their rest were glad
Of precious doctrine nor yet of the lovely songs,
Yet some kept awake. And often, you citizens
Of beautiful towns, they walked among you contented,
At Games, where once in secret the hero
Invisible sat with poets, watched the wrestlers and smiling
Praised—he, the recipient of praise—those idly serious children.
An endless loving it was, and is.
And rightly severed; yet nonetheless we think
Of one another still, you happy ones at the Isthmus,
And by Cephissus and by Taygetus,
And you we think of, vales of the Caucasus,
However ancient, you paradises there,
And of your patriarchs and of your prophets,

O Asia, deiner Starken, o Mutter!
Die furchtlos vor den Zeichen der Welt,
Und den Himmel auf Schultern und alles Schiksaal,
Taglang auf Bergen gewurzelt,
Zuerst es verstanden,
Allein zu reden
Zu Gott. Die ruhn nun. Aber wenn ihr
Und diß ist zu sagen,
Ihr Alten all, nicht sagtet, woher?
Wir nennen dich, heiliggenöthiget, nennen,
Natur! dich wir, und neu, wie dem Bad entsteigt
Dir alles Göttlichgeborne.

Zwar gehn wir fast, wie die Waisen;
Wohl ists, wie sonst, nur jene Pflege nicht wieder;
Doch Jünglinge, der Kindheit gedenk,
Im Hauße sind auch diese nicht fremde.
Sie leben dreifach, eben wie auch
Die ersten Söhne des Himmels.
Und nicht umsonst ward uns
In die Seele die Treue gegeben.
Nicht uns, auch Eures bewahrt sie,
Und bei den Heiligtümern, den Waffen des Worts
Die scheidend ihr den Ungeschikteren uns
Ihr Schiksaalssöhne, zurükgelassen

Ihr guten Geister, da seid ihr auch,
Oftmals, wenn einen dann die heilige Wolk umschwebt,
Da staunen wir und wissens nicht zu deuten
Ihr aber würzt mit Nectar uns den Othem
Und dann frohloken wir oft oder es befällt uns
Ein Sinnen, wenn ihr aber einen zu sehr liebt
Er ruht nicht, bis er euer einer geworden.
Darum, ihr Gütigen! umgebet mich leicht,
Damit ich bleiben möge, denn noch ist manches zu singen,
Jezt aber endiget, seeligweinend,
Wie eine Sage der Liebe,
Mir der Gesang, und so auch ist er
Mir, mit Erröthen, Erblassen,
Von Anfang her gegangen. Doch Alles geht so.

O Asia, of all your mighty ones, Mother,
Who fearless in face of the signs of the world,
The heavens heaped upon shoulders and all manner of fate,
For days were rooted on mountains
And were the first who knew
How to speak alone
To God. These now are at rest. But if,
And this must be said, you ancients
Would never tell us whence it is that
We name you, under a holy compulsion we
Now name you Nature, and new, as from a bath
From you emerges all that's divinely born.

True, like orphans almost we walk;
Though much is what it was, that tutelage now is lacking;
But youths who are mindful of childhood,
These are not strangers now in the house.
Threefold they live, as did
The very first-born of Heaven.
And not for nothing in
Our souls was loyalty fixed.
Not us alone, but that which is yours it preserves
And in those holy relics, the weapons of the word
Which, parting, you sons of Fate,
You left behind for us the less fated,
The less endowed with rightness,

You kindly spirits, in them you are present too,
And often, when the holy cloud is hovering round a man,
We are amazed and do not know the meaning.
But you with nectar spice our breath, and then
We may exult or else a pondering befalls us,
But when too greatly you love a man
He finds no rest till he is one of you.
Therefore, benign ones, surround me lightly,
And let me stay a while, for much remains to be sung;
But now, like a legend of love,
Blissfully weeping, my song
Comes to its end, and so too,
Amid blushing and blanching, it's gone
With me from the start. But that is how all things go.

Michael Hamburger

Die Wanderung

Glükseelig Suevien, meine Mutter,
Auch du, der glänzenderen, der Schwester
Lombarda drüben gleich,
Von hundert Bächen durchflossen!
Und Bäume genug, weißblühend und röthlich,
Und dunklere, wild, tiefgrünenden Laubs voll
Und Alpengebirg der Schweiz auch überschattet
Benachbartes dich; denn nah dem Heerde des Haußes
Wohnst du, und hörst, wie drinnen
Aus silbernen Opferschaalen
Der Quell rauscht, ausgeschüttet
Von reinen Händen, wenn berührt

Von warmen Stralen
Krystallenes Eis und umgestürzt
Vom leichtanregenden Lichte
Der schneeige Gipfel übergießt die Erde
Mit reinestem Wasser. Darum ist
Dir angeboren die Treue. Schwer verläßt,
Was nahe dem Ursprung wohnet, den Ort.
Und deine Kinder, die Städte,
Am weithindämmernden See,
An Nekars Weiden, am Rheine,
Sie alle meinen, es wäre
Sonst nirgend besser zu wohnen.

Ich aber will dem Kaukasos zu!
Denn sagen hört' ich
Noch heut in den Lüften:
Frei sei'n, wie Schwalben, die Dichter.
Auch hat mir ohnediß
In jüngeren Tagen Eines vertraut,
Es seien vor alter Zeit
Die Eltern einst, das deutsche Geschlecht,
Still fortgezogen von Wellen der Donau
Am Sommertage, da diese

The Migration

Blessed Swabia, my mother,
Traversed by a hundred brooks
Like Lombardy, your more luminous
Sister across the way,
And trees enough, with blossoms white and red,
And darker ones, growing wild, full of deep greens,
And the neighborly Swiss Alps
Provide you with shade; for your dwelling place is near
The hearth, and within you hear
The wellspring purl
From silver cups, pure hands
Pouring the libation, as the sun

Thaws ice-crystals and,
Avalanched
By the quickening light,
Snowcaps drench the earth
With the purest water. So loyalty
To origin is innate to you. A place of dwelling
This near the source is hard to leave.
And your offspring, the towns
By shimmering lakes,
By the Neckar's willows, by the Rhine,
All agree there is no
Better spot for home.

Yet I long for the Kaukasos!
Only today I heard
The breezes say
Poets are free as swallows.
And besides, I was told
Long ago that our forefathers,
The German tribe, quietly
Coasted down the Danube
Of a summer's day
And reached the Black Sea,

Sich Schatten suchten, zusammen
Mit Kindern der Sonn'
Am schwarzen Meere gekommen;
Und nicht umsonst sei diß
Das gastfreundliche genennet.

  Denn, als sie erst sich angesehen,
Da nahten die Anderen erst; dann sazten auch
Die Unseren sich neugierig unter den Ölbaum.
Doch als sich ihre Gewande berührt,
Und keiner vernehmen konnte
Die eigene Rede des andern, wäre wohl
Entstanden ein Zwist, wenn nicht aus Zweigen herunter
Gekommen wäre die Kühlung,
Die Lächeln über das Angesicht
Der Streitenden öfters breitet, und eine Weile
Sahn still sie auf, dann reichten sie sich
Die Hände liebend einander. Und bald

  Vertauschten sie Waffen und all
Die lieben Güter des Haußes,
Vertauschten das Wort auch und es wünschten
Die freundlichen Väter umsonst nichts
Beim Hochzeitjubel den Kindern.
Denn aus den heiligvermählten
Wuchs schöner, denn Alles,
Was vor und nach
Von Menschen sich nannt', ein Geschlecht auf. Wo,
Wo aber wohnt ihr, liebe Verwandten,
Daß wir das Bündniß wiederbegehn
Und der theuern Ahnen gedenken?

  Dort an den Ufern, unter den Bäumen
Ionias, in Ebenen des Kaisters,
Wo Kranich, des Aethers froh,
Umschlossen sind von fernhindämmernden Bergen;
Dort wart auch ihr, ihr Schönsten! oder pfleget
Der Inseln, die mit Wein bekränzt,

Meeting with the children
Of the sun
Seeking shade.
Not for nothing
They call this sea Hospitable.

On first catching sight, it was the others
Who drew near; intrigued, our people
Joined them beneath the olive trees.
And as they grazed each other's garments
But could not understand
Each other's speech, there would have
Been a fight, had not a cooling
Come down from the boughs
And spread a smile, as it often does,
Across belligerent faces; for a while
They stared in silence, then offered
Their hands in friendship. And soon

They traded weapons and all
Their precious household goods,
And exchanged the Word, and fathers
Saw that nothing lacked
At their children's wedding feasts.
And from these sacred unions
A race arose, more beautiful than anything
By the name of man
Before or since.
But where can I find you, dear kinsmen,
That we might recelebrate the vows
And honor the memory of our ancestors?

There on the shores beneath the trees
Of Ionia, on the plains of the Cayster,
Where cranes delight in aether,
Bounded by the far-shimmering peaks,
You too were there, O beautiful ones! Or
Tilled islands, garlanded with vines,

Voll tönten von Gesang; noch andere wohnten
Am Tayget, am vielgepriesnen Himettos,
Die blühten zulezt; doch von
Parnassos Quell bis zu des Tmolos
Goldglänzenden Bächen erklang
Ein ewiges Lied; so rauschten
Damals die Wänder und all
Die Saitenspiele zusamt
Von himmlischer Milde gerühret.

O Land des Homer!
Am purpurnen Kirschbaum oder wenn
Von dir gesandt im Weinberg mir
Die jungen Pfirsiche grünen,
Und die Schwalbe fernher kommt und vieles erzählend
An meinen Wänden ihr Haus baut, in
Den Tagen des Mais, auch unter den Sternen
Gedenk' ich, o Ionia, dein! doch Menschen
Ist Gegenwärtiges lieb. Drum bin sich
Gekommen, euch, ihr Inseln, zu sehn, und euch,
Ihr Mündungen der Ströme, o ihr Hallen des Thetis,
Ihr Wälder, euch, und euch, ihr Wolken des Ida!

Doch nicht zu bleiben gedenk ich.
Unfreundlich ist und schwer zu gewinnen
Die Verschlossene, der ich entkommen, die Mutter.
Von ihren Söhnen einer, der Rhein,
Mit Gewalt wollt' er ans Herz ihr stürzen und schwand
Der Zurükgestoßene, niemand weiß, wohin, in die Ferne.
Doch so nicht wünscht' ich gegangen zu seyn,
Von ihr und nur, euch einzuladen,
Bin ich zu euch, ihr Gratien Griechenlands,
Ihr Himmelstöchter, gegangen,
Daß, wenn die Reise zu weit nicht ist,
Zu uns ihr kommet, ihr Holden!

Resounding with song; and others dwelt
By Taygetos, by fabled Hymettos,
And were the last to flower; yet from
The springs of Parnassos to Tmolos'
Gold-glimmering brooks, one everlasting
Hymn rang forth; and the forests
All rustled, every lyre
In unison
At heaven's gentle touch.

Land of Homer!
By the scarlet cherry tree, or when
The young peaches you sent to me
Are still green in the vineyard,
And the swallow arrives from afar and, bringing endless news,
Builds her house in my walls, in
Maytime, and under stars,
Ionia, I think of you. But since men
Are fond of presences, I have come
To visit you, islands, and you,
O rivermouths, halls of Thetis,
And you, O woods, and you, O clouds over Ida!

Yet I do not think I'll linger long.
What I flee is cold and hard
To please, a mystery, my mother.
One of her sons, the Rhine, once tried
To take her heart by force, then disappeared
Into the distance, spurned, who knows where.
I would not wish to leave her thus
And come merely
To invite you, O Graces of Greece,
Daughters of heaven,
To visit us, O lovely ones,
If the journey be not too far.

Wenn milder athmen die Lüfte,
Und liebende Pfeile der Morgen
Uns Allzugedultigen schikt,
Und leichte Gewölke blühn
Uns über den schüchternen Augen,
Dann werden wir sagen, wie kommt
Ihr, Charitinnen, zu Wilden?
Die Dienerinnen des Himmels
Sind aber wunderbar,
Wie alles Göttlichgeborne.
Zum Traume wirds ihm, will es Einer
Beschleichen und straft den, der
Ihm gleichen will mit Gewalt;
Oft überraschet es einen,
Der eben kaum es gedacht hat.

Germanien

Nicht sie, die Seeligen, die erschienen sind,
Die Götterbilder in dem alten Lande,
Sie darf ich ja nicht rufen mehr, wenn aber
Ihr heimatlichen Wasser! jezt mit euch
Des Herzens Liebe klagt, was will es anders,
Das Heiligtrauernde? Denn voll Erwartung liegt
Das Land und als in heißen Tagen
Herabgesenkt, umschattet heut
Ihr Sehnenden! uns ahnungsvoll ein Himmel.
Voll ist er von Verheißungen und scheint
Mir drohend auch, doch will ich bei ihm bleiben,
Und rükwärts soll die Seele mir nicht fliehn
Zu euch, Vergangene! die zu lieb mir sind.
Denn euer schönes Angesicht zu sehn,
Als wärs, wie sonst, ich fürcht' es, tödtlich ists,
Und kaum erlaubt, Gestorbene zu weken.

When breezes blow more sweetly
And dawn releases loving arrows
In our all too patient midst,
And light clouds blossom
Above our bashful eyes,
We shall ask, How, Charites,
Have you come among barbarians?
But the handmaids of heaven
Are miraculous,
As is everything born of the gods.
Try taking it by surprise, and it turns
To a dream; try matching it by force,
And punishment is the reward;
Often, when you've barely given it
A thought, it just happens.

Richard Sieburth

Germania

Not them, the blessed, who once appeared,
Those images of gods in the ancient land,
Them, it is true, I may not now invoke, but if,
You waters of my homeland, now with you
The love of my heart laments, what else does it want, in
Its hallowed sadness? For full of expectation lies
The country, and as though it had been lowered
In sultry dog days, on us a heaven today,
You yearning rivers, casts prophetic shade.
With promises it is fraught, and to me
Seems threatening too, yet I will stay with it,
And backward now my soul shall not escape
To you, the vanished, whom I love too much.
To look upon your beautiful brows, as though
They were unchanged, I am afraid, for deadly
And scarcely permitted it is to awaken the dead.

Entflohene Götter! auch ihr, ihr gegenwärtigen, damals
Wahrhaftiger, ihr hattet eure Zeiten!
Nichts läugnen will ich hier und nichts erbitten.
Denn wenn es aus ist, und der Tag erloschen
Wohl trifts den Priester erst, doch liebend folgt
Der Tempel und das Bild ihm auch und seine Sitte
Zum dunkeln Land und keines mag noch scheinen.
Nur als von Grabesflammen, ziehet dann
Ein goldner Rauch, die Sage drob hinüber,
Und dämmert jezt uns Zweifelnden um das Haupt,
Und keiner weiß, wie ihm geschieht. Er fühlt
Die Schatten derer, so gewesen sind,
Die Alten, so die Erde neubesuchen.
Denn die da kommen sollen, drängen uns,
Und länger säumt von Göttermenschen
Die heilige Schaar nicht mehr im blauen Himmel.

Schon grünet ja, im Vorspiel rauherer Zeit
Für sie erzogen das Feld, bereitet ist die Gaabe
Zum Opfermahl und Thal und Ströme sind
Weitoffen um prophetische Berge,
Daß schauen mag bis in den Orient
Der Mann und ihn von dort der Wandlungen viele bewegen.
Vom Aether aber fällt
Das treue Bild und Göttersprüche reegnen
Unzählbare von ihm, und es tönt im innersten Haine.
Und der Adler, der vom Indus kömmt,
Und über des Parnassos
Beschneite Gipfel fliegt, hoch über den Opferhügeln
Italias, und frohe Beute sucht
Dem Vater, nicht wie sonst, geübter im Fluge
Der Alte, jauchzend überschwingt er
Zulezt die Alpen und sieht die vielgearteten Länder.

Die Priesterin, die stillste Tochter Gottes,
Sie, die zu gern in tiefer Einfalt schweigt,
Sie suchet er, die offnen Auges schaute,
Als wüßte sie es nicht, jüngst, da ein Sturm

Gods who are fled! And you also, present still,
But once more real, you had your time, your ages!
No, nothing here I'll deny and ask no favors.
For when it's over, and Day's light gone out,
The priest is the first to be struck, but lovingly
The temple and the image and the cult
Follow him down into darkness, and none of them now may shine.
Only as from a funeral pyre henceforth
A golden smoke, the legend of it, drifts
And glimmers on around our doubting heads
And no one knows what's happening to him. He feels
The shadowy shapes of those who once were here,
The ancients, newly visiting the earth.
For those who are to come now jostle us,
Nor longer will that holy host of beings
Divinely human linger in azure Heaven.

Already, in the prelude of a rougher age
Raised up for them, the field grows green, prepared
Are offerings for the votive feast and valley
And rivers lie wide open round prophetic mountains,
So that into the very Orient
A man may look and thence be moved by many transformations.
But down from aether falls
The faithful image, and words of gods rain down
Innumerable from it, and the innermost grove resounds.
And the eagle that comes from the Indus
And flies over the snow-covered peaks of
Parnassus, high above the votive hills
Of Italy, and seeks glad booty for
The Father, not as he used to, more practised in flight,
That ancient one, exultant, over the Alps
Wings on at last and sees the diverse countries.

The priestess, her, the quietest daughter of God,
Too fond of keeping silent in deep ingenuousness,
Her now he seeks, who open-eyed looked up
As though she did not know it, lately when a storm,

Todtdrohend über ihrem Haupt ertönte;
Es ahnete das Kind ein Besseres,
Und endlich ward ein Staunen weit im Himmel
Weil Eines groß an Glauben, wie sie selbst,
Die seegnende, die Macht der Höhe sei;
Drum sandten sie den Boten, der, sie schnell erkennend,
Denkt lächelnd so: Dich, unzerbrechliche, muß
Ein ander Wort erprüfen und ruft es laut,
Der Jugendliche, nach Germania schauend:
»Du bist es, auserwählt,
»Alliebend und ein schweres Glük
»Bist du zu tragen stark geworden,

   Seit damals, da im Walde verstekt und blühendem Mohn
Voll süßen Schlummers, trunkene, meiner du
Nicht achtetest, lang, ehe noch auch geringere fühlten
Der Jungfrau Stolz und staunten weß du wärst und woher,
Doch du es selbst nicht wußtest. Ich miskannte dich nicht,
Und heimlich, da du träumtest, ließ ich
Am Mittag scheidend dir ein Freundeszeichen,
Die Blume des Mundes zurük und du redetest einsam.
Doch Fülle der goldenen Worte sandtest du auch
Glükseelige! mit den Strömen und sie quillen unerschöpflich
In die Gegenden all. Denn fast, wie der heiligen,
Die Mutter ist von allem,
Die Verborgene sonst genannt von Menschen,
So ist von Lieben und Leiden
Und voll von Ahnungen dir
Und voll von Frieden der Busen.

   O trinke Morgenlüfte,
Biß daß du offen bist,
Und nenne, was vor Augen dir ist,
Nicht länger darf Geheimniß mehr
Das Ungesprochene bleiben,
Nachdem es lange verhüllt ist;
Denn Sterblichen geziemet die Schaam,
Und so zu reden die meiste Zeit,

Threatening death, rang out above her head;
A better destiny the child divined,
And in the end amazement spread in heaven
Because one being was as great in faith
As they themselves, the blessing powers on high;
Therefore they sent the messenger, who, quick to recognize her,
Smilingly thus reflects: you the unbreakable
A different word must try, and then proclaims,
The youthful, looking towards Germania:
"Yes, it is you, elected
All-loving and to bear
A burdensome good fortune have grown strong,

Since, hidden in the woods and flowering poppies
Filled with drowsiness, you, drunken, did not heed
Me for a long time, before lesser ones even felt
The virgin's pride, and marvelled whose you are and where from,
But you yourself did not know. Yet I did not misjudge you
And secretly, while you dreamed, at noon,
Departing I left a token of friendship,
The flower of the mouth behind, and lonely you spoke.
Yet you, the greatly blessed, with the rivers too
Dispatched a wealth of golden words, and they well unceasing
Into all regions now. For almost as is the holy
The Mother of all things, upholder of the abyss,
Whom men at other times call the Concealed,
Now full of loves and sorrows
And full of presentiments
And full of peace is your bosom.

O drink the morning breezes
Until you are opened up
And name what you see before you;
No longer now the unspoken
May remain a mystery
Though long it has been veiled;
For shame behoves us mortals
And most of the time to speak thus

Ist weise auch von Göttern.
Wo aber überflüssiger, denn lautere Quellen
Das Gold und ernst geworden ist der Zorn an dem Himmel,
Muß zwischen Tag und Nacht
Einsmals ein Wahres erscheinen.
Dreifach umschreibe du es,
Doch ungesprochen auch, wie es da ist,
Unschuldige, muß es bleiben.

    O nenne Tochter du der heiligen Erd'
Einmal die Mutter. Es rauschen die Wasser am Fels
Und Wetter im Wald und bei dem Nahmen derselben
Tönt auf aus alter Zeit Vergangengöttliches wieder.
Wie anders ists! und rechthin glänzt und spricht
Zukünftiges auch erfreulich aus den Fernen.
Doch in der Mitte der Zeit
Lebt ruhig mit geweihter
Jungfräulicher Erde der Aether
Und gerne, zur Erinnerung, sind
Die unbedürftigen sie
Gastfreundlich bei den unbedürftgen
Bei deinen Feiertagen
Germania, wo du Priesterin bist
Und wehrlos Rath giebst rings
Den Königen und den Völkern.

Of gods indeed is wise.
But where more superabundant than purest wellsprings
The gold has become and the anger in Heaven earnest,
For once between Day and Night must
A truth be made manifest.
Now threefold circumscribe it,
Yet unuttered also, just as you found it,
Innocent virgin, let it remain.

    Once only, daughter of holy Earth,
Pronounce your Mother's name. The waters roar on the rock
And thunderstorms in the wood, and at their name
Divine things past ring out from time immemorial.
How all is changed! And to the right there gleam
And speak things yet to come, joy-giving, from the distance.
Yet at the center of Time
In peace with hallowed,
With virginal Earth lives Aether
And gladly, for remembrance, they
The never-needy dwell
Hospitably amid the never-needy,
Amid your holidays,
Germania, where you are priestess and
Defenseless proffer all round
Advice to the kings and the peoples."

Michael Hamburger

Der Rhein
An Isaak von Sinclair

Im dunkeln Epheu saß ich, an der Pforte
Des Waldes, eben, da der goldene Mittag,
Den Quell besuchend, herunterkam
Von Treppen des Alpengebirgs,
Das mir die göttlichgebaute,
Die Burg der Himmlischen heißt
Nach alter Meinung, wo aber
Geheim noch manches entschieden
Zu Menschen gelanget; von da
Vernahm ich ohne Vermuthen
Ein Schiksaal, denn noch kaum
War mir im warmen Schatten
Sich manches beredend, die Seele
Italia zu geschweift
Und fernhin an die Küsten Moreas.

Jezt aber, drinn im Gebirg,
Tief unter den silbernen Gipfeln
Und unter fröhlichem Grün,
Wo die Wälder schauernd zu ihm,
Und der Felsen Häupter übereinander
Hinabschaun, taglang, dort
Im kältesten Abgrund hört'
Ich um Erlösung jammern
Den Jüngling, es hörten ihn, wie er tobt',
Und die Mutter Erd' anklagt',
Und den Donnerer, der ihn gezeuget,
Erbarmend die Eltern, doch
Die Sterblichen flohn von dem Ort,
Denn furchtbar war, da lichtlos er
In den Fesseln sich wälzte,
Das Rasen des Halbgotts.

The Rhine
For Isaak von Sinclair

At the forest's gate I sat among
Dark ivy as the golden noon
Came down visiting the stream, from off
The Alps, their mountain staircase, built
By powers divine, God's Castle as
I call it, in accord
With old opinion, where devolves
To man yet many a thing
Decided in secret; thence
Came to my mind, against expectation,
A destiny, for my soul
Telling itself of this and that in the warm shade
Now was drifting toward Italy
And beyond, to the far coasts of Morea.

But now, in the mountains' midst, deep
Down below the silver peaks, and among
Delighting green, where the forests,
Tremulous, and piled crag heads gaze
All day down at him, there
In the coldest abyss I heard
The stripling moan for liberation,
In floundering rage accuse earth,
His mother, and the thunderer who
Begot him, and they heard him also,
His parents, pitying, yet
Mortals fled the place, for it was terrible,
With him in his chained dark torsions,
The frenzy of the demigod.

Die Stimme wars des edelsten der Ströme,
Des freigeborenen Rheins,
Und anderes hoffte der, als droben von den Brüdern,
Dem Tessin und dem Rhodanus,
Er schied und wandern wollt', und ungeduldig ihn
Nach Asia trieb die königliche Seele.
Doch unverständig ist
Das Wünschen vor dem Schiksaal.
Die Blindesten aber
Sind Göttersöhne. Denn es kennet der Mensch
Sein Haus und dem Thier ward, wo
Es bauen solle, doch jenen ist
Der Fehl, daß sie nicht wissen wohin?
In die unerfahrne Seele gegeben.

Ein Räthsel ist Reinentsprungenes. Auch
Der Gesang kaum darf es enthüllen. Denn
Wie du anfiengst, wirst du bleiben,
So viel auch wirket die Noth,
Und die Zucht, das meiste nemlich
Vermag die Geburt,
Und der Lichtstral, der
Dem Neugebornen begegnet.
Wo aber ist einer,
Um frei zu bleiben
Sein Leben lang, und des Herzens Wunsch
Allein zu erfüllen, so
Aus günstigen Höhn, wie der Rhein,
Und so aus heiligem Schoose
Glüklich geboren, wie jener?

Drum ist ein Jauchzen sein Wort.
Nicht liebt er, wie andere Kinder,
In Wikelbanden zu weinen;
Denn wo die Ufer zuerst
An die Seit ihm schleichen, die krummen,
Und durstig umwindend ihn,
Den Unbedachten, zu ziehn

It was the voice of the most noble river,
The freeborn Rhine,
And as he parted up there from his brothers,
Ticino and Rhodanus, his hopes
Were elsewhere, he meant to travel,
And his royal soul drove him, with impatience,
Toward Asia. But to desire a thing
In destiny's teeth is not prudent.
Yet the blindest of all are
The sons of gods. For man
Knows his house, where to build
Occurs to the animals, but to their soul
Without experience is given the defect
That they know not where to go.

A riddle it is, whatever
Springs from the pure source. Even song
May hardly reveal it. For
As you began so you remain.
And though compulsions leave their mark,
And upbringing, birth performs
The most, and the ray of light encountering
The newborn being. But where is the man
Who can stay free
As long as he lives, and alone
Accomplish his heart's desire
From heights auspicious as the Rhine's,
And born from a womb as holy
With such fortune as his?

Therefore his speech is a shout of joy.
He does not weep and whine
In swaddling clothes like other infants;
For though the shores at first, crooked,
Sidle up to him and coiling
Thirstily are keen to guide him, unawares,
Twixt their teeth and coddle him there, with a laugh
He rends those snakes to tatters, plunges on,

Und wohl zu behüten begehren
Im eigenen Zahne, lachend
Zerreißt er die Schlangen und stürzt
Mit der Beut und wenn in der Eil'
Ein Größerer ihn nich zähmt,
Ihn wachsen läßt, wie der Bliz, muß er
Die Erde spalten, und wie Bezauberte fliehn
Die Wälder ihm nach und zusammensinkend die Berge.

Ein Gott will aber sparen den Söhnen
Das eilende Leben und lächelt,
Wenn unenthaltsam, aber gehemmt
Von heiligen Alpen, ihm
In der Tiefe, wie jener, zürnen die Ströme.
In solcher Esse wird dann
Auch alles Lautre geschmiedet,
Und schön ists, wie er drauf,
Nachdem er die Berge verlassen,
Stillwandelnd sich im deutschen Lande
Begnüget und das Sehnen stillt
Im guten Geschäffte, wenn er das Land baut
Der Vater Rhein und liebe Kinder nährt
In Städten, die er gegründet.

Doch nimmer, nimmer vergißt ers.
Denn eher muß die Wohnung vergehn,
Und die Sazung und zum Unbild werden
Der Tag der Menschen, ehe vergessen
Ein solcher dürfte den Ursprung
Und die reine Stimme der Jugend.
Wer war es, der zuerst
Die Liebesbande verderbt
Und Strike von ihnen gemacht hat?
Dann haben des eigenen Rechts
Und gewiß des himmlischen Feuers
Gespottet die Trozigen, dann erst
Die sterblichen Pfade verachtend
Verwegnes erwählt
Und den Göttern gleich zu werden getrachtet.

Bearing his catch, and if in his haste some
Greater one than he does not tame him,
Nor make him grow, he must split the earth
Like lightning, and the forests hurtle
After him, bewitched, and mountains subsiding.

But a god desires to save his sons
From flitting life, and he smiles
When without restraint, but hemmed in
By holy Alps, the rivers
Rage at him in the depths as this one does.
In such a furnace then
All things freed of dross are shaped
And beauty comes thereafter, when
Leaving the mountains he meanders
Quietly through German lands, content,
And slakes his cravings
In wholesome commerce, in husbandry,
Father Rhine, feeding his beloved
Children in towns that he has founded.

Yet never will he forget, never,
For sooner shall man's dwelling perish,
His laws and his light of day become
Monstrous, than such a one
Forget his origin
And the pure voice of his youth.
Who first tainted the ties
Of love and made
Traps of them? In consequence
Defiant rebels made a mock
Of their own rights and, for sure,
Of heavenly fire, and then
Scorning the ways of mortals
Chose arrogance and ventured
To become the peers of gods.

Es haben aber an eigner
Unsterblichkeit die Götter genug, und bedürfen
Die Himmlischen eines Dings,
So sinds Heroën und Menschen
Und Sterbliche sonst. Denn weil
Die Seeligsten nichts fühlen von selbst,
Muß wohl, wenn solches zu sagen
Erlaubt ist, in der Götter Nahmen
Theilnehmend fühlen ein Andrer,
Den brauchen sie; jedoch ihr Gericht
Ist, daß sein eigenes Haus
Zerbreche der und das Liebste
Wie den Feind schelt' und sich Vater und Kind
Begrabe unter den Trümmern,
Wenn einer, wie sie, seyn will und nicht
Ungleiches dulden, der Schwärmer.

Drum wohl ihm, welcher fand
Ein wohlbeschiedenes Schiksaal,
Wo noch der Wanderungen
Und süß der Leiden Erinnerung
Aufrauscht am sichern Gestade,
Daß da und dorthin gern
Er sehn mag bis an die Grenzen
Die bei der Geburt ihm Gott
Zum Aufenthalte gezeichnet.
Dann ruht er, seeligbescheiden,
Denn alles, was er gewollt,
Das Himmlische, von selber umfängt
Es unbezwungen, lächelnd
Jezt, da er ruhet, den Kühnen.

Halbgötter denk' ich jezt
Und kennen muß ich die Theuern,
Weil oft ihr Leben so
Die sehnende Brust mir beweget.
Wem aber, wie, Rousseau, dir,
Unüberwindlich die Seele

But the gods have enough
Immortality of their own, and if there be
One thing the celestials need
It is heroes and men
And mortals generally. For since
The serenest beings feel nothing at all,
There must come, if to speak
Thus is permitted, another who feels
On their behalf, him
They use and need; but their deposition
Is that he shall destroy
His own house, curse what he loves most
As his enemy, and under the rubble
Bury his father and his child,
If he should seek to be like them and not
Allow inequality, the wild dreamer.

Hence fortune is his who found
A right destiny his own,
Where the surge of wayfaring memories
With sweet recall of hardship known
Whispers on a certain shore,
His gaze may thus extend around
To the limits
Drawn at his birth
By God for his dwelling.
Then he shall come to rest, lowly and
Serene, for all his heart desired,
The heaven he wished for, it is there, effortlessly
Surrounding him, the adventurer,
And smiles at him, now that his quiet has come.

Demigods now I'm thinking of,
And must know them, the dears, because
Their lives have so much stirred
My heart, and often.
Yet to a man, Rousseau, like you,
Whose never daunted soul

Die starkausdauernde ward,
Und sicherer Sinn
Und süße Gaabe zu hören,
Zu reden so, daß er aus heiliger Fülle
Wie der Weingott, thörig göttlich
Und gesezlos sie die Sprache der Reinesten giebt
Verständlich den Guten, aber mit Recht
Die Achtungslosen mit Blindheit schlägt
Die entweihenden Knechte, wie nenn ich den Fremden?

    Die Söhne der Erde sind, wie die Mutter,
Alliebend, so empfangen sie auch
Mühlos, die Glüklichen, Alles.
Drum überraschet es auch
Und schrökt den sterblichen Mann,
Wenn er den Himmel, den
Er mit den liebenden Armen
Sich auf die Schultern gehäufft,
Und die Last der Freude bedenket;
Dann scheint ihm oft das Beste,
Fast ganz vergessen da,
Wo der Stral nicht brennt,
Im Schatten des Walds
Am Bielersee in frischer Grüne zu seyn,
Und sorglosarm an Tönen,
Anfängern gleich, bei Nachtigallen zu lernen.

    Und herrlich ists, aus heiligem Schlafe dann
Erstehen und aus Waldes Kühle
Erwachend, Abends nun
Dem milderen Licht entgegenzugehn,
Wenn, der die Berge gebaut
Und den Pfad der Ströme gezeichnet,
Nachdem er lächelnd auch
Der Menschen geschäfftiges Leben
Das othemarme, wie Seegel
Mit seinen Lüften gelenkt hat,
Auch ruht und zu der Schülerin jezt,
Der Bildner, Gutes mehr
Denn Böses findend,
Zur heutigen Erde der Tag sich neiget.—

Persevered, became invincible,
With certitude of mind
And a sweet gift of listening so,
And speaking, that from holy plenitude
Like the winegod in his folly divine
And all against the rules he gives it,
The language of essences,
That the good may understand, yet strikes
Blind all who do not care and desecrating
Slaves, how shall I speak of the stranger?

The sons of earth, their love comprehends
All, as does their mother's, whence their luck is,
And no effort, likewise all to receive.
And it comes to mortal man as a surprise,
Startling him, when he thinks
Of the heaven that he, with loving arms,
Heaped on his back,
And of the burden of joy;
Often it seems then the best thing
To be there, virtually forgotten,
Where the sun's ray does not burn
In the forest shade
By Lake Bienne among fresh green foliage,
And to be learning, with song notes
Happily indigent, like beginners, from nightingales.

And it is glorious to be standing up then
From holy sleep and waking
Out of the forest cool, to walk
Toward the gentler light in the evening,
When he who built the mountains
And who designed the courses of streams,
Now done with guiding the short-
Breathed busy lives of men with a smile,
Filling them like sails with his winds,
Leans, the artificer, toward his pupil,
Finding more good
Than evil, he, the day,
Leaning toward the earth which is today.—

Dann feiern das Brautfest Menschen und Götter,
Es feiern die Lebenden all,
Und ausgeglichen
Ist eine Weile das Schiksaal.
Und die Flüchtlinge suchen die Heerberg,
Und süßen Schlummer die Tapfern,
Die Liebenden aber
Sind, was sie waren, sie sind
Zu Haußse, wo die Blume sich freuet
Unschädlicher Gluth und die finsteren Bäume
Der Geist umsäuselt, aber die Unversöhnten
Sind umgewandelt und eilen
Die Hände sich ehe zu reichen,
Bevor das freundliche Licht
Hinuntergeht und die Nacht kommt.

Doch einigen eilt
Diß schnell vorüber, andere
Behalten es länger.
Die ewigen Götter sind
Voll Lebens allzeit; bis in den Tod
Kann aber ein Mensch auch
Im Gedächtniß doch das Beste behalten,
Und dann erlebt er das Höchste.
Nur hat ein jeder sein Maas.
Denn schwer ist zu tragen
Das Unglük, aber schwerer das Glük.
Ein Weiser aber vermocht es
Vom Mittag bis in die Mitternacht,
Und bis der Morgen erglänzte,
Beim Gastmahl helle zu bleiben.

Dir mag auf heißem Pfade unter Tannen oder
Im Dunkel des Eichwalds gehüllt
In Stahl, mein Sinklair! Gott erscheinen oder
In Wolken, du kennst ihn, da du kennest, jugendlich,
Des Guten Kraft, und nimmer ist dir
Verborgen das Lächeln des Herrschers

Then men and gods their nuptials celebrate,
All living creatures celebrate
And equilibrium for a time
Makes destinies level,
And fugitives seek a resting place,
And sweet slumber is sought by the brave,
But lovers are
Just what they were, they are
At home where the flower enjoys
Innocuous heat and the spirit rustles
Round dark trees, but enemies are
Transformed and rush
To clasp one another's hands
Before the friendly light descending
Vanishes and the night comes.

Yet some there are
This quickly passes by, others
Retain it longer. At
All times the eternal gods
Are full of life; but into death
Even a man can keep
Stored in memory the best,
And then ultimate experience is his.
Each man has, nonetheless, his measure.
For misfortune is hard
To endure, but fortune even harder.
But at the banquet one wise man
From noon through midnight and until
The gleam of morning came could keep
A steady lucid mind.

To you, on the hot path under pines, or
In the dark of the oak forest hidden
In the steel blade, Sinclair, my friend,
God may appear, or in clouds, you know him,
Having a young cognizance of
The power of good; and the master of men,

Bei Tage, wenn
Es fieberhaft und angekettet das
Lebendige scheinet oder auch
Bei Nacht, wenn alles gemischt
Ist ordnungslos und wiederkehrt
Uralte Verwirrung.

Friedensfeier

Ich bitte dieses Blatt nur gutmüthig zu lesen. So wird es sicher nicht unfaßlich, noch weniger anstößig seyn. Sollten aber dennoch einige eine solche Sprache zu wenig konventionell finden, so muß ich ihnen gestehen: ich kann nicht anders. An einem schönen Tage läßt sich ja fast jede Sangart hören, und die Natur, wovon es her ist, nimmts auch wieder.

Der Verfasser gedenkt dem Publikum eine ganze Sammlung von dergleichen Blättern vorzulegen, und dieses soll irgend eine Probe seyn davon.

Der himmlischen, still wiederklingenden,
Der ruhigwandelnden Töne voll,
Und gelüftet ist der altgebaute,
Seeliggewohnte Saal; um grüne Teppiche duftet
Die Freudenwolk' und weithinglänzend stehn,
Gereiftester Früchte voll und goldbekränzter Kelche,
Wohlangeordnet, eine prächtige Reihe,
Zur Seite da und dort aufsteigend über dem
Geebneten Boden die Tische.
Denn ferne kommend haben
Hieher, zur Abendstunde,
Sich liebende Gäste beschieden.

His smile is never
Concealed from you, by day
When the vivid world seems
Febrile or shackled, nor yet
By night, when all is blent
And orderless, and age-old
Confusion comes again.

Christopher Middleton

Celebration of Peace

All I ask is that the reader be kindly disposed towards these pages. In that case he will certainly not find them incomprehensible, far less objectionable. But if, nonetheless, some should think such a language too unconventional, I must confess to them: I cannot help it. On a fine day—they should consider—almost every mode of song makes itself heard; and Nature, whence it originates, also receives it again.

The author intends to offer the public an entire collection of such pieces, and this one should be regarded as a kind of sample.

With heavenly, quietly echoing,
With calmly modulating music filled,
And aired is the anciently built,
The sweetly familiar hall; upon green carpets wafts
The fragrant cloud of joy and, casting their brightness far,
Full of most mellow fruit and chalices wreathed with gold,
Arranged in seemly order, a splendid row,
Erected here and there on either side above
The leveled floor, stand the tables.
For, come from distant places,
Here, at the evening hour,
Loving guests have forgathered.

Und dämmernden Auges denk' ich schon,
Vom ernsten Tagwerk lächelnd,
Ihn selbst zu sehn, den Fürsten des Fests.
Doch wenn du schon dein Ausland gern verläugnest,
Und als vom langen Heldenzuge müd,
Dein Auge senkst, vergessen, leichtbeschattet,
Und Freundesgestalt annimmst, du Allbekannter, doch
Beugt fast die Knie das Hohe. Nichts vor dir,
Nur Eines weiß ich, Sterbliches bist du nicht.
Ein Weiser mag mir manches erhellen; wo aber
Ein Gott noch auch erscheint,
Da ist doch andere Klarheit.

Von heute aber nicht, nicht unverkündet ist er;
Und einer, der nicht Fluth noch Flamme gescheuet,
Erstaunet, da es stille worden, umsonst nicht, jezt,
Da Herrschaft nirgend ist zu sehn bei Geistern und Menschen.
Das ist, sie hören das Werk,
Längst vorbereitend, von Morgen nach Abend, jezt erst,
Denn unermeßlich braußt, in der Tiefe verhallend,
Des Donnerers Echo, das tausendjährige Wetter,
Zu schlafen, übertönt von Friedenslauten, hinunter.
Ihr aber, theuergewordne, o ihr Tage der Unschuld,
Ihr bringt auch heute das Fest, ihr Lieben! und es blüht
Rings abendlich der Geist in dieser Stille;
Und rathen muß ich, und wäre silbergrau
Die Loke, o ihr Freunde!
Für Kränze zu sorgen und Mahl, jezt ewigen Jünglingen ähnlich.

Und manchen möcht' ich laden, aber o du,
Der freundlichernst den Menschen zugethan,
Dort unter syrischer Palme,
Wo nahe lag die Stadt, am Brunnen gerne war;
Das Kornfeld rauschte rings, still athmete die Kühlung
Vom Schatten des geweiheten Gebirges,
Und die lieben Freunde, das treue Gewölk,
Umschatteten dich auch, damit der heiligkühne
Durch Wildniß mild dein Stral zu Menschen kam, o Jüngling!

And already with eyes dusk-dim,
With solemn day-labor smiling,
I think that I see him in person, the prince of the feast day.
But though you like to disavow your foreign land,
And weary, it seems, with long heroic war,
Cast down your eyes, oblivious, lightly shaded,
Assuming the shape of a friend, you known to all men, yet
Almost it bends our knees, such loftiness. Nothing in
Your presence I know; but one thing: mortal you are not.
A wise man could elucidate much for me; but where
A God as well appears,
A different clarity shines.

Yet not sprung up today, nor unproclaimed he comes;
And one who did not balk at either flood or flame
Not without reason astonishes us, now that all is quiet,
Dominion nowhere to be seen among spirits or mortals.
That is, only now do they hear
The work that long has prepared them, from Orient to Occident,
For now immeasurably, fading away in the deeps,
The Thunderer's echo, the millennial storm
Rolls down to sleep, intermingled with peaceful music.
But you, grown dear to us, O days of innocence,
It's you, beloved, that bring this feast-day too, and round us
The spirit flowers, vespertine in this quiet;
And, friends, I must advise you, though
Our hair had turned silver-grey,
To see to garlands and banquet, now like men immortally young.

And many there are I would invite, but you,
O you that benignly, gravely disposed to men
Down there beneath the Syrian palm tree, where
The town lay near, by the well were glad to be;
Round you the cornfield rustled, quietly coolness breathed
From shadows of the hallowed mountainsides,
And your dear friends, the faithful cloud
Cast shade upon you too, so that the holy, the bold,
The beam through wilderness gently should fall on men, O youth.

Ach! aber dunkler umschattete, mitten im Wort, dich
Furchtbarentscheidend ein tödtlich Verhängniß. So ist schnell
Vergänglich alles Himmlische; aber umsonst nicht;

Denn schonend rührt des Maases allzeit kundig
Nur einen Augenblik die Wohnungen der Menschen
Ein Gott an, unversehn, und keiner weiß es, wenn?
Auch darf alsdann das Freche drüber gehn,
Und kommen muß zum heilgen Ort das Wilde
Von Enden fern, übt rauhbetastend den Wahn,
Und trift daran ein Schiksaal, aber Dank,
Nie folgt der gleich hernach dem gottgegebnen Geschenke;
Tiefprüfend ist es zu fassen.
Auch wär' uns, sparte der Gebende nicht
Schon längst vom Seegen des Heerds
Uns Gipfel und Boden entzündet.

Des Göttlichen aber empfiengen wir
Doch viel. Es ward die Flamm' uns
In die Hände gegeben, und Ufer und Meersfluth.
Viel mehr, denn menschlicher Weise
Sind jene mit uns, die fremden Kräfte, vertrauet.
Und es lehret Gestirn dich, das
Vor Augen dir ist, doch nimmer kannst du ihm gleichen.
Vom Alllebendigen aber, von dem
Viel Freuden sind und Gesänge,
Ist einer ein Sohn, ein Ruhigmächtiger ist er,
Und nun erkennen wir ihn,
Nun, da wir kennen den Vater
Und Feiertage zu halten
Der hohe, der Geist
Der Welt sich zu Menschen geneigt hat.

Denn längst war der zum Herrn der Zeit zu groß
Und weit aus reichte sein Feld, wann hats ihn aber erschöpfet?
Einmal mag aber ein Gott auch Tagewerk erwählen,
Gleich Sterblichen und theilen alles Schiksaal.
Schiksaalgesez ist diß, daß Alle sich erfahren,

But oh, more darkly, even as you spoke,
And dreadfully determining a deadly doom overshadowed you
   there.

                                   So all
That's heavenly fleets on; but not for nothing;

   For sparingly, at all times knowing the measure,
A God for a moment only will touch the dwellings
Of men, by none foreseen, and no one knows when.
And over it then all insolence may pass,
And to the holy place must come the savage
From ends remote, and roughly fingering works out his
Delusion, so fulfilling a fate, but thanks
Will never follow at once upon the god-sent gift;
Probed deeply, this can be grasped.
And were not the giver sparing
The wealth of our hearth long ago would
Have fired both the roof and the floor.

   Yet much that's divine nonetheless we
Received. The flame was entrusted
To us, and shore and ocean flood.
Much more than humanly only
Are these, the alien powers, familiar with us.
And you are taught by the stars
In front of your eyes, but never you can be like them.
Yet to the All-Living from whom
Many joys and songs have sprung
There's one who is a son, and quietly powerful is he,
And now we recognize him,
Now that we know the Father
And to keep holidays
The exalted, the Spirit of
The World has inclined towards men.

   For long now he had been too great to rule
As Lord of Time, and wide his field extended, but when did it
   exhaust him?
For once, however, even a God may choose
Mere daily tasks, like mortals, and share all manner of fate.
This is a law of fate, that each shall know all others,

Daß, wenn die Stille kehrt, auch eine Sprache sei.
Wo aber wirkt der Geist, sind wir auch mit, und streiten,
Was wohl das Beste sei. So dünkt mir jezt das Beste,
Wenn nun vollendet sein Bild und fertig ist der Meister,
Und selbst verklärt davon aus seiner Werkstatt tritt,
Der stille Gott der Zeit und nur der Liebe Gesez,
Das schönausgleichende gilt von hier an bis zum Himmel.

Viel hat von Morgen an,
Seit ein Gespräch wir sind und hören voneinander,
Erfahren der Mensch; bald sind wir aber Gesang.
Und das Zeitbild, das der große Geist entfaltet,
Ein Zeichen liegts vor uns, daß zwischen ihm und andern
Ein Bündniß zwischen ihm und andern Mächten ist.
Nicht er allein, die Unerzeugten, Ew'gen
Sind kennbar alle daran, gleichwie auch an den Pflanzen
Die Mutter Erde sich und Licht und Luft sich kennet.
Zulezt ist aber doch, ihr heiligen Mächte, für euch
Das Liebeszeichen, das Zeugniß
Daß ihrs noch seiet, der Festtag,

Der Allversammelnde, wo Himmlische nicht
Im Wunder offenbar, noch ungesehn im Wetter,
Wo aber bei Gesang gastfreundlich untereinander
In Chören gegenwärtig, eine heilige Zahl
Die Seeligen in jeglicher Weise
Beisammen sind, und ihr Geliebtestes auch,
An dem sie hängen, nicht fehlt; denn darum rief ich
Zum Gastmahl, das bereitet ist,
Dich, Unvergeßlicher, dich, zum Abend der Zeit,
O Jüngling, dich zum Fürsten des Festes; und eher legt
Sich schlafen unser Geschlecht nicht,
Bis ihr Verheißenen all,
All ihr Unsterblichen, uns
Von eurem Himmel zu sagen,
Da seid in unserem Hauße.

That when the silence returns there shall be a language too.
Yet where the Spirit is active, we too will stir and debate
What course might be the best. So now it seems best to me
If now the Master completes his image and, finished,
Himself transfigured by it, steps out of his workshop,
The quiet God of Time, and only the law of love,
That gently resolves all difference, prevails from here up to Heaven.

Much, from the morning onwards,
Since we have been a discourse and have heard from one another,
Has human kind learnt; but soon we shall be song.
That temporal image too, which the great Spirit reveals,
As a token lies before us that between him and others,
Himself and other powers, there is a pact of peace.
Not he alone, the Unconceived, Eternal
Can all be known by this, as likewise by the plants
Our Mother Earth and light and air are known.
Yet ultimately, you holy powers, our token
Of love for you, and the proof
That still you are holy to us, is the feast day.

The all-assembling, where heavenly beings are
Not manifest in miracles, nor unseen in thunderstorms,
But where in hymns hospitably conjoined
And present in choirs, a holy number,
The blessèd in every way
Meet and forgather, and their best-beloved,
To whom they are attached, is not missing; for that is why
You to the banquet now prepared I called,
The unforgettable, you, at the Evening of Time,
O youth, called you to the prince of the feast day; nor shall
Our nation ever lie down to sleep until
All you that were prophesied,
Every one of you Immortals,
To tell us about your Heaven
Are here with us in our house.

Leichtathmende Lüfte
Verkünden euch schon,
Euch kündet das rauchende Thal
Und der Boden, der vom Wetter noch dröhnet,
Doch Hoffnung röthet die Wangen,
Und vor der Thüre des Haußes
Sizt Mutter und Kind,
Und schauet den Frieden
Und wenige scheinen zu sterben
Es hält ein Ahnen die Seele,
Vom goldnen Lichte gesendet,
Hält ein Versprechen die Ältesten auf.

Wohl sind die Würze des Lebens,
Von oben bereitet und auch
Hinausgeführet, die Mühen.
Denn Alles gefällt jezt,
Einfältiges aber
Am meisten, denn die langgesuchte,
Die goldne Frucht,
Uraltem Stamm
In schütternden Stürmen entfallen,
Dann aber, als liebstes Gut, vom heiligen Schiksaal selbst,
Mit zärtlichen Waffen umschüzt,
Die Gestalt der Himmlischen ist es.

Wie die Löwin, hast du geklagt,
O Mutter, da du sie,
Natur, die Kinder verloren.
Denn es stahl sie, Allzuliebende, dir
Dein Feind, da du ihn fast
Wie die eigenen Söhne genommen,
Und Satyren die Götter gesellt hast.
So hast du manches gebaut,
Und manches begraben,
Denn es haßt dich, was
Du, vor der Zeit
Allkräftige, zum Lichte gezogen.
Nun kennest, nun lässet du diß;
Denn gerne fühllos ruht,
Bis daß es reift, furchtsamgeschäfftiges drunten.

Winds lightly breathing
Already announce you,
The vapor that drifts from the valley
And the ground still resounding with thunder,
But hope now flushes our cheeks,
In front of the door of their house
Sit mother and child,
And look upon peace,
And few now seem to be dying;
The souls of the oldest even
Held back by a hint, a promise
Conveyed by the golden light.

Indeed it is travails, designed from
Above and there carried out,
That are the spice of life.
For now all things are pleasing
But most of all the
Ingenuous, because the long-sought,
The golden fruit,
In shattering gales fallen down from
An age-old bough
But then, as the dearest possession, by Fate herself
Protected with tender weapons,
The shape of the Heavenly it is.

Like the lioness you lamented,
O Mother, when you lost
Your children, Nature,
For they were stolen from you, the all too loving, by
Your enemy, when almost
Like your own sons you had nursed him
And with satyrs made gods consort.
So there is much you built
And much you buried,
For you are hated by
That which too soon
All-powerful, you raised to the light.
Now you know the fault, and desist;
For, till grown ripe, unfeeling
What's timidly busy likes to rest down below.

Michael Hamburger

Der Einzige
Erste Fassung

Was ist es, das
An die alten seeligen Küsten
Mich fesselt, daß ich mehr noch
Sie liebe, als mein Vaterland?
Denn wie in himmlische
Gefangenschaft verkauft
Dort bin ich, wo Apollo gieng
In Königsgestalt,
Und zu unschuldigen Jünglingen sich
Herablies Zevs und Söhn' in heiliger Art
Und Töchter zeugte
Der Hohe unter den Menschen?

Der hohen Gedanken
Sind nemlich viel
Entsprungen des Vaters Haupt
Und große Seelen
Von ihm zu Menschen gekommen.
Gehöret hab' ich
Von Elis und Olympia, bin
Gestanden oben auf dem Parnaß,
Und über Bergen des Isthmus,
Und drüben auch
Bei Smyrna und hinab
Bei Ephesos bin ich gegangen;

Viel hab' ich schönes gesehn,
Und gesungen Gottes Bild,
Hab' ich, das lebet unter
Den Menschen, aber dennoch
Ihr alten Götter und all
Ihr tapfern Söhne der Götter
Noch Einen such ich, den
Ich liebe unter euch,
Wo ihr den lezten eures Geschlechts
Des Haußes Kleinod mir
Dem fremden Gaste verberget.

The Only One
First Version

What is it that
Binds me to these ancient
Blessed shores, that I love
Them more than my country?
As if sold into
Heavenly bondage,
I am where Apollo
Walked in the guise of a king
And Zeus descended
On innocent youths
And sired sons and daughters
Among mortals by holy means.

Many lofty thoughts
Have sprung from
The Father's brow,
From him great souls
Have come to men.
I have heard
Of Elis and Olympia, have
Stood atop Parnassos
And above the mountains of the Isthmos
And over toward
Smyrna and down
By Ephesos have I walked;

I have seen much beauty
And sung the image of God
Which lives among men,
And yet, O ancient gods
O brave sons of gods,
There is One among you
Whom I love and seek,

The last of your race,
The jewel of your house
Whom you hide from me,
A passing stranger.

Mein Meister und Herr!
O du, mein Lehrer!
Was bist du ferne
Geblieben? und da
Ich fragte unter den Alten,
Die Helden und
Die Götter, warum bliebest
Du aus? Und jezt ist voll
Von Trauern meine Seele
Als eifertet, ihr Himmlischen, selbst
Daß, dien' ich einem, mir
Das andere fehlet.

Ich weiß es aber, eigene Schuld
Ists! Denn zu sehr,
O Christus! häng' ich an dir,
Wiewohl Herakles Bruder
Und kühn bekenn' ich, du
Bist Bruder auch des Eviers, der
An den Wagen spannte
Die Tyger und hinab
Bis an den Indus
Gebietend freudigen Dienst
Den Weinberg stiftet und
Den Grimm bezähmte der Völker.

Es hindert aber eine Schaam
Mich dir zu vergleichen
Die weltlichen Männer. Und freilich weiß
Ich, der dich zeugte, dein Vater,
Derselbe der,

Denn nimmer herrscht er allein.

My Master and Lord,
My Teacher,
Why have you kept
So far away? When I
Inquired among the ancients,
Among heroes and
Gods, why did you fail
To appear? And now
My soul is filled with grief,
As if, O gods, you jealously decreed
That serving the one, I
Thereby lose the other.

But I know, the fault
Is all mind. For I cling
Too close to you, Christ,
Though you are Heracles' brother
And, I must confess, the brother
Of Euios too, who
Harnassed tigers to his
Chariot and, commanding
Joyous worship down
To the Indus,
Founded vineyards and
Tamed the wrath of nations.

Yet some sense of shame
Keeps me from comparing
Worldly men to you. And of course
I know who sired you, your Father,
The very one who

For he never reigns alone.

* * *

Es hänget aber an Einem
Die Liebe. Diesesmal
Ist nemlich von eigenen Herzen
Zu sehr gegangen der Gesang,
Gut machen will ich den Fehl
Wenn ich noch andere singe.
Nie treff ich, wie ich wünsche,
Das Maas. Ein Gott weiß aber
Wenn kommet, was ich wünsche das Beste.
Denn wie der Meister
Gewandelt auf Erden
Ein gefangener Aar,

Und viele, die
Ihn sahen, fürchteten sich,
Dieweil sein Äußerstes that
Der Vater und sein Bestes unter
Den Menschen wirkete wirklich,
Und sehr betrübt war auch
Der Sohn so lange, bis er
Gen Himmel fuhr in den Lüften,
Dem gleich ist gefangen die Seele der Helden.
Die Dichter müssen auch
Die geistigen weltlich seyn.

* * *

But love clings
To One. This time
The song has come too deep
From my heart,
Let me mend the error
By singing others.
I never achieve the measure
I wish. But a god knows
When the best I wish comes true.
For like the Master
Who wandered the earth,
A captive eagle,

(And many who saw him
Took fright,
While the Father did
His utmost to realize
His best among men,
And the Son was dark
With grief until he rose
To heaven on the breeze),
Like him, heroes' souls are captive.
Poets, too, men of the spirit,
Must keep to the world.

Richard Sieburth

Patmos
Dem Landgrafen von Homburg

Nah ist
Und schwer zu fassen der Gott.
Wo aber Gefahr ist, wächst
Das Rettende auch.
Im Finstern wohnen
Die Adler und furchtlos gehn
Die Söhne der Alpen über den Abgrund weg
Auf leichtgebaueten Brüken.
Drum, da gehäuft sind rings
Die Gipfel der Zeit, und die Liebsten
Nah wohnen, ermattend auf
Getrenntesten Bergen,
So gieb unschuldig Wasser,
O Fittige gieb uns, treuesten Sinns
Hinüberzugehn und wiederzukehren.

So sprach ich, da entführte
Mich schneller, denn ich vermuthet
Und weit, wohin ich nimmer
Zu kommen gedacht, ein Genius mich
Vom eigenen Hauß'. Es dämmerten
Im Zwielicht, da ich gieng
Der schattige Wald
Und die sehnsüchtigen Bäche
Der Heimath; nimmer kannt' ich die Länder;
Doch bald, in frischem Glanze,
Geheimnißvoll
Im goldenen Rauche, blühte
Schnellaufgewachsen,
Mit Schritten der Sonne,
Mit tausend Gipfeln duftend,

Mir Asia auf, und geblendet sucht'
Ich eines, das ich kennete, denn ungewohnt
War ich der breiten Gassen, wo herab

Patmos
For the Landgrave of Homburg

    Near is
And difficult to grasp, the God.
But where danger threatens
That which saves from it also grows.
In gloomy places dwell
The eagles, and fearless over
The chasm walk the sons of the Alps
On bridges lightly built.
Therefore, since round about
Are heaped the summits of Time
And the most loved live near, growing faint
On mountains most separate,
Give us innocent water,
O pinions give us, with minds most faithful
To cross over and to return.

    So I spoke, when more swiftly
Than ever I had expected,
And far as I never thought
I should come, a Genius carried me
From my own house. There glimmered
In twilight, as I went,
The shadowy wood
And the yearning streams of
My homeland; no longer I knew those regions;
But soon, in a radiance fresh,
Mysteriously,
In the golden haze,
Quickly grown up,
With strides of the sun,
And fragrant with a thousand peaks,

    Now Asia burst into flower for me, and dazzled
I looked for one thing there I might know, being unaccustomed
To those wide streets where down

Vom Tmolus fährt
Der goldgeschmükte Pactol
Und Taurus stehet und Messogis,
Und voll von Blumen der Garten,
Ein stilles Feuer; aber im Lichte
Blüht hoch der silberne Schnee;
Und Zeug unsterblichen Lebens
An unzugangbaren Wänden
Uralt der Epheu wächst und getragen sind
Von lebenden Säulen, Cedern und Lorbeern
Die feierlichen,
Die göttlichgebauten Palläste.

    Es rauschen aber um Asias Thore
Hinziehend da und dort
In ungewisser Meeresebene
Der schattenlosen Straßen genug,
Doch kennt die Inseln der Schiffer.
Und da ich hörte
Der nahegelegenen eine
Sei Patmos,
Verlangte mich sehr,
Dort einzukehren und dort
Der dunkeln Grotte zu nahn.
Denn nicht, wie Cypros,
Die quellenreiche, oder
Der anderen eine
Wohnt herrlich Patmos,

    Gastfreundlich aber ist
Im ärmeren Hauße
Sie dennoch
Und wenn vom Schiffbruch oder klagend
Um die Heimath oder
Den abgeschiedenen Freund
Ihr nahet einer
Der Fremden, hört sie es gern, und ihre Kinder
Die Stimmen des heißen Hains,

From Tmolus drives
The golden-bedded Pactolus,
And Taurus stands, and Messogis,
And full of flowers the garden,
A quiet fire; but in the light, high up
There blossoms the silver snow;
And, witness to life immortal,
On inaccessible walls
Pristine the ivy grows, and supported
On living pillars, cedars and laurels,
There stand the festive,
The palaces built by gods.

But around Asia's gates there murmur,
Extending this way and that
In the uncertain plain of the sea,
Shadowless roads enough;
Yet the boatman knows the islands.
And when I heard
That of the near islands one
Was Patmos,
I greatly desired
There to be lodged, and there
To approach the dark grotto.
For not like Cyprus,
The rich in wellsprings,
Nor any of the others
Magnificently does Patmos dwell,

Hospitable nonetheless
In her poorer house
She is,
And when, after shipwreck or lamenting for
His homeland or else for
The friend departed from him,
A stranger draws near
To her, she is glad to hear it, and her children,
The voices of the hot noonday copse,

Und wo der Sand fällt, und sich spaltet
Des Feldes Fläche, die Laute
Sie hören ihn und liebend tönt
Es wieder von den Klagen des Manns. So pflegte
Sie einst des gottgeliebten,
Des Sehers, der in seeliger Jugend war

   Gegangen mit
Dem Sohne des Höchsten, unzertrennlich, denn
Es liebte der Gewittertragende die Einfalt
Des Jüngers und es sahe der achtsame Mann
Das Angesicht des Gottes genau,
Da, beim Geheimnisse des Weinstoks, sie
Zusammensaßen, zu der Stunde des Gastmals,
Und in der großen Seele, ruhigahnend den Tod
Aussprach der Herr und die lezte Liebe, denn nie genug
Hatt' er von Güte zu sagen
Der Worte, damals, und zu erheitern, da
Ers sahe, das Zürnen der Welt.
Denn alles ist gut. Drauf starb er. Vieles wäre
Zu sagen davon. Und es sahn ihn, wie er siegend blikte
Den Freudigsten die Freunde noch zulezt,

   Doch trauerten sie, da nun
Es Abend worden, erstaunt,
Denn Großentschiedenes hatten in der Seele
Die Männer, aber sie liebten unter der Sonne
Das Leben und lassen wollten sie nicht
Vom Angesichte des Herrn
Und der Heimath. Eingetrieben war,
Wie Feuer im Eisen, das, und ihnen gieng
Zur Seite der Schatte des Lieben.
Drum sandt' er ihnen
Den Geist, und freilich bebte
Das Haus und die Wetter Gottes rollten
Ferndonnernd über
Die ahnenden Häupter, da, schwersinnend
Versammelt waren die Todeshelden,

And where the sand falls, and the field's
Flat surface cracks, the sounds—
These hear him, and lovingly all is loud
With the man's re-echoed lament. So once
She tended the God-beloved,
The seer who in blessèd youth

   Had walked with
The son of the Highest, inseparable, for
The bearer of thunder loved the disciple's
Ingenuousness, and the attentive man
Saw the face of the God exactly
When over the mystery of the vine
They sat together at the hour of the communal meal
And in his great soul, calmly foreknowing,
The Lord pronounced death and the ultimate love, for never
He could find words enough
To say about kindness, then, and to soothe, when
He saw it, the wrath of the world.
For all things are good. After that he died. Much could
Be said of it. And the friends at the very last
Saw him, the gladdest, looking up triumphant,

   Yet they were sad, now that
The evening had come, amazed,
For the souls of these men contained
Things greatly predetermined, but under the sun they loved
This life and were loath to part from
The visible face of the Lord
And their homeland. Driven in,
Like fire into iron, was this, and beside them
The loved one's shadow walked.
Therefore he sent them
The Spirit, and mightily trembled
The house, and God's thunderstorms rolled
Distantly rumbling above
Their heads foreknowledge bowed, when deep in thought
Assembled were the heroes of death,

Izt, da er scheidend
Noch einmal ihnen erschien.
Denn izt erlosch der Sonne Tag
Der Königliche und zerbrach
Den geradestralenden,
Den Zepter, göttlichleidend, von selbst,
Denn wiederkommen sollt es
Zu rechter Zeit. Nicht wär es gut
Gewesen, später, und schroffabbrechend, untreu,
Der Menschen Werk, und Freude war es
Von nun an,
Zu wohnen in liebender Nacht, und bewahren
In einfältigen Augen, unverwandt
Abgründe der Weisheit. Und es grünen
Tief an den Bergen auch lebendige Bilder,

Doch furchtbar ist, wie da und dort
Unendlich hin zerstreut das Lebende Gott.
Denn schon das Angesicht
Der theuern Freunde zu lassen
Und fernhin über die Berge zu gehn
Allein, wo zweifach
Erkannt, einstimmig
War himmlischer Geist; und nicht geweissagt war es, sondern
Die Loken ergriff es, gegenwärtig,
Wenn ihnen plözlich
Ferneilend zurük blikte
Der Gott und schwörend,
Damit er halte, wie an Seilen golden
Gebunden hinfort
Das Böse nennend, sie die Hände sich reichten—

Wenn aber stirbt alsdenn
An dem am meisten
Die Schönheit hieng, daß an der Gestalt
Ein Wunder war und die Himmlischen gedeutet
Auf ihn, und wenn, ein Räthsel ewig füreinander
Sie sich nicht fassen können

Now that, departing,
Once more he appeared to them.
For now the kingly one extinguished
The day of the sun and broke
The straightly beaming, the scepter,
Divinely suffering, yet of his own free will,
For it was to come back when
The time was due. To have done so later
Would not have been good, and the work of men
Abruptly broken off, disloyally, and from now on
A joy it was
To dwell in loving Night and in fixed,
Ingenuous eyes to preserve
Abysses of wisdom. And low down at
The foot of mountains, too, will living images thrive,

Yet dreadful it is how here and there
Unendingly God disperses whatever lives.
For only to part from the sight
Of their dear friends
And far across the mountains to go
Alone, when doubly
Perceived, heavenly spirit before had been
Unanimous; and not predicted was this,
But seized them by the hair, on the instant,
When suddenly the God
Far off in haste looked back
At them, and vowing,
So that he would stay, from now on goldenly
Bound fast as to ropes,
Calling the evil by name, they linked hands—

But when thereupon he dies
To whom beauty most adhered, so that
A miracle was wrought in his person and
The Heavenly had pointed at him,
And when, an enigma to one another
For ever, they cannot understand

Einander, die zusammenlebten
Im Gedächtniß, und nicht den Sand nur oder
Die Weiden es hinwegnimmt und die Tempel
Ergreifft, wenn die Ehre
Des Halbgotts und der Seinen
Verweht und selber sein Angesicht
Der Höchste wendet
Darob, daß nirgend ein
Unsterbliches mehr am Himmel zu sehn ist oder
Auf grüner Erde, was ist diß?

Es ist der Wurf des Säemanns, wenn er faßt
Mit der Schaufel den Waizen,
Und wirft, dem Klaren zu, ihn schwingend über die Tenne.
Ihm fällt die Schaale vor den Füßen, aber
Ans Ende kommet das Korn,
Und nicht ein Übel ists, wenn einiges
Verloren gehet und von der Rede
Verhallet der lebendige Laut,
Denn göttliches Werk auch gleichet dem unsern,
Nicht alles will der Höchste zumal.
Zwar Eisen träget der Schacht,
Und glühende Harze der Aetna,
So hätt' ich Reichtum,
Ein Bild zu bilden, und ähnlich
Zu schaun, wie er gewesen, den Christ,

Wenn aber einer spornte sich selbst,
Und traurig redend, unterweges, da ich wehrlos wäre
Mich überfiele, daß ich staunt' und von dem Gotte
Das Bild nachahmen möcht' ein Knecht—
Im Zorne sichtbar sah' ich einmal
Des Himmels Herrn, nicht, daß ich seyn sollt etwas, sondern
Zu lernen. Gütig sind sie, ihr Verhaßtestes aber ist,
So lange sie herrschen, das Falsche, und es gilt
Dann Menschliches unter Menschen nicht mehr.
Denn sie nicht walten, es waltet aber
Unsterblicher Schiksaal und es wandelt ihr Werk

One another who lived together
Conjoined by remembrance, and not only
The sand or the willows it takes away,
And seizes the temples, when even
The demigod's honor and that of his friends
Is blown away by the wind, and the Highest
Himself averts his face
Because nowhere now
An immortal is to be seen in the skies or
On our green earth, what is this?

   It is the sower's cast when he scoops up
The wheat in his shovel
And throws it, towards clear space, swinging it over the thrashing-
   floor.
The husk falls at his feet, but
The grain reaches its end,
And there's no harm if some of it
Is lost, and of the speech
The living sound dies away,
For the work of gods, too, is like our own,
Not all things at once does the Highest intend.
The pit bears iron, though,
And glowing resins Etna,
And so I should have wealth
With which to form an image and see
The Christ as he truly was,

   But if someone spurred himself on
And, talking sadly, on the road, when I was
Defenseless, attacked me, so that amazed I tried
To copy the God's own image, I, a servant—
In anger visible once I saw
The Lord of Heaven, not that I should be something, but
To learn. Benign they are, but what they most abhor,
While their reign lasts, is falsehood, and then
What's human no longer counts among human kind.
For they do not govern, the fate

Von selbst, und eilend geht es zu Ende.
Wenn nemlich höher gehet himmlischer
Triumphgang, wird genennet, der Sonne gleich
Von Starken der frohlokende Sohn des Höchsten,

   Ein Loosungszeichen, und hier ist der Stab
Des Gesanges, niederwinkend,
Denn nichts is gemein. Die Todten weket
Er auf, die noch gefangen nicht
Vom Rohen sind. Es warten aber
Der scheuen Augen viele
Zu schauen das Licht. Nicht wollen
Am scharfen Strale sie blühn,
Wiewohl den Muth der goldene Zaum hält.
Wenn aber, als
Von schwellenden Augenbraunen
Der Welt vergessen
Stilleuchtende Kraft aus heiliger Schrift fällt, mögen
Der Gnade sich freuend, sie
Am stillen Blike sich üben.

   Und wenn die Himmlischen jezt
So, wie ich glaube, mich lieben
Wie viel mehr Dich,
Denn Eines weiß ich,
Daß nemlich der Wille
Des ewigen Vaters viel
Dir gilt. Still ist sein Zeichen
Am donnernden Himmel. Und Einer stehet darunter
Sein Leben lang. Denn noch lebt Christus.
Es sind aber die Helden, seine Söhne
Gekommen all und heilige Schriften
Von ihm und den Bliz erklären
Die Thaten der Erde bis izt,
Ein Wettlauf unaufhaltsam. Er ist aber dabei. Denn seine
                                        Werke sind
Ihm all bewußt von jeher.

It is of immortals that governs, and their work
Proceeds by its own force and hurrying seeks its end.
For when heavenly triumph goes higher
The jubilant son of the Highest
Is called like the sun by the strong,

    A secret token, and here is the wand
Of song, signaling downward,
For nothing is common. The dead
He reawakens whom coarseness has not
Made captive yet. But many timid eyes
Are waiting to see the light.
They are reluctant to flower
Beneath the searing beam, though it is
The golden bridle that curbs their courage.
But when, as if
By swelling eyebrows made
Oblivious of the world
A quietly shining strength falls from holy scripture,
Rejoicing in grace, they
May practice upon the quiet gaze.

    And if the Heavenly now
Love me as I believe,
How much more you
They surely love,
For one thing I know:
The eternal Father's will
Means much to you. Now silent is
His sign on thundering heaven. And there is one who stands
Beneath it his whole life long. For Christ lives yet.
But all the heroes, his sons,
Have come, and holy scriptures
About him, and lightning is explained by
The deeds of the world until now,
A race that cannot be stopped. But he is present in it. For known
To him are all his works from the beginning.

Zu lang, zu lang schon ist
Die Ehre der Himmlischen unsichtbar.
Denn fast die Finger müssen sie
Uns führen und schmählich
Entreißt das Herz uns eine Gewalt.
Denn Opfer will der Himmlischen jedes,
Wenn aber eines versäumt ward,
Nie hat es Gutes gebracht.
Wir haben gedienet der Mutter Erd'
Und haben jüngst dem Sonnenlichte gedient,
Unwissend, der Vater aber liebt,
Der über allen waltet,
Am meisten, daß gepfleget werde
Der veste Buchstab, und bestehendes gut
Gedeutet. Dem folgt deutscher Gesang.

Patmos
Bruchstücke der späteren Fassung

Voll Güt' ist; keiner aber fasset
Allein Gott.
Wo aber Gefahr ist, wächst
Das Rettende auch.
Im Finstern wohnen
Die Adler, und Furchtlos gehn
Die Söhne der Alpen über den Abgrund weg
Auf leichtgebaueten Brüken.
Drum, da gehäuft sind rings, um Klarheit,
Die Gipfel der Zeit,
Und die Liebsten nahe wohnen, ermattend auf
Getrenntesten Bergen,
So gieb unschuldig Wasser,
O Fittige gieb uns, treuesten Sinns
Hinüberzugehn und wiederzukehren.

Too long, too long now
The honor of the Heavenly has been invisible.
For almost they must guide
Our fingers, and shamefully
A power is wresting our hearts from us.
For every one of the Heavenly wants sacrifices, and
When one of these was omitted
No good ever came of it.
We have served Mother Earth
And lately have served the sunlight,
Unwittingly, but what the Father
Who reigns over all loves most
Is that the solid letter
Be given scrupulous care, and the existing
Be well interpreted. This German song observes.

Michael Hamburger

Patmos
Fragments of the Later Version

Most kind is; but no one by himself
Can grasp God.
But where danger threatens
That which saves from it also grows.
In gloomy places dwell
The eagles, and fearless over
The chasm walk the sons of the Alps
On bridges lightly built.
Therefore, since round about are heaped, around clearness,
The summits of Time,
And the most loved live near, growing faint
On mountains most separate,
Give us innocent water,
O pinions give us, with minds most faithful
To cross over and to return.

So sprach ich, da entführte
Mich künstlicher, denn ich vermuthet
Und weit, wohin ich nimmer
Zu kommen gedacht, ein Genius mich
Vom eigenen Hauß'. Es kleideten sich
Im Zwielicht, Menschen ähnlich, da ich **gieng**
Der schattige Wald
Und die sehnsüchtigen Bäche
Der Heimath; nimmer kannt' ich die Länder.
Viel aber mitgelitten haben wir, viel Maale. So
In frischem Glanze, geheimnißvoll,
In goldenem Rauche blühte
Schnellaufgewachsen,
Mit Schritten der Sonne,
Von tausend Tischen duftend, jezt,

Mir Asia auf und geblendet ganz
Sucht' eins ich, das ich kennete, denn ungewohnt
War ich der breiten Gassen, wo herab
Vom Tmolus fährt
Der goldgeschmükte Pactol
Und Taurus stehet und Messogis,
Und schläfrig fast von Blumen der Garten,

O Insel des Lichts!
Denn wenn erloschen ist der Ruhm die Augenlust und gehalten
   nicht mehr
Von Menschen, schattenlos, die Pfade zweifeln und die Bäume,
Und Reiche, das Jugendland der Augen sind vergangen
Athletischer
Im Ruin,   und Unschuld angeborne
Zerrissen ist. Von Gott aus nemlich kommt gediegen
Und gehet das Gewissen, Offenbarung, die Hand des Herrn
Reich winkt aus richtendem Himmel, dann und eine Zeit ist
Untheilbar Gesez, und Amt, und die Hände
Zu erheben, das, und das Niederfallen
Böser Gedanken, los, zu ordnen. Grausam nemlich hasset

So I spoke when more ingeniously
Than ever I had expected
And far as I never thought
I should come, a Genius carried me
From my own house. There clothed themselves,
Like men, in the twilight, as I went,
The shadowy wood
And the yearning streams of
My homeland; no longer I knew those regions.
Yet much we have suffered with them, many times.
So, in a radiance fresh, mysteriously,
In the golden haze
Quickly grown up,
With strides of the sun,
And fragrant with a thousand tables,

Now, Asia burst into flower for me, and wholly dazzled
I looked for one thing there I might know, being unaccustomed
To those wide streets where down
From Tmolus drives
The golden-bedded Pactolus,
And Taurus stands, and Messogis,
And drowsy almost with flowers the garden,

O island of light!
For when extinguished is fame, the delight in seeing, and no longer
    maintained
By human kind, shadowless, the paths succumb to doubt, and the
    trees,
And kingdoms, the youthful land of eyes, are perished,
More athletic
In ruin,   and inborn innocence
Is torn to shreds. For from God unalloyed
Does conscience come and go, revelation, the hand of the Lord
Richly beckons from judging Heaven, then and for a time there
Is indivisible law, and office, and hands to
Be raised, both this and to control
The falling of evil thoughts, loose. For cruelly

Allwissende Stirnen Gott. Rein aber bestand
Auf ungebundnem Boden Johannes. Wenn einer
Für irrdisches prophetisches Wort erklärt

      Vom Jordan und von Nazareth
Und fern vom See, an Capernaum,
Und Galiläa die Lüfte, und von Cana.
Eine Weile bleib ich, sprach er. Also mit Tropfen
Stillt er das Seufzen des Lichts, das durstigem Wild
War ähnlich in den Tagen, als um Syrien
Jammert der getödteten Kindlein heimatliche
Anmuth im Sterben, und das Haupt
Des Täuffers gepflükt, war unverwelklicher Schrift gleich
Sichtbar auf weilender Schüssel. Wie Feuer
Sind Stimmen Gottes. Schwer ists aber
Im Großen zu behalten das Große.
Nich eine Waide. Daß einer
Bleibet im Anfang. Jezt aber
Geht dieses wieder, wie sonst.

     Johannes. Christus. Diesen möcht'
Ich singen, gleich dem Herkules, oder
Der Insel, welche vestgehalten und gerettet, erfrischend
Die benachbarte mit kühlen Meereswassern aus der Wüste
Der Fluth, der weiten, Peleus. Das geht aber
Nicht. Anders ists ein Schiksaal. Wundervoller.
Reicher, zu singen. Unabsehlich
Seit jenem die Fabel. Und jezt
Möcht' ich die Fahrt der Edelleute nach
Jerusalem, und das Leiden irrend in Canossa,
Und den Heinrich singen. Daß aber
Der Muth nicht selber mich aussezze. Begreiffen müssen
Diß wir zuvor. Wie Morgenluft sind nemlich die Nahmen
Seit Christus. Werden Träume. Fallen, wie Irrtum
Auf das Herz und tödtend, wenn nicht einer

God hates omniscient brows. But pure
On a site unbound did John remain. When someone
Declares that a prophetic word is earthly

From Jordan and from Nazareth
And far from the lake, at Capernaum,
And Galilee the breezes, and from Canaan.
A little while I shall stay, he said. So with drops
He quenched the sighing of the light that was
Like thirsty wild beasts in those days, when for Syria
Lamented the native grace in dying of
Small children killed, and the Baptist's head,
Just picked, was visible like an unwithering script
On the abiding platter. Like fire
Are voices of God. Yet it is hard
In great events to preserve what is great.
Not a pasture. So that one shall
Abide in the beginning. But now
This goes on again, as before.

John. Christ. This latter now I wish
To sing, like Hercules or the island which
Was held and saved, refreshing
The neighbouring one with cool sea waters drawn
From ocean's desert, the vast, Peleus. But that's
Impossible. Differently it is a fate. More marvelous.
More rich to sing. Immeasurable
The fable ever since. And now
I wish to sing the journey of the nobles to
Jerusalem, and anguish wandering at Canossa,
And Heinrich himself. If only
My very courage does not expose me. This first we
Must understand. For like morning air are the names
Since Christ. Become dreams. Fall on the heart
Like error, and killing, if one does not

Erwäget, was sie sind und begreift.
Es sah aber der achtsame Mann
Das Angesicht des Gottes,
Damals, da, beim Geheimnisse des Weinstoks sie
Zusammensaßen, zu der Stunde des Gastmals,
Und in der großen Seele, wohlauswählend, den Tod
Aussprach der Herr, und die lezte Liebe, denn nie genug
Hatt er, von Güte, zu sagen
Der Worte, damals, und zu bejahn bejahendes. Aber sein Licht war
Tod. Denn karg ist das Zürnen der Welt.
Das aber erkannt' er. Alles ist gut. Drauf starb er.
Es sahen aber, gebükt, deß ungeachtet, vor Gott die Gestalt
Des Verläugnenden, wie wenn
Ein Jahrhundert sich biegt, nachdenklich, in der Freude der
    Wahrheit
Noch zulezt die Freunde,

    Doch trauerten sie, da nun
Es Abend worden. Nemlich rein
Zu seyn, ist Geschik, ein Leben, das ein Herz hat,
Vor solchem Angesicht', und dauert über die Hälfte.
Zu meiden aber ist viel. Zu viel aber
Der Liebe, wo Anbetung ist,
Ist gefahrreich, triffet am meisten. Jene wollten aber
Vom Angesichte des Herrn
Nicht lassen und der Heimath. Eingeboren
Wie Feuer war in dem Eisen das, und ihnen
Zur Seite gieng, wie eine Seuche, der Schatte des Lieben.
Drum sandt er ihnen
Den Geist, und freilich bebte
Das Haus und die Wetter Gottes rollten
Ferndonnernd, Männer schaffend, wie wenn Drachenzähne,
                              prächtigen Schiksaals,

Consider what they are and understand.
But the attentive man saw
The face of God,
At that time, when over the mystery of the vine
They sat together, at the hour of the communal meal,
And in his great soul, carefully choosing, the Lord
Pronounced death, and the ultimate love, for never
He could find words enough
To say about kindness, then, and to affirm the affirmative. But his
    light was
Death. For niggardly is the wrath of the world.
Yet this he recognized. All is good. Thereupon he died.
But nevertheless, bowed down, the friends at the very last
Before God saw the denier's presence, as when
A century bends, thoughtfully, in
The joy of truth,

    Yet they were sad, now that
The evening had come. For to
Be pure is a skill, a life that has a heart, in
The presence of such a face, and outlasts the middle.
But much is to be avoided. Too much
Of love, though, where there is idolatry,
Is dangerous, strikes home most. But those men were loath
To part from the face of the Lord
And from their homeland. Inborn
Like fire in iron was this, and beside them
Walked, like a plague, the loved one's shadow.
Therefore he sent them
The Spirit, and mightily trembled
The house and God's thunderstorms rolled
Distantly rumbling, creating men, as when dragons' teeth,
                                        of glorious fate,

Michael Hamburger

Andenken

Der Nordost wehet,
Der liebste unter den Winden
Mir, weil er feurigen Geist
Und gute Fahrt verheißet den Schiffern.
Geh aber nun und grüße
Die schöne Garonne,
Und die Gärten von Bourdeaux
Dort, wo am scharfen Ufer
Hingehet der Steg und in den Strom
Tief fällt der Bach, darüber aber
Hinschauet ein edel Paar
Von Eichen und Silberpappeln;

Noch denket das mir wohl und wie
Die breiten Gipfel neiget
Der Ulmwald, über die Mühl',
Im Hofe aber wächset ein Feigenbaum.
An Feiertagen gehn
Die braunen Frauen daselbst
Auf seidnen Boden,
Zur Märzenzeit,
Wenn gleich ist Nacht und Tag,
Und über langsamen Stegen,
Von goldenen Träumen schwer,
Einwiegende Lüfte ziehen.

Es reiche aber,
Des dunkeln Lichtes voll,
Mir einer den duftenden Becher,
Damit ich ruhen möge; denn süß
Wär' unter Schatten der Schlummer.
Nicht ist es gut,
Seellos von sterblichen
Gedanken zu seyn. Doch gut
Ist ein Gespräch und zu sagen
Des Herzens Meinung, zu hören viel
Von Tagen der Lieb',
Und Thaten, welche geschehen.

Remembrance

The northeasterly blows in,
My favorite among winds,
Since it promises fire
And safe passage to sailors.
But go now and greet
The lovely Garonne
And the gardens of Bordeaux,
There, where the path cuts
Along the shore and the stream dives
Riverward, but a noble pair
Of oaks and white poplars
Looks on from above;

All this still comes to mind and how
The broad tops of elms
Bend over the mill,
But a figtree is growing in the courtyard.
There, on feastdays,
Brown women walk
The silky ground,
Toward March,
When night and day are equal,
And down leisurely paths
Heavy with golden dreams,
Drift lulling breezes.

But someone reach me
A fragrant cupful
Of dark light, that
I might rest; it would be sweet
To drowse in the shade.
It is no good
To let mortal thoughts
Rob you of your soul. Yet
Dialogue is good and to speak
The heart, to hear all
About the days of love
And deeds that have taken place.

Wo aber sind die Freunde? Bellarmin
Mit dem Gefährten? Mancher
Trägt Scheue, an die Quelle zu gehn;
Es beginnet nemlich der Reichtum
Im Meere. Sie,
Wie Mahler, bringen zusammen
Das Schöne der Erd' und verschmähn
Den geflügelten Krieg nicht, und
Zu wohnen einsam, jahrlang, unter
Dem entlaubten Mast, wo nicht die Nacht durchglänzen
Die Feiertage der Stadt,
Und Saitenspiel und eingeborener Tanz nicht.

Nun aber sind zu Indiern
Die Männer gegangen,
Dort an der luftigen Spiz'
An Traubenbergen, wo herab
Die Dordogne kommt,
Und zusammen mit der prächt'gen
Garonne meerbreit
Ausgehet der Strom. Es nehmet aber
Und giebt Gedächtniß die See,
Und die Lieb' auch heftet fleißig die Augen,
Was bleibet aber, stiften die Dichter.

Der Ister

Jezt komme, Feuer!
Begierig sind wir
Zu schauen den Tag,
Und wenn die Prüfung
Ist durch die Knie gegangen,
Mag einer spüren das Waldgeschrei.

But where are my friends? Bellarmin
With his companion? There are those
Who shy from the source;
Since riches begin
At sea. Like
Painters, they gather
The beauty of the earth, nor refuse
Wings of war or years lived
Alone beneath a mast
Without leaves, where the night is not
Brightened by the feast days of the city,
Nor by lyre or native dances.

But now the men are gone
To the Indies,
From that breezy spit of land
And hillsides of grapes, where
The Dordogne descends
Toward the majestic Garonne
And the two flow out
As one wide sea. But memory
Is taken and given by the ocean,
And the eyes of love do not waver in their gaze,
But poets establish what remains.

Richard Sieburth

The Ister

Now come, fire!
We are impatient
To look upon Day,
And when the trial
Has passed through the knees
One may perceive the cries in the wood.

Wir singen aber vom Indus her
Fernangekommen und
Vom Alpheus, lange haben
Das Schikliche wir gesucht,
Nicht ohne Schwingen mag
Zum Nächsten einer greifen
Geradezu
Und kommen auf die andere Seite.
Hier aber wollen wir bauen.
Denn Ströme machen urbar
Das Land. Wenn nemlich Kräuter wachsen
Und an denselben gehn
Im Sommer zu trinken die Thiere,
So gehn auch Menschen daran.

  Man nennet aber diesen den Ister.
Schön wohnt er. Es brennet der Säulen Laub,
Und reget sich. Wild stehn
Sie aufgerichtet, untereinander; darob
Ein zweites Maas, springt vor
Von Felsen das Dach. So wundert
Mich nicht, daß er
Den Herkules zu Gaste geladen,
Fernglänzend, am Olympos drunten,
Da der, sich Schatten zu suchen
Vom heißen Isthmos kam,
Denn voll des Muthes waren
Daselbst sie, es bedarf aber, der Geister wegen,
Der Kühlung auch. Darum zog jener lieber
An die Wasserquellen hieher und gelben Ufer,
Hoch duftend oben, und schwarz
Vom Fichtenwald, wo in den Tiefen
Ein Jäger gern lustwandelt
Mittags, und Wachstum hörbar ist
An harzigen Bäumen des Isters,

But, as for us, we sing from the Indus,
Arrived from afar, and
From the Alpheus, long we
Have sought what is fitting,
Not without wings may one
Reach out for that which is nearest
Directly
And get to the other side.
But here we wish to build.
For rivers make arable
The land. For when herbs are growing
And to the same in summer
The animals go to drink,
There too will human kind go.

    This one, however, is called the Ister.
Beautifully he dwells. The pillars' foliage burns,
And stirs. Wildly they stand
Supporting one another; above,
A second measure, juts out
The roof of rocks. No wonder, therefore,
I say, this river
Invited Hercules,
Distantly gleaming, down by Olympus,
When he, to look for shadows,
Came up from the sultry isthmus,
For full of courage they were
In that place, but, because of the spirits,
There's need of coolness too. That is why that hero
Preferred to come here to the wellsprings and yellow banks,
Highly fragrant on top, and black
With fir woods, in whose depths
A huntsman loves to amble
At noon, and growth is audible
In resinous trees of the Ister,

Der scheinet aber fast
Rükwärts zu gehen und
Ich mein, er müsse kommen
Von Osten.
Vieles wäre
Zu sagen davon. Und warum hängt er
An den Bergen gerad? Der andre
Der Rhein ist seitwärts
Hinweggegangen. Umsonst nicht gehn
Im Troknen die Ströme. Aber wie? Ein Zeichen braucht es
Nichts anderes, schlecht und recht, damit es Sonn
Und Mond trag' im Gemüth', untrennbar,
Und fortgeh, Tag und Nacht auch, und
Die Himmlischen warm sich fühlen aneinander.
Darum sind jene auch
Die Freude des Höchsten. Denn wie käm er
Herunter? Und wie Hertha grün,
Sind sie die Kinder des Himmels. Aber allzugedultig
Scheint der mir, nicht
Freier, und fast zu spotten. Nemlich wenn

Angehen soll der Tag
In der Jugend, wo er zu wachsen
Anfängt, es treibet ein anderer da
Hoch schon die Pracht, und Füllen gleich
In den Zaum knirscht er, und weithin hören
Das Treiben die Lüfte,
Ist der zufrieden;
Es brauchet aber Stiche der Fels
Und Furchen die Erd',
Unwirthbar wär es, ohne Weile;
Was aber jener thuet der Strom,
Weis niemand.

Yet almost this river seems
To travel backwards and
I think it must come from
The East.
Much could
Be said about this. And why does
It cling to the mountains, straight? The other,
The Rhine, has gone away
Sideways. Not for nothing rivers flow
Through dry land. But how? A sign is needed,
Nothing else, plain and honest, so that
Sun and moon it may bear in mind, inseparable,
And go away, day and night no less, and
The Heavenly feel warm one beside the other.
That also is why these are
The joy of the Highest. For how
Would he get down? And like Hertha green
They are the children of Heaven. But all too patient
He seems to me, not
More free, and nearly derisive. For when

Day is due to begin
In youth, where it starts
To grow, another already there
Drives high the splendour, and like foals
He grinds the bit, and far off the breezes
Can hear the commotion,
If he is contented;
But the rock needs incisions
And the earth needs furrows,
Would be desolate else, unabiding;
Yet what that one does, the river,
Nobody knows.

Michael Hamburger

Mnemosyne

Ein Zeichen sind wir, deutungslos
Schmerzlos sind wir und haben fast
Die Sprache in der Fremde verloren.
Wenn nemlich über Menschen
Ein Streit ist an dem Himmel und gewaltig
Die Monde gehn, so redet
Das Meer und Ströme müssen
Den Pfad sich suchen. Zweifellos
Ist aber Einer, der
Kann täglich es ändern. Kaum bedarf er
Gesez. Und es tönet das Blatt und Eichbäume wehn dann neben
Den Firnen. Denn nicht vermögen
Die Himmlischen alles. Nemlich es reichen
Die Sterblichen eh' an den Abgrund. Also wendet es sich, das Echo
Mit diesen. Lang ist
Die Zeit, es ereignet sich aber
Das Wahre.

Wie aber liebes? Sonnenschein
Am Boden sehen wir und trokenen Staub
Und tief mit Schatten die Wälder und es blühet
An Dächern der Rauch, bei alter Krone
Der Thürme, friedsam; gut sind nemlich,
Hat gegenredend die Seele
Ein Himmlisches verwundet, die Tageszeichen.
Denn Schnee, wie Majenblumen
Das Edelmüthige, wo
Es seie, bedeutend, glänzet auf der grünen Wiese
Der Alpen, hälftig
Da, vom Kreuze redend, das
Gesezt ist unterwegs einmal
Gestorbenen, auf hoher Straß'
Ein Wandersmann geht zornig,
Fernahnend mit
Dem andern, aber was ist diß?

Mnemosyne

A sign we are, without meaning
Without pain we are and have nearly
Lost our language in foreign lands,
For when the heavens quarrel
Over humans and moons proceed
In force, the sea
Speaks out and rivers must find
Their way. But there is One,
Without doubt, who
Can change this any day. He needs
No law. The rustle of leaf and then the sway of oaks
Beside glaciers. Not everything
Is in the power of the gods. Mortals would sooner
Reach toward the abyss. With them
The echo turns. Though the time
Be long, truth
Will come to pass.

But what we love? We see sunshine
On the floor and motes of dust
And the shadows of our native woods and smoke
Blooms from rooftops, at peace beside
Turrets' ancient crowns; for the signs
Of day are good if a god has scarred
The soul in response.
Snow, like lilies of the valley,
Signifying a site
Of nobility, half gleams
With the green of the Alpine meadow
Where, talking of a wayside cross
Commemorating the dead,
A traveler climbs in a rage,
Sharing distant premonitions with
The other, but what is this?

Am Feigenbaum ist mein
Achilles mir gestorben,
Und Ajax liegt
An den Grotten der See,
An Bächen, benachbart dem Skamandros.
An Schläfen Sausen ist, nach
Der unbewegten Salamis steter
Gewohnheit, in der Fremd' ist groß
Ajax gestorben.
Patroklos aber in des Königes Harnisch. Und es starben
Noch andere viel. Am Kithäron aber lag
Elevtherä, der Mnemosyne Stadt. Der auch, als
Ablegte den Mantel Gott, das abendliche nachher löste
Die Loken. Himmlische nemlich sind
Unwillig, wenn einer nicht
Die Seele schonend sich
Zusammengenommen, aber er muß doch; dem
Gleich fehlet die Trauer.

Reif sind. . .

Reif sind, in Feuer getaucht, gekochet
Die Frücht und auf der Erde geprüfet und ein Gesez ist
Daß alles hineingeht, Schlangen gleich,
Prophetisch, träumend auf
Den Hügeln des Himmels. Und vieles
Wie auf den Schultern eine
Last von Scheitern ist
Zu behalten. Aber bös sind
Die Pfade. Nemlich unrecht,
Wie Rosse, gehn die gefangenen
Element' und alten
Geseze der Erd. Und immer

By the figtree
My Achilles died,
And Ajax lies
By the grottoes of the sea,
By streams, with Scamandros as neighbor.
In the persisting tradition of Salamis,
Great Ajax died
Of the roar in his temples
And on foreign soil, unlike
Patroclos, dead in king's armor. And many
Others also died. On Kithairon
Lay Eleutherai, city of Mnemosyne. And when
God cast off his cloak, the darkness came to cut
Her lock of hair. For the gods grow
Indignant if a man
Not gather himself to save
His soul, yet he has no choice; like-
Wise, mourning is in error.

Richard Sieburth

The fruits are ripe . . .

The fruits are ripe, dipped in fire, cooked
And tested here on earth, and it is a law,
Prophetic, that all things pass
Like snakes, dreaming on
The hills of heaven. And as
A load of logs upon
The shoulders, there is much
To bear in mind. But the paths
Are evil. For like horses,
The captive elements
And ancient laws
Of the earth go astray. Yet always

Ins Ungebundene gehet eine Sehnsucht. Vieles aber ist
Zu behalten. Und Noth die Treue.
Vorwärts aber und rükwärts wollen wir
Nicht sehn. Uns wiegen lassen, wie
Auf schwankem Kahne der See.

Wenn nemlich der Rebe Saft . . .

Wenn nemlich der Rebe Saft,
Das milde Gewächs suchet Schatten
Und die Traube wächset unter dem kühlen
Gewölbe der Blätter,
Den Männern eine Stärke,
Wohl aber duftend den Jungfraun,
Und Bienen,
Wenn sie, vom Wohlgeruche
Des Frühlings trunken, der Geist
Der Sonne rühret, irren ihr nach
Die Getriebenen, wenn aber
Ein Stral brennt, kehren sie
Mit Gesumm, vielahnend
   darob
  die Eiche rauschet,

The longing to reach beyond bounds. But much
To be retained. And loyalty a must.
But we shall not look forward
Or back. Let ourselves rock, as
On a boat, lapped by the waves.

Richard Sieburth

When the sap . . .

When the sap of the vine,
This gentle plant, seeks out shade
And the grape grows beneath the cool
Vault of leaves,
A source of strength to men
But fragrant to young girls
And bees
When, drunk on the scent
Of Spring, they are stirred
By the spirit of the sun, driven
Erratic in its pursuit, but when
Burnt by a ray, they all veer back
Abuzz, filled with premonition
      above
    The oak tree rustles,

Richard Sieburth

Meinest du es solle gehen . . .

                              meinest du
Es solle gehen,
Wie damals? Nemlich sie wollten stiften
Ein Reich der Kunst. Dabei ward aber
Das Vaterländische von ihnen
Versäumet und erbärmlich gieng
Das Griechenland, das schönste, zu Grunde.
Wohl hat es andere
Bewandtniß jezt.
Es sollten nemlich die Frommen

                              und alle Tage wäre
Das Fest.
                              Also darf nicht
Ein ehrlich Meister

                              und wie mit Diamanten
In die Fenster machte, des Müßiggangs wegen
Mit meinen Fingern, hindert

                              so hat mir
Das Kloster etwas genüzet,

Do you think . . .

                     do you think
Things will go
As they once did? They wanted to found
A kingdom of art. But in the process
Neglected what was native
To them, and Greece, fairest of all,
Went down pitifully.
The case is certainly
Different now.
Indeed the devout should

                     and every day would be
A feast.
                     A respected teacher
Thus should not

                     and as with diamonds
Etched in windows by my idle
Fingers, hinders

                     so the cloister
Was of help to me,

                     Richard Sieburth

Vom Abgrund nemlich . . .

Vom Abgrund nemlich haben
Wir angefangen und gegangen
Dem Leuen gleich, in Zweifel und Ärgerniß,
Denn sinnlicher sind Menschen
In dem Brand
Der Wüste
Lichttrunken und der Thiergeist ruhet
Mit ihnen. Bald aber wird, wie ein Hund, umgehn
In der Hizze meine Stimme auf den Gassen der Gärten
In denen wohnen Menschen
In Frankreich
Der Schöpfer
Frankfurt aber, nach der Gestalt, die
Abdruk ist der Natur zu reden
Des Menschen nemlich, ist der Nabel
Dieser Erde, diese Zeit auch
Ist Zeit, und deutschen Schmelzes.
Ein wilder Hügel aber stehet über dem Abhang
Meiner Gärten. Kirschenbäume. Scharfer Othem aber wehet
Um die Löcher des Felses. Allda bin ich
Alles miteinander. Wunderbar
Aber über Quellen beuget schlank
Ein Nußbaun und   sich. Beere, wie Korall
Hängen an dem Strauche über Röhren von Holz,
Aus denen
Ursprünglich aus Korn, nun aber zu gestehen, bevestigter
        Gesang von Boumen als
Neue Bildung aus der Stadt, wo
Bis zu Schmerzen aber der Nase steigt
Citronengeruch auf und das Öl, aus der Provence, und es haben
        diese
Dankbarkeit mir die Gasgognischen Lande
Gegeben. Gezähmet aber, noch zu sehen, und genährt hat mich
Die Rappierlust und des Festtags gebraten Fleisch
Der Tisch und braune Trauben, braune
                        und mich leset o
Ihr Blüthen von Deutschland, o mein Herz wird
Untrügbarer Krystall an dem
Des Licht sich prüfet wenn   Deutschland

We set out from the abyss . . .

We set out from the abyss
And proceeded like the lion,
Vexed with doubt,
Since men sense more
In the scorch
Of deserts,
Drunk with light, and the spirit of animals
Rests with them. But soon, like a dog in hot weather,
My voice shall amble through the alleys of gardens
In which people live
In France.
The Creator.
But Frankfurt, to speak of man
By nature's stamp upon
The human shape, is the navel
Of this earth, and this age
Is time of German fusion.
A wild hill looms over the slope
Of my gardens. Cherry trees. And sharp breath blows
Through rock's holes. Here I am everything
At once. A lovely
Nut tree bends slender
Over springs and   itself. Berries, like coral,
Hang from shrubs over wooden pipes
Out of which
First from grain, now from flowers, fortified song
As new culture from the city, where nostrils
Nearly ache with the rising
Scent of lemon and oil from Provence, such gratitude
Have the lands of Gascogne
Granted me. I have been tamed (still to be seen) and nourished
By love of rapier and festivals' roasted meats,
The table, the brown grapes, brown
                        and you gather me, O
Flowers of Germany, O my heart turns
Into unerring crystal, touchstone
Of light when   Germany

Richard Sieburth

Griechenland
Dritte Fassung

O ihr Stimmen des Geschiks, ihr Wege des Wanderers
Denn an der Schule Blau,
Fernher, am Tosen des Himmels
Tönt wie der Amsel Gesang
Der Wolken heitere Stimmung gut
Gestimmt vom Daseyn Gottes, dem Gewitter.
Und Rufe, wie hinausschauen, zur
Unsterblichkeit und Helden;
Viel sind Erinnerungen. Wo darauf
Tönend, wie des Kalbs Haut
Die Erde, von Verwüstungen her, Versuchungen der Heiligen
Denn anfangs bildet das Werk sich
Großen Gesezen nachgehet, die Wissenschaft
Und Zärtlichkeit und den Himmel breit lauter Hülle nachher
Erscheinend singen Gesangeswolken.
Denn fest ist der Erde
Nabel. Gefangen nemlich in Ufern von Gras sind
Die Flammen und die allgemeinen
Elemente. Lauter Besinnung aber oben lebt der Aether. Aber
     silbern
An reinen Tagen
Ist das Licht. Als Zeichen der Liebe
Veilchenblau die Erde.
Zu Geringem auch kann kommen
Großer Anfang.
Alltag aber wunderbar zu lieb den Menschen
Gott an hat ein Gewand.
Und Erkentnissen verberget sich sein Angesicht
Und deket die Lüfte mit Kunst.
Und Luft und Zeit dekt
Den Schröklichen, daß zu sehr nicht eins
Ihn liebet mit Gebeten oder
Die Seele. Denn lange schon steht offen
Wie Blätter, zu lernen, oder Linien und Winkel
Die Natur

Greece
Third Version

O you voices of fate, you ways of the wanderer!
For amid the blue of the school,
From afar, amid the uproar of heaven
Rings out like the blackbird's song
The clouds' happy mood, well
Tempered by the existence of God, the thunderstorm.
And calls, like looking out, for
Immortality and heroes;
Memories are many. Where ringing out
On it, as on the calf's hide,
The earth, proceeding from devastations, temptations of the saints,
For at the beginning the work is shaped,
Pursues great laws, and knowledge
And tenderness and the width of heaven, all wrapping, later
    becoming
Visible, sing clouds of song.
For firmly fixed is the navel
Of Earth. For captive in banks of grass are
The flames and the common
Elements. But above, all reflection, lives Aether. But silver
On pure days
Is light. As a sign of love
Violet-blue the earth.
A great beginning can come
Even to humble things.
Everyday but marvellous, for the sake of men,
God has put on a garment.
And his face is withheld from the knowing
And covers the winds with art.
And air and time cover
The terrible one, so that not too much a man
With prayers shall love him.
Or else the soul. For long already like leaves,
To learn, or like lines and angles,
Nature lies open

Und gelber die Sonnen und die Monde,
Zu Zeiten aber
Wenn ausgehn will die alte Bildung
Der Erde, bei Geschichten nemlich
Gewordnen, muthig fechtenden, wie auf Höhen führet
Die Erde Gott. Ungemessene Schritte
Begränzt er aber, aber wie Blüthen golden thun
Der Seele Kräfte dann der Seele Verwandtschaften sich zusammen,
Daß lieber auf Erden
Die Schönheit wohnt und irgend ein Geist
Gemeinschaftlicher sich zu Menschen gesellet.

Süß ists, dann unter hohen Schatten von Bäumen
Und Hügeln zu wohnen, sonnig, wo der Weg ist
Gepflastert zur Kirche. Reisenden aber, wem,
Aus Lebensliebe, messend immerhin,
Die Füße gehorchen, blühn
Schöner die Wege, wo das Land

Der Frühling

Wenn aus der Tiefe kommt der Frühling in das Leben,
Es wundert sich der Mensch, und neue Worte streben
Aus Geistigkeit, die Freude kehret wieder
Und festlich machen sich Gesang und Lieder.

Das Leben findet sich aus Harmonie der Zeiten,
Daß immerdar den Sinn Natur und Geist geleiten,
Und die Vollkommenheit ist Eines in dem Geiste,
So findet vieles sich, und aus Natur das Meiste.

Mit Unterthänigkeit
Scardanelli.

d. 24 Mai
1758.

And more yellow the suns and the moons,
But at times
When the ancient knowledge of earth is in danger
Of going out, amid histories, that is, grown, come to pass
And boldly fencing, as on high places God
Leads on the Earth. Unmeasured paces, though,
He limits, but like blossoms golden then
The faculties, affinities of the soul consort
So that more willingly
Beauty dwells on earth and one or the other spirit
More communally joins in human affairs.

Sweet it is then to dwell under the high shade
Of trees and hills, sunny, where the road
Is paved to church. To travelers, though,
To him whose feet, from love of life,
Measuring all along, obey him,
More beautifully blossom the roads, where the land

Michael Hamburger

Spring

When springtime from the depth returns to life,
Men are amazed, and from their minds aspire
New words, and happiness once more is rife,
And festive music rings from house and choir.

Life finds itself in seasonal harmonies,
That ever Nature, Spirit might attend our thought,
And *one* within our minds perfection is;
So, most of all from Nature, much to itself is brought.

Your humble and obedient servant
May 24th   Scardanelli
   1758.

Michael Hamburger

Endnotes

In preparing these notes I have drawn on the commentaries of a number of scholars. I am especially indebted to the extensive notes provided by Friedrich Beissner in his *Grosse Stuttgarter Ausgabe* as well as in his smaller Insel Edition (1969), prepared with Jochen Schmidt. I have also made use of the notes in D. E. Sattler's *Frankfurter Ausgabe* and the commentaries published by Middleton, Hamburger, and Sieburth in their respective editions of the poems. The spelling of some Greek and German names varies from translator to translator.

Hyperion

Hölderlin first mentions his plan to write a novel as a student in 1792 and works on various versions of the novel for the next seven years. Schiller publishes a first fragmentary draft in his *Neuer Thalia* in 1794 and on his recommendation the first volume of the final version is published by Cotta in 1797. The second volume follows in 1799. Other versions of the novel exist in fragmentary form, including a verse draft composed in Jena and one entitled "Hyperion's Youth." For his descriptions of Greek landscape Hölderlin most likely consulted German translations of Richard Chandler's *Travels in Asia Minor and Greece* and Count Choiseul-Gouffier's *Voyage pittoresque de la Grèce.*

Hyperion has often been compared with Goethe's *Sufferings of Young Werther* and, though the two works exhibit a number of similar formal aspects and thematic preoccupations, the reader will find a more complex emplotment of the dialectic of desire, so central to both novels, in the work of the younger poet. In the preface to the "Fragment of Hyperion," the shape of this dialectic is characterized as the "eccentric path" leading man from a condition of "more or less pure simplicity" to one of "more or less completed cultivation." In the preface to the final version, the eccentric path is described as the movement toward the "resolution of dissonances in a particular character." In the novel this movement takes place at two levels: that of the life story told by the "hermit in Greece" and that of the narration itself. That is, in *Hyperion* the eccentric path signifies not only the lived life of joys and sorrows, communion and conflict, in the realms of politics and

Eros, but the work of narration itself. For the author of these letters, the elegiac procedures of anamnesis and narration prove to be as important and transformative as any other life experience.

"When I was a boy. . ." / "Da ich ein Knabe war. . ."

1797–98 (dates given for composition of poems are in large measure conjectural). Hölderlin's mythology of childhood seems to have been largely influenced by Rousseau. This mythology is familiar from *Hyperion:* "The child is wholly what it is, and that is why it is so beautiful. The pressure of Law and Fate touches it not; only in the child is freedom. In the child is peace; it has not yet come to be at odds with itself."

"Empedokles"

1798. The fifth-century B.C. poet-philosopher was the subject of Hölderlin's unfinished tragedy, "The Death of Empedocles" which occupied him from 1797 to 1799. Empedocles's suicide was for Hölderlin a powerful reminder of the dangers of the longing for unmediated contact with the sacred element. The "queen" is an allusion to Cleopatra, who, according to Plinius, melted pearls in vinegar and drank them to win a bet with Anthony that she could consume ten million sestertia at one meal.

"Sophokles"

Probably written in the summer of 1799 while working on plans for his ill-fated literary journal *Iduna*. The epigram expresses the deep affinity between tragedy, sacrifice, and elegy in Hölderlin's writings. In his notes to *Antigone*, Hölderlin writes: "The tragic representation has as its premise . . . the merging of the fully present God with man . . . such that the infinite enthusiasm gathers itself infinitely, that is, . . . in a consciousness that cancels itself as consciousness, . . . and the God becomes manifest in the figure of death."

"The Root of All Evil" / "Wurzel alles Übels"

1799. In the poem Hölderlin distances himself from the totalitarian potential in philosophies and politics that overemphasize identity at the expense of heterogeneity. Hyperion remarks to Alabanda: "The state has always been made a hell by man's wanting to make it his heaven."

"My Possessions" / "Mein Eigentum"

1799. Hölderlin wrote a large number of odes in classical meters, limiting himself primarily to alcaic and asclepiadic strophic forms. This one is alcaic (translations only approximate to the original measures):

$$\cup - \cup - \cup - \cup \cup - \cup -$$
$$\cup - \cup - \cup - \cup \cup - \cup -$$
$$\cup - \cup - \cup - \cup - \cup$$
$$- \cup \cup - \cup \cup - \cup - \cup$$

Hölderlin wrote the poem a year after his painful separation from the Gontard household and at a time when he was struggling with various plans to support himself as a writer. Hölderlin's precarious existence in a politically and economically oppressive civil society resonates here with the transcendental homelessness that was to become one of the central themes of his elegies and hymns. As this ode already suggests, a condition of material and spiritual desolation can make one vulnerable to the self-destructive impulse to seek unmediated contact with the gods.

"Heidelberg"

1798–1800. The ode is asclepiadic:

$$- \cup - \cup \cup - - \cup \cup - \cup -$$
$$- \cup - \cup \cup - - \cup \cup - \cup -$$
$$- \cup - \cup \cup - \cup$$
$$- \cup - \cup \cup - \cup -$$

Hölderlin was in Heidelberg on at least two occasions. The central strophes most likely allude to his visit in 1795 after his sudden departure from Jena in a state of great emotional distress.

"The Course of Life" / "Lebenslauf"

1798–99. Asclepiadic. In April 1797 Hölderlin writes to his sister: "It's not a bad thing if a young man strives beyond himself; but a more mature life curves back once more to what is human and serene."

"The Farewell" / "Der Abschied"

1798–1800. Asclepiadic. The labor of mourning performed in the poem is particularly harsh, even violent: the lily at the end of the poem—in Hölderlin flowers are often associated with poetic language—appears to be linked to a bleeding away of desire.

"Nature and Art" / "Natur und Kunst"

1800–01. Alcaic. Saturn, the god of the golden age, was dethroned by his son Jupiter. Hölderlin identifies Kronos (Saturn) with Chronos (time), which makes Jupiter both "the son of Kronos" (Kronion) and of time. The relation between the gods (and what they represent) anticipates the relation between the Dionysian and the Apollinian principles in Nietzsche's *Birth of Tragedy*.

"The Poet's Vocation" / "Dichterberuf"

1800–01 (expansion of shorter poem, "To Our Great Poets" written 1798). Alcaic. One of the central questions of Hölderlin's mature writings concerns the task of the poet in desolate times, which are associated here with the predominance of instrumental reason in human affairs. In the final lines the poet's unique relation to God's absence displaces the emphasis in an earlier version on the relation of mortals in general to God's proximity ("And neither honors nor weapons are / Needed, as long as the God remains near.") It is unclear whether in the final version Hölderlin is being ironic or suggesting, rather, that the poet's vocation is precisely to discover, by way of a certain negative theology, the spiritual resources of an absent God.

"Voice of the People" / "Stimme des Volks"

1799–1800. Alcaic. The origin of the proverb that informs the poem, "vox populi, vox dei," is uncertain. The city of Xanthos was twice besieged: by the Persians between 546 and 539 B.C. and by Brutus in 42 B.C. The ode contains the most explicit reference in all of Hölderlin's writings to a suicidal (repetition) compulsion to undo individuation, particularly at moments of great danger.

"Chiron"

Between 1802 and early 1804, Hölderlin revised three earlier odes and included them among the nine poems he sent to Friedrich Wilmans for publication in his *Taschenbuch für das Jahr 1805*. Hölderlin referred to these poems as *Nachtgesänge* (Nightsongs). The three odes were: "Chiron," a reworking of "Der blinde Sänger" (The blind poet); "Blödigkeit," a reworking of "Dichtermut" (The poet's courage); and "Ganymed," a reworking of "Der gefesselte Strom" (The fettered river). Chiron was the wise and just among the centaurs and, having been instructed in the arts of medicine, music, prophecy, and hunting by Apollo and Artemis, became the teacher of various Achaen heroes such as Jason and Achilles. While hunting, he was inadvertently struck by one of Heracles's poisoned arrows. Rather than bear the pain, Chiron agreed to give up his immortality to Prometheus, thus fulfilling the prophecy that the latter would be redeemed only if a god would die for him. Heracles kills the eagle that had fed on Prometheus' liver and tells Zeus of Chiron's desire to die for Prometheus. The word "clouds" in the penultimate strophe may be a translation of the Greek *néphos*, meaning "cloud" as well as "horde" or "band."

"Timidness" / "Blödigkeit"

See note to "Chiron." In the final strophe Hölderlin creates a series of puns using derivations of the verb *schicken* (to send). *Geschickt,* the past participle of *schicken,* can also mean skillful; the noun *Geschick* denotes skill as well as fate or destiny (related to *Schicksal*). *Schicklich* connotes suitable, becoming, within the limits of propriety.

"Ganymed"

See note to "Chiron." Ganymede was the legendary Trojan prince whose beauty so captivated Zeus that the god assumed the form of an eagle and carried him off to Olympus to be his cupbearer.

"Menon's Lament for Diotima" / "Menons Klage um Diotima"

Hölderlin's elegies, written 1799–1801, are "elegiac" in both form and content. That is, they are poems of lament and they are written in elegiac distichs (alternating dactylic hexameters and pentameters; sometimes thought of as coupled hexameters, the second with a masculine caesura after the third beat), one of the oldest Greek verse forms, naturalized in Germany in the eighteenth century. Hölderlin developed his conception of the theme and tone of elegiac poetry within the framework of Schiller's notion of the genre as a subclass of sentimental poetry. As performed by Hölderlin, the elegist's lament often takes on hymnic character: the work of mourning a lost state of erotic or spiritual fulfillment (and thereby of renewing one's attachments to the world of the living) may open up to visionary projections of a future state of fulfillment and unity to be achieved, at least in part, in and through the language of poetry.

"Bread and Wine" / "Brod und Wein"

In July, 1796, Hölderlin, Susette Gontard, and her four children arrived in Kassel as refugees from Frankfurt, which had been overrun by Napoleon's army. Their host in Kassel was Wilhelm Heinse, a friend of the Gontard family and author of the novel *Ardinghello* (1787). Both the novel and its author influenced Hölderlin's own novel *Hyperion*. The first strophe was published separately by Leo von Seckendorf in his *Musenalmanach für das Jahr 1807* under the title "Die Nacht" and is known to have had a powerful impact on, among others, Clemens Brentano, who cites several lines from the poem nearly verbatim in his own "Märchen von Gockel, Hinkel und Gackeleia." The poem, which was first published in its entirety in 1894 (and at an earlier stage was called "Der Weingott"), mixes together allusions to Dionysus and to Christ. As gods who experienced death and rebirth and whose presence is furthermore preserved in a symbolic form—in bread and wine—providing comfort in the promise of later renewal, they are particularly well suited to be the patron deities of elegiac poetry. (This mixing of Hellenic and biblical traditions is typical of Hölderlin's later work.) In the poem Hölderlin achieves the mythopoetic vision of history that will dominate the later hymns; according to this vision, the poet's vocation is to prepare his community for a new epiphany, which will bring to an ecstatic conclusion the spiritual darkness that has plagued humankind since the withdrawal of the gods at the end of the Golden Age of Greek antiquity. To accomplish this task the poet must draw upon the salvific resources of the present moment of danger.

Thebe: a river nymph.

Ismenos: river near the city of Thebes.

Cadmus: founder of Thebes; his daughter, Semele, was the mother of

Dionysus. Cithaeron, a mountain near Thebes, was the site of Dionysian rites.

The Syrian: perhaps a condensation of Dionysus and Christ; both bring consolation to a nocturnal (under)world.

"Half of Life" / "Hälfte des Lebens"

One of the "Nightsongs" written in late 1802 and 1803 for Wilman's *Taschenbuch für das Jahr 1805*. The first drafts of the poem appear to have grown out of Hölderlin's efforts to complete his first large hymnic work after Pindar, "As on a Holiday. . . ."

"The Shelter at Hahrdt" / "Der Winkel von Hahrdt"

One of the "Nightsongs." According to a Swabian legend, in 1519 Duke Ulrich of Württemberg hid from enemy nobles in the "Ulrich Stone," a natural shelter formed by two large slabs of sandstone in the woods near Nürtigen.

"Ages of Life" / "Lebensalter"

One of the "Nightsongs." The city of Palmyra was decimated by the Romans in 273. Hölderlin's vision of the ruins of Palmyra was perhaps influenced by the poem "Die Ruinen von Palmyra" published in the first volume of the *Englische Blätter* (1793) edited by Ludwig Schubart, and the description of the deserted city in the first chapter of Volney's *Les Ruines, ou méditations sur les révolutions des empires* (1791). The contrast between the worlds separated in the poem by the semicolon resonates with Hölderlin's vision of the fundamental differences between Greek antiquity and modern Germany elaborated in his letter to Böhlendorff of December 4, 1801 (see introduction). Sieburth's translation follows D. E. Sattler's reconstruction of the poem in the *Einleitung* to the *Frankfurter Ausgabe*.

"As on a holiday. . ." / "Wie wenn am Feiertage. . ."

End of 1799. The first of the late hymnic works in which Hölderlin tries to adapt the triadic construction of the Pindaric ode—the progression from strophe to antistrophe to epode—to the historical and spiritual experience of Hesperidean man. In this first and, as it turned out, fragmentary attempt, Hölderlin also tries to imitate Pindar's patterns of metrical responsion. In the first prose drafts of the poem Hölderlin draws upon his translation of the prologue of Euripides's *Bacchae,* the first lines of which refer to the mythic birth of Dionysus from the union of Zeus and Semele.

"At the Source of the Danube" / "Am Quell der Donau"

1801. Hölderlin's major hymns were written for the most part between 1801 and 1803. Hölderlin characterized the tone of his hymnic work as the "high and pure jubilation of patriotic songs" *(das hohe und reine Frohlocken vaterländischer Gesänge)* in contrast to the "tired flight" of love songs that were more typical of the period. Some commentators have suggested that "As on a holiday. . . ." remained a fragment (and should not even be included among the *vaterländische Gesänge*) because Hölderlin had not yet worked through to this more public poetic attitude and voice. The triadic structure of "At the Source of the Danube" would be completed by two missing strophes, which, judging from prose drafts, would have contained an invocation to Mother Asia: (12, 12), 15; 12, 12, 16; 12, 12, 14. The late hymns make frequent reference to geography (for example, the course of rivers or the placement of mountains), to illustrate the westerly migration of a world-historical spirit from Asia, to Greece and Rome, and finally to Northern Europe. The Danube, which flows from Swabia to the Black Sea, may thereby become the locus of a mediation between the primordial site of an inspired humanity and a modernity awaiting spiritual renewal.

Parnassus: mountain above Delphi, sacred to Apollo and the muses.
Cithaeron: mountain near Thebes; site of Dionysian rites.
Capitol: site of the temple of Jupiter in Rome.
Ionia: region along the western coast of Asia Minor.
Isthmus: Isthmus at Corinth, site of the Isthmian Games.
Cephissus: river near Athens.
Taygetus: mountain range overlooking Sparta.
Caucasus: mountain range marking for Hölderlin the boundary between Asia and Europe.

"The Migration" / "Die Wanderung"

1801. The boundaries of Swabia evoked in the first strophe reflect the dimensions of the medieval duchy of Swabia under the Hohenstaufer. The

thic union of the German tribe with the "children of the sun" may allude
a wave of Swabian emigration toward the lower basin of the Danube in
70.
Lombardy: region of northern Italy bordering on Switzerland.
Neckar: major river in Swabia.
They called this sea Hospitable: previously referred to as "desolate," the
reeks called the Black Sea "hospitable" after colonization.
Cayster: river in Ionia.
Taygetos: mountain range overlooking Sparta.
Hymettos: mountain range southeast of Athens famous for its honey and
ıarble.
Tmolos: the river Paktolos in Asia Minor, known for its gold, runs down
:om Mount Tmolos.
Land of Homer: Ionia.
The young peaches: the peach, was introduced to Europe from Asia
Vinor.
Thetis: sea nymph, mother of Achilles.
Ida: mountain range south of Troy.
Graces of Greece: the Charites: Euphrosyne ("joy"), Aglaia ("brilliance"),
and Thalia ("bloom").

"Germanien"

1801. The flight of the eagle follows much the same path of the "voice that
moulds and makes human" in "At the Source of the Danube." The "storm,
threatening death", is perhaps an allusion to the Napoleonic wars. The
"lesser ones" of the fifth strophe might be an allusion to the Romans
defeated by Germanic warriors in the Teutoburger Wald. The strophe as a
whole appears to have been influenced by Tacitus's *Germania*.

"Der Rhein"

1801. Isaac von Sinclair, to whom the poem is dedicated, was one of
Hölderlin's closest and most loyal friends. His "Jacobin" politics led to his
expulsion from the university of Jena in 1795 and to his arrest and brief
incarceration in 1805 (see chronology). In a marginal note on one of the
manuscripts of the poem, Hölderlin characterized the structure of the hymn
as follows (in Christopher Middleton's translation): "The law of this poem
[*dieses Gesanges*] is that the first two parts are formally opposed as pro-
gression and regression, but are alike in subject matter; the two succeeding

parts are formally alike but are opposed as regards subject matter; the last part, however, balances everything out with a continuous metaphor." Hölderlin thus grouped the fifteen strophes of the hymn into five sets of three strophes each (triad). The terms "progression" and "regression" may refer to the movement of thought and voice through the three major poetic tonalities as conceived by Hölderlin: naive, heroic, ideal. Each tonality gives voice to a different position, attitude, and existential mood vis-à-vis the heroic destiny that is the central theme of the poem.

Morea: the Peloponnesus (southern part of Greece).

Ticino, Rhodanus: rivers that rise near the source of the Rhine in the Swiss Alps.

Toward Asia: the Rhine flows eastward from its source before turning northward in the Graubünden mountains.

He rends the snakes: allusion to Heracles struggling with the snakes placed in his cradle by Hera.

Rousseau: Hölderlin wrote an (unfinished) ode to Rousseau around the turn of the century. He was important to Hölderlin as the first great modern psychologist of alienation and as prophet of revolutionary change.

Lake Bienne: Rousseau took refuge on the Peterinsel in this lake in 1765.

One wise man: an allusion to Socrates at the symposium.

In the steel blade: perhaps an allusion to Sinclair's revolutionary politics.

"Celebration of Peace" / "Friedensfeier"

1801–02. The final version of this hymn was discovered in 1954 in a private collection in London. The twelve strophes are divisible into four triads (Hölderlin left extra spaces after every third strophe to mark the divisions). The first drafts were composed in the euphoria following the Treaty of Lunéville in February 1801 (see chronology). Since its publication, commentators have suggested a number of possible identities of the prince of the feast day: the genius of the people; Napoleon; Christ; the God of Peace; the World Spirit; Helios; Dionysus; Heracles. Still others have argued that Hölderlin has been quite careful to suspend the question of identity in the hymn.

"The Only One" / "Der Einzige"

1802; further versions 1803. The fragmentary hymn is one of Hölderlin's ambivalent attempts to integrate Christ into the lineage of Greek gods as part of his effort to establish a proper measure of distance (and proximity) to him without compromising his uniqueness.

Elis: region in the western Peloponnesus where Olympia lies; site of the panhellenic games.

Smyrna . . . Ephesos: Greek settlements in Ionia, on the western coast of Asia Minor.

Euios: cult name of Dionysus.

"Patmos"

1802. In 1802, the Landgrave Friedrich of Hessen-Homburg, a critic of the "false freedom and Jacobinism" he saw as the legacy of the Enlightenment and the French Revolution, commissioned Klopstock to write a poem reaffirming traditional biblical values. When Klopstock was unable to oblige him, Hölderlin, who met the Landgrave in Regensburg in October 1802, took on the task. Sinclair handed the poem with Hölderlin's dedication to the Landgrave on February 6, 1803, on the occasion of the latter's fifty-fifth birthday. Patmos is the island in the Sporades (Aegean archipelago) where St. John the Divine is said to have written the Book of Revelations. Hölderlin shared the common assumption that this John was identical with the apostle John. A later version merges John the Baptist with this composite figure. The poem is perhaps Hölderlin's most powerful evocation of the primal scene of dispersion and fragmentation that marks the advent of modernity for the poet, which, he suggests, is a time when the divine is only available in the form of signs to be recollected and interpreted.

Give us innocent water: the line recalls Hölderlin's translation (1799) of Leander's letter to Hero—i.e., from antiquity's most famous swimmer to his beloved—from the eighteenth epistle in Ovid's Heroides.

Tmolus, Taurus, Messogis: mountains in Asia Minor, now Turkey.

Bearer of thunder; mystery of the vine: here as in "Bread and Wine," Hölderlin sometimes mingles the attributes of Christ and Dionysus.

The evening had come: the world-historical night brought on by Christ's absence.

The loved one's shadow: perhaps an allusion to Christ's appearance to the disciples on the way to Emmaus (Luke 24:13–17.). In a later version this shadow is compared to a plague.

He sent them / The Spirit: cf. Acts 2: 1–4.

To have done so later: these difficult lines are rendered by Sieburth as follows: "Far worse, had it / Happened later, brutally tearing men / From their work." Beissner suggests the following reading: Later, life would not have been good, would have been the mere work of men (and moreover a sign of God's infidelity), had Christ not sent the disciples the Spirit that consoles them during the period of darkness before Parousia.

God disperses whatever lives: in a later version this is changed to "God destroys whatever lives."

The sower's cast: a condensation of two New Testament parables: cf. Matthew 3: 11–12; Mark 4: 3–9 and 11–20.

To copy God's own image: the warning against graven images contained in these difficult lines is made more explicit in Sieburth's translation: "I once saw the lords of heaven / Visibly furious that I wanted to *be* something / Rather than learn."

How much more you: The Landgrave Friedrich

For known / To him are all his works: cf. Acts 15: 18.

"Patmos" [Fragments of the Later Version]

1803.
From Jordan: cf. Matthew 4: 23–25; Luke: 4: 14–37; John 4: 43–54.
A little while I shall stay: cf. John, 13: 33.
Small children killed: cf. Matthew 2: 16–18.
The Baptist's head: cf. Matthew 14: 8–11; Mark 6: 25–28.
Peleus: king of the Myrmidons at Phthia in Thessaly and father of Achilles. He was shipwrecked on the island of Kos, near Patmos.
The nobles: the Crusaders.
Heinrich: the German Emperor Heinrich IV (1056–1106); under pressure from the German princes, he did penance at Canossa in 1077 to absolve himself from excommunication by Pope Gregory VII.
Dragons' teeth: allusion to Cadmus's sowing of armed soldiers from the teeth of a dragon (cf. Ovid, *The Metamorphoses*, 3, 99–130); with five of these soldiers Cadmus built the city of Thebes.

"Remembrance" / "Andenken"

1803 (perhaps as late as 1805). One of the first poems to incorporate details of the French landscape Hölderlin witnessed during his brief employment as a private tutor in Bordeaux (see chronology).

The northeasterly: the wind that blows from Germany toward Bordeaux (and to the West Indies).

Garonne: river that flows from the southeast into the Atlantic near Bordeaux after joining with the Dordogne, which flows from east to west.

But a noble pair: Hölderlin's use of the conjunction *aber* here and throughout the late hymns reflects a tendency in the later hymns toward parataxis.

Bellarmin: the addressee of Hyperion's letters in Hölderlin's epistolary novel.

To the Indies: the manuscript version reads *Indien,* while the printed text reads *Indiern.*

But poets establish what remains: Middleton renders the last line: "But poets alone ordain what abides."

"Der Ister"

1803 (perhaps as late as 1805). Ister is the ancient Greek name for the Danube.

Indus: river associated with the sacred origins of culture.

Alpheus: river that runs by Olympia.

What is fitting: see note to the ode "Timidness."

Hercules (Heracles): according to Pindar's Third Olympian (translated by Hölderlin), Hercules brought back olive trees from the source of the Danube to provide shade for the Olympic fields.

To travel backwards: for Hölderlin the Danube mediates between the ancient origins of culture in the east and Hesperidean modernity.

The Rhine, has gone away / Sideways: allusion to the easterly course of the river at its source.

Hertha: according to Tacitus, this fertility goddess was the Mother Earth of the ancient Germans.

"Mnemosyne"

1803 (perhaps as late as 1805). The Sieburth translation published here follows D. E. Sattler's reconstruction of the poem in the *Einleitung* to the *Frankfurter Ausgabe.* The strophe that Beissner presents as the first strophe of a "third version" of the poem (replacing "A sign we are. . . ." is published here separately as the fragment "The fruits are ripe. . . ." According to Beissner, Hölderlin's work on the poem was contemporary with his translations from Sophocles's *Ajax.* Mnemosyne is the Greek goddess of memory and mother of the Muses.

Eleutherai: city on the slopes of Mt. Kithairon; according to Hesiod, Mnemosyne reigned over the hills of Eleuther.

Cut / Her lock of hair: in Greek mythology this is to mark one for death.

Mourning is in error: this last line has been the subject of debate among scholars. If one reads *fehlet* to signify a lack rather than error and *gleich* to mean "soon," one might read the line as: "For him mourning will soon pass," that his, for him who gathers himself and lets go of an obsessive, melancholic mode of memory.

"The fruits are ripe. . ." / "Reif sind. . ."

The dates of composition of the five drafts of hymns published here are generally taken to be 1801 to 1806. Before Sattler's reconstruction of "Mnemosyne" most scholars accepted Beissner's reading of "Reif sind. . . ." as the first strophe of a third version of that hymn. Sattler includes the fragment as part of a larger collection of fragments he has entitled "Apriorität des Individuellen." According to Paracelsus, "The ripening of fruit is natural cookery: therefore what nature has in her, she cooks, and when it is cooked, then nature is whole" (Hamburger's translation).

"When the sap. . ." / "Wenn nemlich der Rebe Safe. . ."

A sort of miniature of the dialectic of light and shade—the Greek fires from heaven and Hesperidean sobriety—which is a central motif in all the late hymns.

"Do you think . . ." / "Meinest du es solle gehen . . ."

On September 28, 1803, in a letter to his publisher regarding his translations of Sophocles, Hölderlin writes: "I hope to bring Greek art, which is foreign to us, more to life . . . by highlighting the Oriental quality [*das Orientalische*] which they denied." What is meant here is the passionate, "aorgic" excess that, as Hölderlin writes in his first letter to Böhlendorff, was innate to the Greeks (see chronology).

"We set out from the abyss. . ." / "Vom Abgrund nemlich. . ."

Much of the imagery derives from Hölderlin's sojourn in Bordeaux. It would appear that Frankfurt, the site of Hölderlin's love affair with Susette Gontard, is being equated with Delphi, which the Greeks thought to be the naval of the earth.

"Greece" / "Griechenland"

Hamburger's translation of the line *Wenn ausgehn will die alte Bildung* has been challenged by Middleton, who renders the line as: "When the old shaping images / Of earth launch forth." Middleton construes the passage to "mean that earth contains an occult vein of *Urbilder,* primordial images, which emerge spontaneously in times of historical crisis and shape events (metaphysical patterns of history)." Sieburth's translation generally corresponds with Hamburger's, though he reduces much of the ambiguity of the original: "At times / When the ancient civilization of the world / Threatens to go out, amid the blaze of battle, / And the old stories all come true, God then leads / The earth onto heights."

"Spring" / "Der Frühling"

During his last thirty-six years in Tübingen, Hölderlin continued to write poetry, often at the request of visitors. These poems, of which fifty remain, are for the most part rhymed (typically with feminine rhyme), written in iambic meter, and treat a narrow spectrum of subjects: the seasons, a view of a landscape, "man," Greece, the zeitgeist. Hölderlin signed a number of these small poems with the name Scardanelli.

Bibliography

Listed below is a brief selection of book-length studies of Hölderlin (including several volumes with significant chapters on Hölderlin) published in English since 1960.

Benn, Maurice. *Hölderlin and Pindar.* The Hague: Mouton, 1962.
Constantine, David. *The Significance of Locality in the Poetry of Friedrich Hölderlin.* London: MHRA Texts and Dissertations, 1979.
———. *Hölderlin.* Oxford: Clarendon Press, 1988.
De Man, Paul. *The Rhetoric of Romanticism.* New York: Columbia University Press, 1984. [several essays relevant to Hölderlin]
Fehervary, Helen. *Hölderlin and the Left.* Heidelberg: Carl Winter Universitätsverlag, 1977.
Gaskill, Howard. *Hölderlin's Hyperion.* Durham: University of Durham, 1984.
George, Emery. *Hölderlin's "Ars Poetica": A Part-Rigorous Analysis of Information Structure in the Late Hymns.* The Hague: Mouton, 1973.
———, ed. *Friedrich Hölderlin: An Early Modern.* Ann Arbor: University of Michigan Press, 1972.
Harrison, R. B. *Hölderlin and Greek Literature.* Oxford: Clarendon Press, 1975.
Kuzniar, Alice. *Delayed Endings: Nonclosure in Novalis and Hölderlin.* Athens: University of Georgia Press, 1987.
Nägele, Rainer. *Reading after Freud: Essays on Goethe, Hölderlin, Habermas, Nietzsche, Brecht, Celan, and Freud.* New York: Columbia University Press, 1987. [several essays relevant to Hölderlin]
Ryan, Thomas. *Hölderlin's Silence.* New York: Peter Lang, 1988.
Santner, Eric. *Friedrich Hölderlin: Narrative Vigilance and the Poetic Imagination.* New Brunswick: Rutgers University Press, 1986.
Shelton, Roy. *The Young Hölderlin.* Bern: Peter Lang, 1973.
Silz, Walter. *Hölderlin's Hyperion: A Critical Reading.* Philadelphia: University of Pennsylvania Press, 1969.
Simon, Martin. *Friedrich Hölderlin. The Theory and Practice of Religious Poetry: Studies in the Elegies.* Stuttgart: H. D. Heinz Akademischer Verlag, 1988

Szondi, Peter. *On Textual Understanding and Other Essays.* Trans. Harvey Mendelsohn. Minneapolis: University of Minnesota Press, 1986. [several essays relevant to Hölderlin]

Unger, Richard. *Hölderlin's Major Poetry.* Bloomington: Indiana University Press, 1975.

———. *Friedrich Hölderlin.* Boston: Twayne, 1984.

Warminski, Andrzej. *Readings in Interpretation: Hölderlin, Hegel, Heidegger.* Minneapolis: University of Minnesota Press, 1987.

Acknowledgments

Every reasonable effort has been made to locate the owners of rights to previously published translations printed here. We gratefully acknowledge permission to reprint the following material:

University of Chicago Press for permission to reprint translations of "Da ich ein Knabe war," "Heidelberg," "Dichterberuf," "Ganymed," and "Der Rhein" from Christopher Middleton, translator, *Friedrich Hölderlin, Eduard Morike: Selected Poems*. Copyright © 1972.

Princeton University Press for permission to reprint translations from Richard Sieburth, trans. and intro., *Hymns and Fragments by Friedrich Hölderlin*. Copyright © 1984 by Princeton University Press. Excerpts reprinted with permission of Princeton University Press.

Cambridge University Press and Michael Hamburger for permission to reprint translations from *Friedrich Hölderlin: Poems and Fragments* (translated by Michael Hamburger). Reprinted by permission of Michael Hamburger.